The Last Trump Shall Sound

***

Michael Stands!

Author: Henry Carroll Hills

Loud Cry Publishing
222 Ensley Rd., S.E.
Cleveland, TN 37323

Unless otherwise noted Bible texts are
from the King James Bible

Cover design by Henry Hills
with Frank Strack

For bulk purchases of this book
henry.hills@gmail.com
(423) 584-0220

February 13, 2020

(Enhanced Edition 6 October 2020)

ISBN: 978-1-7343261-1-6

Will something of global importance happen on:
Valentine's Day 14 February 2020?
Yes...Bomb Cyclone struck Iceland and Europe
Yes...COVID-19 identified as a global pandemic
2 April 2020?
Yes...D.J. Trump said: We control our own fate!
Yes...US Paycheck Protection Program started!
Yes...Israel troops besieged
Bethlehem's Church of the Nativity!
17 May 2020?
Yes...COVID-19 stopped Pope Francis I's global
conference called for May 2020!

Though we may not know the day or hour of specific events, Jesus is able to secure us in His care no matter what! But neglecting to study His word sets us up to fail!

"God's purposes know no haste and no delay"

Desire of Ages

They did not possess that faith that is the substance of things hoped for, the evidence of things unseen. (See Hebrews 11:1.) They did not want to move by faith, but to walk out by sight, and no farther. Therefore, they were easily turned aside from the work. This history will be repeated. There will be religious failures because men have not faith. When they look at the things that are seen, impossibilities present themselves, but God knows nothing of impossibilities. The great work of God will advance only by the push of faith... (10MR 122.3).

Table of Contents

Prophecy Meets History

We have also a more sure word of prophecy; whereunto ye do well that ye take heed, as unto a light that shineth in a dark place, until the day dawn, and the day star arise in your hearts: Knowing this first, that no prophecy of the scripture is of any private interpretation. For the prophecy came not in old time by the will of man: but holy men of God spake as they were moved by the Holy Ghost (2 Peter 1:19-21).

People who disagree with a prophetic warning may justify their skepticism by claiming that the prophecy in question is being skewed by a private interpretation. That may be true. But it may also be a pretext to protect a cherished traditional belief. The word *idios* that is translated as *private* is also the root for the word *idiotic*. *True interpretations are not idiotic!*

Having then gifts differing according to the grace that is given to us, whether prophecy, let us prophesy according to the proportion of faith (Romans 12:6).

But if all prophesy, and there come in one that believeth not, or one unlearned, he is convinced...
(1 Corinthians 1:24)

Bible prophecy assures us of God's love. Consider the 333 prophecies in the Bible predicting Christ's first coming. Adrian Rogers has said that if only eight of them were considered (for example: Jesus being born at a certain time, at a certain place; His mother being a virgin; babies being killed in an attempt to kill Him; Jesus would heal the sick; and then be rejected, crucified, and rise from the dead), if only eight prophecies were merely left to chance, (by the law of probability) it would be impossible for them to happen. Just to get eight prophecies correct would be like covering the entire state of Texas with a two-foot pile of silver dollars and then placing a man at a random location within the state tasked with finding a specific coin in the pile. He finds it! According to Rogers: Peter Stoner, a statistician, calculated the probability of all of the 333 prophecies that predicted Christ's First Advent being fulfilled by chance precisely as predicted as astronomically impossible!

Just eight prophecies prove that God's prophetic word is true and trustworthy. Based on getting the 333 prophecies about Christ's First Advent correct, God's accuracy in the past proves that He knows the future and that God has left nothing up to chance. Thus, we are sure that the prophecies about Christ's Second Advent will be fulfilled as well!

In 1997, God impressed me to study Bible prophecy. I began studying to find out for myself if God is, and if His word is trustworthy. I did not know at that time that millennia before the fact God gave 333 incredible revelations that have been confirmed. God accurately foretold the future! He exists! His word is trustworthy!

My quest: To find out what the Bible really said about Christ's Second Advent. I began with studies from Daniel and Revelation. When the lessons prepared by various churches were compared, they did not agree. If the Bible is the source of the lessons, how can they have contradictions? I learned that the people who prepared them subscribed to schools of prophetic interpretation that had been invented to give Bible students a framework to facilitate understanding. But the tools are not the prophecies. The tools must not replace the prophecies. Failing to allow the Bible to explain itself is a recipe for confusion, disputes, and misunderstanding.

When the Bible speaks for itself, I learned without any doubt that God reveals things that He wants His people to understand before they happen. As with preparing for a disaster: Folks on a flood plain hope to be ready for floods that may never come. But it is also possible that they may encounter fires, tornadoes, earthquakes, or other disasters that they never imagined. Is it better to prepare for a disaster that may never come or to assume that it is not worthwhile and to be taken by surprise? Disaster preparedness saves lives! Likewise, heeding Bible prophecy saves souls!

The Nearness of Time

My study encountered the nearness of Christ's Advent. But time is not the message. What is happening now is the message that must be heard aright! We must prepare for the coming chaotic conflict between our world and the unseen supernatural world! Self-perpetuating wars, displaced populations, border insecurity, unparalleled global disasters, rampant drug abuse, antibiotic resistant epidemics, entrenched political wrangling, the prophesied loss of our moral compass (at endtime Babylon's fall because of her fornication), and the pending time of trouble. It is not business as usual. What is happening? Why is it happening?

> *Though no man knoweth the day nor the hour of His coming, we are instructed and required to know when it is near. We are further taught that to disregard His warning, and refuse or neglect to know when His Advent is near, will be as fatal for us, as it was for those who lived in the days of Noah not to know when the flood was coming* (GC88 370.2).

The nations shall rush like the rushing of many waters: but *God* shall rebuke them, and they shall flee far off, and shall be chased as the chaff of the mountains before the wind, and like a rolling thing before the whirlwind (Isaiah 17:13).

And then shall appear the sign of the Son of man in heaven: and then shall all the tribes of the earth mourn, and they shall see the Son of man coming in the clouds of heaven with power and great glory (Matthew 24:30).

Jesus also warned, "How dreadful it will be in those days for pregnant women and nursing mothers!" (Matthew 24:19, NIV). Has that time past? If not, when? Why did Jesus give this warning? Is He teaching family planning?

Your gold and silver...shall be a witness against you, and shall eat your flesh as it were fire. Ye have heaped treasure together for the last days (James 5:3).

With retirement funds, 401Ks and financial planning for the purpose of having a secure future, will there be a time that our possessions will curse us? What about having a house mortgage, car payments, and unpaid debts? Will these monitory issues hinder our Christian life?

How do we know when it is time to give our offerings to the LORD to finish His work as Israel gave in the wilderness? Instead of having our possessions consume our flesh, it would be better to use them for God like the poor widow.

This poor widow hath cast more in, than all they which have cast into the treasury: For all *they* did cast in of their abundance; but she of her want did cast in all that she had, *even* all her living (Matthew 12:42-43).

Jesus forewarns us of pending danger because He wants us to understand and to prepare for the coming conflict. With the dreaded 666 *Mark of the beast* coming, it will be dangerous for people to be in the military. After the Mark of the Beast that deceives the world is enforced, being in the armed services will not merely be *having a secure government job*. Being in the military will be a curse for God's people when the Mark is enforced! It is dangerous to wait and see. Now is the time to understand the Three Angels' Messages.

While discussing the endtimes with a religion major at the non-denominational University of Tennessee at Chattanooga, Ellen White was mentioned. He told me: "You cannot study Christianity in America without encountering Ellen White." Since the encounter is inevitable, let's do it.

Ellen G. White

Was she a prophetess? Or a charlatan? She began life as Ellen G. Harmon. Hearing the Baptist Minister, William Miller, who had preached in the early1800's that Christ's

Advent would happen in 1843 (and then 1844), she believed his message and awaited Christ's Second Advent twice. But she was disappointed: Christ had not Come! Then she began having visions in 1845. She learned that Jesus had not come at the times that Miller had calculated because the book of Daniel was not predicting Christ's Advent at those times. Miller had the right times from his study of Daniel, but the wrong event. The correct event was the cleansing of Heaven's Sanctuary when the books in heaven were opened to confirm the saints' identity in preparation for Christ's Advent. For Christ had promised: "He that overcometh...I will not blot out his name out of the book of life, but I will confess his name before My Father, and before His angels." "And behold, I come quickly; and My reward is with Me, to give every man according as his work shall be" (Revelation 3:5; 22:12).

Ellen Harmon married James White. They published her writings as the *Spirit of Prophecy*. Thus, Ellen G. White wrote for 70 years (1845 to 1915). Though she is virtually unknown (you have not seen her on Oprah's book club), she is undeniably, America's most prolific woman author.

> In the city of Portland, the Lord ordained me as His messenger, and here my first labors were given to the cause of present truth. After a period of despair, the blessed Saviour revealed to me His love, and brought joy and happiness to my soul. When I was but a child, the Lord placed upon me a burden for souls. I worked earnestly for the conversion of my playmates, and at times ministers of some of the churches would send for me to bear testimony before their congregations. After the great disappointment, the Lord revealed Himself to me in a special manner, and bade me bear His messages to His people (RH, May 18, 1911 par. 3).

> I was asked several times, Are you a prophet? I have ever responded; I am the Lord's messenger. *I know that many have called me a prophet*, but I have made no claim to this title. My Saviour declared me to be His messenger. "Your work," He instructed me, "is to bear My word.

Strange things will arise, and in your youth, I set you apart to bear the message to the erring ones, to carry the word before unbelievers, and with pen and voice to reprove from the Word actions that are not right. Exhort from the Word. I will make My Word open to you. It shall not be as a strange language. In the true eloquence of simplicity, with voice and pen, the messages that I give shall be heard from one who has never learned in the schools. My Spirit and My power shall be with you" (RH, July 26, 1906 par. 5).

Does the Bible forbid Ellen White from being a prophetess? Though White never claimed to be a prophet, she never rebuked anyone, who called her a prophet.

God has put prophets and prophetesses in His church: "He [is] a prophet" (Genesis 20:7), "a prophetess...judged Israel" (Judges 4:4), and "Anna, a prophetess" (Luke 2:36). Paul said: "And He gave some, apostles; and some, prophets; and some, evangelists; and some, pastors and teachers...Till we all come in the unity of the faith, and of the knowledge of the Son of God" (Ephesians 4:11, 13). Is the church *now in the unity of the faith*? No! Did God do away with apostles, prophets, or prophetesses, while keeping pastors, teachers, and evangelists in the church; before the church came to *the unity of the faith* promised by Paul? No!

Prophesying was withdrawn from God's people from the time of Malachi to Matthew (450 years). The gift of prophecy reappeared in the Apostles Day. But prophesying has been rare in the past 2100 years. Was that gift to be entirely withdrawn from the church after Christ ascended to Heaven?

I [am] the LORD your God...My people shall never be ashamed. And it shall come to pass afterward, [that] I will pour out My Spirit upon all flesh; and your sons and *your daughters shall prophesy*, your old men shall dream dreams, your young men shall see visions: And also upon the servants and *upon the handmaids in those days will I pour out My Spirit*. And I will shew wonders in the heavens and in the earth (Joel 2:27-30).

I had known of Ellen White before I met that religion major in Chattanooga. In 1970, Ellen's grandson, Arthur White, showed me the large family Bible that Ellen had held up while in vision. How could a sickly weak teenager, hold an 18½ pound Bible aloft with one hand for a long time? Imagine holding a jug with more than 2 gallons of milk in it high up in the air with one hand while pointing to the label with the other and quoting it verbatim while looking in a different direction. It sounds impossible. But eye witnesses report that a similar event happened. Here is the backstory:

"By invitation of Brother and Sister Nichols, my sister and myself again went to Massachusetts, and made their house our home. There was in Boston and vicinity a company of fanatical persons, who held that it was a sin to labor. Their principal message was, 'Sell that ye have, and give alms.' They said they were in the jubilee, the land should rest, and the poor must be supported without labor. Sargent, Robbins, and some others, were leaders. They denounced my visions as being of the devil, because I had been shown their errors. They were severe upon all who did not believe with them. While we were visiting at the house of Brother S. Nichols, Sargent and Robbins came from Boston to obtain a favor of Brother Nichols, and said they had come to have a visit, and tarry over night with him. Brother Nichols replied that he was glad they had come, for Sisters Sarah and Ellen were in the house, and he wished them to become acquainted with us. They changed their minds at once, and could not be persuaded to come into the house. Brother Nichols asked if I could relate my message in Boston, and if they would hear, and then judge. "Yes," said they, "Come into Boston next Sabbath, we would like the privilege of hearing her" (LS80 231.1).

"We accordingly designed to visit Boston, but in the evening, at the commencement of the Sabbath, while engaged in prayer, I was shown in vision that we must not go into Boston, but in an opposite direction to

Randolph; that the Lord had a work for us to do there. We went to Randolph, and found a large room full collected, and among them those who said they would be pleased to hear my message in Boston. As we entered, Robbins and Sargent looked at each other in surprise and began to groan. They had promised to meet me in Boston, but thought they would disappoint us by going to Randolph, and while we were in Boston, warn the brethren against us. They did not have much freedom. During intermission one of their number remarked that good matter would be brought out in the afternoon. Robbins told my sister that I could not have a vision where he was (LS80 231.2).

J. N. Loughborough wrote of this meeting at Randolph to which the Lord miraculously sent Ellen. Loughborough reported the details about this supernatural Bible study in his book, "The Great Second Advent Movement." This incredible event was God's response to skeptics, who claimed that Ellen was not God's prophet. Loughborough wrote:

Remarkable Demonstrations

Sister Ellen was taken off in vision with extraordinary manifestations, and continued talking in vision with a clear voice, which could be distinctly understood by all present, until about sundown. Sargent, Robbins, and French were much exasperated, as well as excited, to hear Sister Ellen talk in vision, which they declared was of the devil; they exhausted all their influence and bodily strength to destroy the effect of the vision. They would unite in singing very loud, and then alternately would talk and read from the Bible in a loud voice, in order that Ellen might not be heard, until their strength was exhausted. And their hands would shake so they could not read from the Bible, but amidst all this confusion and noise, Ellen's clear and shrill voice, as she talked in vision, was distinctly heard by all present. The opposition of these men continued as long as they could talk and sing, notwithstanding some of their own friends rebuked them, and requested them to stop. But said Robbins, "You are bowed to an idol: you are worshiping a golden calf."

Mr. Thayer, the owner of the house was not fully satisfied that her vision was of the devil, as Robbins declared it to be. He wanted it tested in some way. He had heard that visions of Satanic power were arrested by opening the Bible and laying it on the person in vision, and asked Sargent if he would test it in that way, which he declined to do. Then Mr. Thayer took a heavy, large quarto family Bible which was lying on the table, and seldom used, opened it, and laid it open upon the breast of Ellen while in vision, as she was then inclined backward against the wall in the corner of the room. Immediately after the Bible was laid upon her, she arose upon her feet, and walked into the middle of the room, with the Bible open in one hand, and lifted up as high as she could reach, with her eyes steadily looking upward, declared in a solemn manner, "The inspired testimony from God," or words of the same import. And then, while the Bible was extended in one hand, and her eyes looking upward, and not on the Bible, she continued for a long time to turn over the leaves with her other hand, and place her finger upon certain passages, and correctly utter their words with a solemn voice. Many present looked at the passages where her finger was pointed, to see if she spoke them correctly, for her eyes at the same time were looking upward. Some of the passages were judgments against the wicked and blasphemers; and others were admonitions and instructions relative to our present condition" (The Great Second Advent Movement).

Ellen's prophetic insights have been accompanied by manifestations that testify that God is the Originator of her Bible based messages. Failing to read and heed her writings is like ignoring the speed limit while passing a police car.

In every place God is working to bring us to a knowledge of Christ and His righteousness. He speaks to us in His Word. The Bible is the key that unlocks the mysteries which it is essential for us to understand in order to know what we must do to gain eternal life. The Bible is its own expositor. Its bright beams are to shine into all parts of the world, that sin may be revealed. The Bible is a chart, pointing out the waymarks of truth. Those who are acquainted with this chart will be enabled to tread with certainty the path of duty, wherever we may be called to go (cf 7MR 236.2).

White's Christian character, writings, and good works have blessed humanity as God planned: "I wish above all things that thou mayest prosper and be in health, even as thy soul prospereth" (3 John 1:2). She exalted Jesus thru sound Bible teachings, promoted education globally, taught sound health principles, established hospitals like Loma Linda, and taught folks how to better themselves. Google her. Critics may belittle her looks, but they cannot fault her godly life and character: "Whereas they speak against you as evildoers, they may by your good works, which they shall behold, glorify God in the day of visitation" (1 Peter 2:12).

God Prepares His People

The Lord is testing His people to see who will be loyal to the principles of His truth. *Our work is to proclaim to the world the first, second, and third angels' messages.* In the discharge of our duties we are neither to despise nor to fear our enemies. ... We are to treat with kindness and courtesy those who refuse to be loyal to God, but we are never, never to unite with them in counsel regarding the vital interests of His work. Putting our trust in God, we are to move steadily forward, doing His work with unselfishness, in humble dependence upon Him, committing to His providence ourselves and all that concerns our present and future, holding the beginning of our confidence firm unto the end, remembering that we receive the blessings of heaven, not because of our worthiness, but because of Christ's worthiness and our acceptance, through faith in Him, of God's abounding grace (7T 107.2).

It is possible to be a formal, partial believer, and yet be found wanting, and lose eternal life. It is possible to practice some of the Bible injunctions, and be regarded as a Christian, and yet perish because you are lacking in essential qualifications that constitute Christian character. The destroying angels have the commission from the Lord, "Begin at My sanctuary." And "they began at the ancient men which were before the house." If the warnings which God has given are neglected or regarded with indifference, if you suffer sin to be cherished, you are sealing your soul's destiny; you will be weighed in the balances and found wanting. Grace, peace, and pardon will be withdrawn forever; Jesus will have passed by, never again to come within the reach of your prayers and entreaties. While mercy still lingers, while Jesus is making intercession for us, let us make thorough work for eternity (RH, January 11, 1887 par. 24).

Fulfilled prophecy assures us that God is and that He is in control! He knows everything before it happens. It builds our faith and confidence, not because someone said so, but because our own experience with God has taught us that He is able to keep us thru the trials. While heeding His prophetic warnings: We will be safe in the arms of Jesus.

When the day dawns, the light is faint and subdued; but as the sun rises, its light increases and strengthens, until its rays reach the perfect day. This is the way in which the Christian's light is to increase. We are to know more of Christ today than we knew yesterday; we are to grow in grace and in the knowledge of our Lord and Saviour; we are to trust Him more in trial and difficulty, looking to Him as the Author and Finisher of our faith. In sorrow and temptation, we are to realize that He is touched with the feeling of our infirmities; that He was a man of sorrows and acquainted with grief; that He was wounded for our transgressions, and by His stripes we are healed (RH, April 14, 1891 par. 12).

The present generation have trusted their bodies with the doctors, and their souls with the ministers. Do they not pay the minister well for studying the Bible for them, that they need not be to the trouble? And is it not his business to tell them what they must believe, and to settle all doubtful questions of theology without special investigation on their part? (HR, August 1, 1866 par. 3)

The astonishing indifference and carelessness which many now feel, is because they are separated in their thoughts from God, and really ignorant of their own peril. If the truth does not have a sanctifying influence upon your life and character, you will be like the foolish virgins, whose lamps were gone out at the very time when the bridegroom came to go in to the marriage. A theory of the truth is not enough. There is a high standard for us to reach. Our conflict is a continual conflict with the powers of darkness, and we must put on the whole armor of God, fight the good fight of faith, and lay hold on eternal life. But how few are willing to urge their way heavenward against every opposing force of evil in the world! (ST, July 27, 1888 par. 8).

When Bibles were chained to pulpits, people relied on priests to teach God's word. It was so misconstrued that rituals replaced it. Religious confusion stifled the intellect for 1260 years: Those were the Dark Ages.

We are to engage in no work that will make us indifferent to the dangers that threaten our salvation. All that we do in this life is to be done with reference to the eternal well-being of ourselves and those who are connected with us (https://egwwritings.org/Ms121-1902.23).

When the appeals of the Holy Spirit come to the heart, our only safety lies in responding to them without delay... "Today if ye will hear His voice, harden not your hearts." Hebrews 4:7. It is unsafe to delay obedience. You may never hear the invitation again (COL 280.4).

The "time of trouble, such as never was," is soon to open upon us; and we shall need an experience which we do not now possess and which many are too indolent to obtain. It is often the case that trouble is greater in anticipation than in reality; but this is not true of the crisis before us. The most vivid presentation cannot reach the magnitude of the ordeal. In that time of trial, every soul must stand for himself before God. "Though Noah, Daniel, and Job" were in the land, "as I live, saith the Lord God, they shall deliver neither son nor daughter; they shall but deliver their own souls by their righteousness." Ezekiel 14:20 (GC 622.4).

Revelations

[Daniel's] wonderful prophecies, as recorded by him in chapters 7 to 12 of the book bearing his name, were not fully understood even by the prophet himself; but before his life labors closed, he was given the blessed assurance that "at the end of the days"--in the closing period of this world's history--he would again be permitted to stand in his lot and place. It was not given him to understand all that God had revealed of the divine purpose. "Shut up the words, and seal the book," he was directed concerning his prophetic writings; these were to be sealed "even to the time of the end" (PK 547.1).

Daniel begins with God giving the king of Israel, the city of Jerusalem, and eventually the Temple to Nebuchadnezzar. But why did God give His people to be ruled by heathens?

I have made the earth, the man and the beast that *are* upon the ground, by My great power and by My outstretched arm, and have given it unto whom it seemed meet unto Me. And now have I given all these lands into the hand of Nebuchadnezzar the king of Babylon, My servant (Jeremiah 27:5-6).

The LORD had promised Abram "I will make of thee a great nation" (cf Genesis 12:1-2; 18:17-18). But the Jews repeatedly flourished for a season only to fall away after a while. When they rejected the LORD, He "afflicted her for the multitude of her transgressions: her children are gone into captivity before the enemy" (Lamentations 1:5). As a consequence of their refusing to obey God, "every reformation was followed by deeper apostasy" (DA 28.1).

God established the Jews as His chosen people. They were the guardians 1) of His Commandments (God's Law); 2) of His statutes that supplement the commandments; 3) of God's prophetic word and His health requirements that ensure a healthy lifestyle, longevity, and prosperity; and 4) of the world's Savior, who was to arise from among them.

God is love and longsuffering. Even though He wants to bless us more than we can receive, He will not compel anyone to obey Him! Nor will God continue to shower blessings upon His people if they choose to rebel against Him! The fact that God means and does what He says testifies that He is faithful to His word. This was evident in the fall of Judaism and the rise of Christianity: God turned from those who turn from Him to those who choose to follow Christ.

> "Not everyone that saith unto Me, Lord, Lord, shall enter into the kingdom of heaven; but he that doeth the will of My Father which is in heaven. Many will say to Me in that day, Lord, Lord, have we not prophesied in Thy name? and in Thy name have cast out devils? and in Thy name done many wonderful works? And then will I profess unto them, *I never knew you:* depart from Me, ye that work iniquity." "Whosoever shall not receive you, nor hear your words {i.e., The kingdom of heaven is at hand} ...It shall be more tolerable for the land of Sodom and Gomorrah in the day of judgment, than for that city" (cf Matthew 7:21-23; 10:7, 14-15).

> Except the LORD of hosts had left unto us a very small remnant, we should have been as Sodom, *and* we should have been like unto Gomorrah (Isaiah 1:9).

The Apostolic Church became God's chosen people after the Jews rejected Jesus. It eventually became synonymous with the Roman Church. After it was subjugated by the state, it was allotted 1260 years. During that time, Mohammed claimed that God chose Islam. Though the transition from Judaism to Christianity is biblical, God did not choose Islam. In spite of God's rejection of Ishmael, Muslims believe that his descendants were ordained to replace Christianity.

> Abraham said unto God, O that Ishmael might live before thee! And God said, Sarah thy wife shall bear thee

a son indeed; and thou shalt call his name Isaac: and I will establish My covenant with him for an everlasting covenant, and with his seed after him. And as for Ishmael, I have heard thee: Behold, I have blessed him, and will make him fruitful, and will multiply him exceedingly...and I will make him a great nation. *But My covenant will I establish with Isaac* (cf Genesis 17:18-21).

Abraham's early teachings had not been without effect upon Ishmael, but the influence of his wives resulted in establishing idolatry in his family... In his latter days he repented of his evil ways and returned to his father's God, but the stamp of character given to his posterity remained. *The powerful nation descended from him were a turbulent, heathen people...* (PP 174.1).

The principle that man can save himself by his own works lay at the foundation of every heathen religion; it had now become the principle of the Jewish religion. Satan had implanted this principle. Wherever it is held, men have no barrier against sin (DA 35.2).

Muslims believe in good works as the way to Heaven (http://www.justaskislam.com/23/salvation-in-islam/), and that Jesus was a prophet, but not as significant a prophet as Mohammad; and not the only begotten *Son of God*. Islam considers Christ's sacrificial death to be worthless; even denying that it happened. Like Judaism, they reject Christ while propagating their religion: "A YAZIDI sex slave has described how ISIS terrorists would tell the captives they had to rape them to convert them to Islam" (www.thesun.co.uk/news/4666880/yazidi-sex-slaves-tell-how-sick-isis-predators-raped-them-to-make-them-muslim/).

The book of Revelation states: "Babylon is fallen is fallen...because...of her fornication" (Revelation 14:8). "*The term Babylon, derived from Babel, and signifying confusion, is applied in Scripture to the various forms of false or apostate religion*" (4SP 232.2).

In the endtime, it may be difficult for people who believe in these three great religions or the Protestant Churches to see that they are part of spiritual Babylon: Apostate Religion. But even if the spiritual condition of these religions is concealed, the fornication scandals take away all doubt!

The Roman Church, eventually completely apostatized. It is identified in the endtimes by its fornicating priests' sex scandals. Many Protestant churches are now also embroiled in fornication scandals of their own as is Islam.

Today, Judaism is also linked to major sex scandals in America and Israel. Judaism rejected Jesus, the One who came, as God had promised: "The Lord Himself shall give you a sign; Behold, a virgin shall conceive, and bear a son, and shall call his name Immanuel" (Isaiah 7:14). "And she shall bring forth a son, and thou shalt call His name JESUS: for He shall save His people from their sins... Behold, a virgin shall be with child, and shall bring forth a son, and they shall call his name Emmanuel, which being interpreted is, God with us" (Matthew 1:21, 23). "For unto you is born this day ...a Saviour, which is Christ the Lord" (cf Luke 2:11). Jesus was the promised Messiah, the Christ.

Christ means *anointed*. It was prophesied of the Messiah, "Thou lovest righteousness, and hatest wickedness: therefore God, *Thy God, hath anointed Thee...*" (Psalm 45:7).

Jesus...asked... whom say ye that I am? And Simon Peter answered... *Thou art the Christ, the Son of the living God.* And Jesus answered and said... *flesh and blood hath not revealed it unto thee, but My Father which is in heaven* (cf Matthew 16:13-17).

Jesus saith...I am the Way, the Truth, and the Life: *No man cometh unto the Father, but by Me* (cf John 14:6).

He that receiveth Me receiveth Him that sent Me (Matthew 10:40).

Enter ye in at the strait gate: for wide is the gate, and broad is the way, that leadeth to destruction, and many there be which go in thereat: Because strait is the gate, and narrow is the way, which leadeth unto life, and few there be that find it (Matthew 7:13-14).

Jesus also warned of the importance of staying faithful. Failure has consequences. In a parable, Jesus forewarned:

He sent unto them his son ... They said among themselves, This is the heir; come, let us kill him... Therefore, say I unto you, The kingdom of God shall be taken from you, and given to a nation bringing forth the fruits thereof (Matthew 21:37, 38, 43).

The leaders of the Jews led them to reject Jesus: The One who is able to say, *Depart from Me, ye that work iniquity*!

They cried out, Away with Him, away with Him, crucify Him. Pilate saith unto them, Shall I crucify your King? The chief priests answered, We have no king but Caesar (John 19:15).

The Jews' rejection of Jesus (*God with us*, the One who *saves His people from their sins*) thrust them into Spiritual Babylon. They cut themselves off from the community of believers, as Christ had forewarned:

Many shall come from the east and west, and shall sit down with Abraham, and Isaac, and Jacob, in the kingdom of heaven. *But the children of the kingdom shall be cast out into outer darkness...*

Whosoever therefore shall confess Me before men, him will I confess also before My Father which is in heaven. But *whosoever shall deny Me before men, him will I also deny before My Father which is in heaven...*

All things are delivered unto Me of My Father: and no man knoweth the Son, but the Father; neither knoweth any man the Father, save the Son, and he to whomsoever the Son will reveal Him (cf Matthew 8:11-12; 10:32-33; 11:24).

Three and a half years after Christ's crucifixion, after the Jews rejected Jesus, disobeyed God's Commandments and His statutes, and yielded to worldly ambitions instead of Heaven centered goals, God appointed that the gospel go to the Gentiles. The Blessings that God had entrusted to the Jews were then bestowed upon the Christian Church.

And He said unto them, Go ye into all the world, and preach the gospel to every creature (Mark 16:15).

Thus, the Christian Church was set up by Christ. It took up His work on earth for the salvation of humanity. But all is not lost to the Jews:

The branches were broken off...because of unbelief... God spared not the natural branches...If they abide not still in unbelief, shall be grafted in: for God is able to graft them in again (cf Romans 11:19-23).

Until the Jews choose to be grafted back into God's Church, they remain part of Babylon. Thus, we must pray for Israel that they will return to God. But what about Christendom? It too has become part of spiritual Babylon.

In this scripture the announcement of the fall of Babylon, as made by the second angel, [Revelation 14:8.] is repeated, with the additional mention of the corruptions which have been entering the churches since 1844. *A terrible condition of the religious world is here described. With every rejection of truth, the minds of the people have become darker, their hearts more stubborn, until they are entrenched in an infidel hardihood. In defiance of the warnings which God has given, they continue to trample upon one of the precepts of the decalogue, and they persecute those who hold it sacred.* Christ is set at naught in the contempt placed upon his word and His people. As the teachings of Spiritualism are accepted by the churches, **no real restraint is imposed upon the carnal heart, and the profession of religion becomes a cloak to conceal the basest iniquity. A belief in spiritual manifestations opens the door to seducing spirits and doctrines of devils. The influence of evil angels is felt in the churches throughout the land** (4SP 421.2).

The uncontrolled indulgence and consequent disease and degradation that existed at Christ's first advent will again exist, with intensity of evil, before His Second Coming. Christ declares that the condition of the world will be as in the days before the Flood, and as in Sodom and Gomorrah. Every imagination of the thoughts of the heart will be evil continually. Upon the very verge of that fearful time we are now living, and to us should come home the lesson of the Saviour's fast. Only by the inexpressible anguish which Christ endured can we estimate the evil of unrestrained indulgence. His example declares that our only hope of eternal life is through bringing the appetites and passions into subjection to the will of God (DA 122.2).

Babylon is fallen: "Come out of her, My people, that ye be not partakers of her sins, and that ye receive not of her plagues (Revelation 18:4). Obey the command! Discern if your beloved church has become Babylon. *Flee from her*!

The prophecies of Daniel and of John are to be understood; they interpret each other. They give to the world truths which everyone should understand. These prophecies are to be witnesses in the world. *By their fulfillment in these last days, they will explain themselves* (PH135 5.1).

Daniel and Revelation are explaining themselves! Her fornications are headlining! There is no doubt: Fallen

Babylon is identified by her *fornication*. The Roman Catholic Church has obviously fallen as have Protestant churches!

Prophecy is being fulfilled today: Pope Benedict XVI's resignation linked to Babylon's priests' fornication scandal. How so? Prior to becoming Pope Benedict XVI, as Cardinal Joseph Ratzinger, he was authorized to "handle abuse cases directly," but he was "part of a culture of nonresponsibility, denial, legalistic foot-dragging and outright obstruction" (http://www.nytimes.com/2010/07/02/world/europe/02pope.html?pagewanted=all&_r=0).

He "leaves behind a Church grappling with a global fallout from sex abuse and a personal legacy marred by allegations that he was instrumental in covering up that abuse" (http://abcnews.go.com/Blotter/pope-benedicts-legacy-marred-sex-abuse-scandal/story?id=18466726).

He had known about the priests' fornications. Prior to becoming pope, Cardinal Ratzinger did not deal with this sin. As pope, his ritual usher was "implicated in a gay prostitution ring...on the heels of major pedophilia scandals involving the abuse of children by priests in Ireland, Germany and the United States" (http://www.nydailynews.com/news/world/sex-scandal-rocks-vatican-papal-usher-chorister-linked-gay-prostitution-ring-article-1.172149). His failure to correct the pedophile priests' overt fornications contradicted his pious profession of morality: "The Church cannot cease to proclaim that in accordance with God's plans (cf. Mt 19: 3-9), marriage and the family are irreplaceable and permit no other alternatives" (www.vatican.va/holy_father/benedict_xvi/letters/2005/documents/hf_ben-xvi_let_20050517_famiglia-valencia_en.html). Benedict XVI's reign ended in 2013 when the priests' sex scandal repeated the Second Angel's Message of Revelation 14: *Babylon is fallen because of her fornication!* Revelation 18 was fulfilled in 2013 when it repeated the message. The Roman church's priests' fornication identified her as fallen Babylon. God calls His people: *Come out of Babylon!*

There is no doubt that God is calling His people to flee fornicating Babylon. The Roman Catholic Church's blatant gay orgies cannot be denied (https://www.breitbart.com/

national-security/2017/07/06/vatican-police-raid-drug-in fused-gay-orgy-at-home-of-cardinals-aide/). Their fornication is ongoing: On 6 February 2019, Pope Francis I disclosed that Babylon's priests have been and may still be using nuns as sex slaves (www.nation.co.ke/news/world/ Pope-says-priests-kept-nuns-as-sex-slaves/1068-4969764-yoy24xz/ index.html). On 16 February, Francis defrocked Cardinal McCarrick for sexually abusing children and seminarians (https://jeffreysalkin.religionnews.com/2019/02/16/vatica n-defrocks-former-us-cardinal-mccarrick-over -sex-abuse/). On the 21st through the 24th, a global bishop's conference was convened by Pope Francis I to address the Roman Catholic Church's ongoing clergy sex abuse scandal (https://www.dosp.org/accountability/blog/protection-of-minors-in-the-church-meeting-in-the-vatican-to-be-held-february-21-24-2019/).

Babylon is the Roman Church and so much more. Protestant Churches must hear and heed God's command: Come out of her My people! But many of them are reuniting with the Roman Mother Church. Worse yet, many of them are approving and indulging in her fornication. The 12 June 2019 Southern Baptist Convention addressed sex abuse of boys by ministers in 750 of its churches (http:// bpnews.net/issue-06/12/2019).

As spiritual leaders led God's people away from Christ (the Light of the world) in His day, it is happening now in Protestant Churches. Because of the deception of Babylon's fornications, the Methodists, are on the verge of splitting (https://www.npr.org/2019/03/02/699506797/united-methodists-face-fractured-future).

Much of Christendom is setting Truth aside for the Roman Church's fornication and its doctrines of devils. Many people see nothing wrong with her or her doctrines in spite of the priests' blatant sexual fornication. God's word declares licentious heterosexuality and homosexuality is sin.

False teachings about abortion and the male priesthood are deceiving others. No one who understands the love of God wants to kill babies or deny the gender that God wired into them. Zealous to maintain a godly profession, many seek to compel others to yield their conscience to the will of a majority though compulsion abolishes freedom of choice!

So, it will be again. The authorities will make laws to restrict religious liberty. They will assume the right that is God's alone. They will think they can force the conscience, which God alone should control. Even now they are making a beginning; this work they will continue to carry forward till they reach a boundary over which they cannot step. God will interpose in behalf of His loyal, commandment-keeping people (DA 630.1).

Shall we exalt human wisdom, and point to finite, changeable, erring men as a dependence in time of trouble? Or shall we exemplify our faith by our trust in God's power, revealing the net of false theories, religions, and philosophies which Satan has spread to catch unwary souls? (SpTA06 30.1)

"There is no real standard of righteousness apart from God's law. By obedience to this law the intellect is strengthened, and the conscience is enlightened and made sensitive." We "need to gain a clear understanding of God's law." We "are not left to follow blindly the guidance of men. The great prophetic waymarks which God Himself has set up show the path of obedience to be the only path that can be followed with certainty" (YI, September 22, 1903 par. 8). Our salvation depends on a knowledge of the truth contained in the Scriptures. It is God's will that we should possess this. Search, O search the precious Bible with hungry hearts. Explore God's word... Never give up the search until you have ascertained your relation to God and His will in regard to you. Christ declared, "Whatsoever ye shall ask in My name, that will I do, that the Father may be glorified in the Son. If ye shall ask anything in My name, I will do it." John 14:13, 14 (COL 111.3).

God speaks in His word, and fulfills this word in the world. We need now to seek to understand the movements of God's providence. Said Paul, "Ye, brethren, are not in darkness, that that day should overtake you as a thief. Ye are all the children of light, and the children of the day: we are not of the night nor of darkness." God's people are not left to depend on man's wisdom. With prophetic guideposts God has marked out the way He wishes them to take. These great waymarks show us that the path of obedience is the only path we can follow with certainty. Men break their word, and prove themselves untrustworthy, but God changes not. His word will abide the same forever. Those who love and obey the law of Jehovah will meet with trial and temptation; but these are only what Jesus met, and He declares: "My sheep hear My voice, and I know them, and they follow Me: and I give unto them eternal life; and they shall never perish, neither shall any man pluck them out of My hand." If we hope and pray, and by faith trust His word, we shall be able to say, with Paul, "I am persuaded, that neither death nor life nor angels, nor principalities, nor powers, nor things present, nor things to come, nor height, nor depth, nor any other creature, shall be able to separate us from the love of God, which is in Christ Jesus our Lord" (Loyalty or Disloyalty? RH, Feb. 6, 1900 par. 11).

Daniel 1

¹In the third year of the reign of Jehoiakim king of Judah came Nebuchadnezzar king of Babylon unto Jerusalem, and besieged it. ²And the Lord gave Jehoiakim king of Judah into his hand, with part of the vessels of the house of God: which he carried into the land of Shinar to the house of his god; and he brought the vessels into the treasure house of his god.

³And the king spake unto Ashpenaz the master of his eunuchs, that he should bring [certain] of the children of Israel, and of the king's seed, and of the princes; ⁴Children in whom [was] no blemish, but well favored, and skillful in all wisdom, and cunning in knowledge, and understanding science, and such as [had] ability in them to stand in the king's palace, and whom they might teach the learning and the tongue of the Chaldeans. ⁵And the king appointed them a daily provision of the king's meat, and of the wine which he drank: so, nourishing them three years, that at the end thereof they might stand before the king.

⁶Now among these were of the children of Judah, Daniel, Hananiah, Mishael, and Azariah: ⁷Unto whom the prince of the eunuchs gave names: for he gave unto Daniel [the name] of Belteshazzar; and to Hananiah, of Shadrach; and to Mishael, of Meshach; and to Azariah, of Abednego. ⁸But Daniel purposed in his heart that he would not defile himself with the portion of the king's meat, nor with the wine which he drank: therefore, he requested of the prince of the eunuchs that he might not defile himself.

⁹Now God had brought Daniel into favor and tender love with the prince of the eunuchs. ¹⁰And the prince of the eunuchs said unto Daniel, I fear my lord the king, who hath appointed your meat and your drink: for why

should he see your faces worse liking than the children which [are] of your sort? then shall ye make [me] endanger my head to the king. ¹¹Then said Daniel to Melzar, whom the prince of the eunuchs had set over Daniel, Hananiah, Mishael, and Azariah, ¹²Prove thy servants, I beseech thee, ten days; and let them give us pulse to eat, and water to drink. ¹³Then let our countenances be looked upon before thee, and the countenance of the children that eat of the portion of the king's meat: and as thou seest, deal with thy servants. ¹⁴So he consented to them in this matter, and proved them ten days.

¹⁵And at the end of ten days their countenances appeared fairer and fatter in flesh than all the children which did eat the portion of the king's meat. ¹⁶Thus, Melzar took away the portion of their meat, and the wine that they should drink; and gave them pulse. ¹⁷As for these four children, God gave them knowledge and skill in all learning and wisdom: and Daniel had understanding in all visions and dreams.

¹⁸Now at the end of the days that the king had said he should bring them in, then the prince of the eunuchs brought them in before Nebuchadnezzar. ¹⁹And the king communed with them; and among them all was found none like Daniel, Hananiah, Mishael, and Azariah: therefore, stood they before the king. ²⁰And in all matters of wisdom [and] understanding, that the king inquired of them, he found them ten times better than all the magicians [and] astrologers that [were] in all his realm. ²¹And Daniel continued [even] unto the first year of king Cyrus.

Points to Ponder

1. The Lord gave the king and Judah to the Babylonians
2. Daniel's diet was important to God
3. Daniel continued until Cyrus ruled Babylon

God Gave Israel to Babylon

The dealings of God with His people should be often repeated. He has worked as a wonder-working God. He has baptized His chosen messengers with the Holy Spirit. The past history of the cause of God needs often to be brought before the people, young and old, that they may be familiar with it. How frequently were the waymarks set up by the Lord in His dealing with ancient Israel, lest they should forget the history of the past? (9MR 134.3)

God warned Israel that their *faithfulness* depended on their obedience. Consider His warning in Deuteronomy.

27:9O Israel; this day thou art become the people of the LORD thy God. 10Thou shalt therefore obey the voice of the LORD thy God, and do His commandments and His statutes, which I command thee this day...

28:1And it shall come to pass, if thou shalt hearken diligently unto the voice of the LORD thy God, to observe and to do all His commandments which I command thee this day, that the LORD thy God will set thee on high above all nations of the earth: 2And all these blessings shall come on thee, and overtake thee, if thou shalt hearken unto the voice of the LORD thy God...

9The LORD shall establish thee an holy people unto Himself, as He hath sworn unto thee, if thou shalt keep the commandments of the LORD thy God, and walk in His ways. 10And all people of the earth shall see that thou art called by the name of the LORD; and they shall be afraid of thee...

14And thou shalt not go aside from any of the words which I command thee this day, to the right hand, or to the left, to go after other gods to serve them. 15But it shall come to pass, if thou wilt not hearken unto the voice of the LORD thy God, to observe to do all His commandments and His statutes which I command thee this day; that all these curses shall come upon thee, and overtake thee...

20The LORD shall send upon thee cursing, vexation, and rebuke, in all that thou settest thine hand unto for to do, until thou be destroyed, and until thou perish quickly; because of the wickedness of thy doings, whereby thou hast forsaken Me...

45Moreover, all these curses shall come upon thee, and shall pursue thee, and overtake thee, till thou be destroyed; because thou hearkenedst not unto the voice of the LORD thy God, to keep His commandments and His statutes which He commanded thee: 46And they shall be upon thee for a sign and for a wonder, and upon thy seed forever. 47Because thou servedst not the LORD thy God with joyfulness, and with gladness of heart, for the abundance of all things; 48Therefore, shalt thou serve thine enemies which the LORD shall send against thee, in hunger, and in thirst, and in nakedness, and in want of all things: and He shall put a yoke of iron upon thy neck, until He have destroyed thee...

58If thou wilt not observe to do all the words of this law that are written in this book, that thou mayest fear this glorious and fearful name, THE LORD THY GOD; 59Then the LORD will make thy plagues wonderful, and the plagues of thy seed, even great plagues, and of long continuance, and sore sicknesses, and of long continuance. 60Moreover, He will bring upon thee all the diseases of Egypt, which thou wast afraid of; and they shall cleave unto thee. 61Also, every sickness, and every plague, which is not written in the book of this law, them will the LORD bring upon thee, until thou be destroyed. 62And ye shall be left few in number, whereas ye were as the stars of heaven for multitude; because thou wouldest not obey the voice of the LORD thy God...

63As the LORD rejoiced over you to do you good, and to multiply you; so, the LORD will rejoice over you to destroy you, and to bring you to nought; and ye shall be plucked from off the land whither thou goest...

29:1These are the words of the covenant, which the LORD commanded Moses to make with the children of Israel in the land of Moab, beside the covenant which He made with them in Horeb.

Read the entire warning (Deuteronomy 27-29) in a translation of your choosing. And see that *God is love and longsuffering.* But even though the Lord wants to bless more than we can receive, God faithfully keeps His word to bless, and to curse as seen at the Babylonian Captivity, the Roman destruction of Jerusalem, Judaism's replacement by Christianity, and even the Holocaust. They were not flukes!

God will not compel anyone to obey Him! Nor will He shower blessings upon people, who persist in rebellion! In spite of God's great love for Israel, He allowed those unspeakable chapters in their history. God's blessing and cursing of His chosen people, is an example that all nations and people must hear and heed. God's turning from those who turn from Him is a fact that Christianity will also soon encounter. We also have Noah's example: A profession of faith did not save anyone who did not enter the ark.

Therein shall be left a remnant that shall be brought forth, [both] sons and daughters: behold, they shall come forth unto you, and ye shall see their way and their doings: and ye shall be comforted concerning the evil that I have brought upon Jerusalem, [even] concerning all that I have brought upon it (Ezekiel 14:22).

Diet

Of Daniel and his fellows, the Scripture states: "As for these four children, God gave them knowledge and skill in all learning and wisdom: and Daniel had understanding in all visions and dreams." **In what manner are you fitting yourselves to co-operate with God? "Draw nigh to God, and He will draw nigh to you" "Resist the devil, and he will flee from you."** Let the diet be carefully studied; it is not healthful. The various little dishes concocted for desserts are injurious instead of helpful and healthful...there should be a decided change in the preparation of food... The dishes of soft foods, the soups and liquid foods, or the free use of meat, are not the best to give healthful muscles, sound digestive organs, or clear brains....The diet question is to be studied; no one person's appetite, or tastes, or fancy, or notion is to be followed; but there is need of great reform; for lifelong injury will surely be the result of the present manner of cooking... if this work is neglected, the mind will not be prepared to do its work, because the stomach has been treated unwisely and cannot do its work properly. Strong minds are needed. The human intellect must gain expansion and vigor and acuteness and activity. It must be taxed to do hard work, or it will become weak and inefficient. Brain power is required to think most earnestly; it must be put to the stretch to solve hard problems and master them; else the mind decreases in power and aptitude to think. The mind must invent, work, and wrestle, in order to give hardness and vigor to the intellect; and if the physical organs are not kept in the most healthful condition by substantial, nourishing food, the brain does not receive its portion of nutrition to work. Daniel understood this, and he brought himself to a plain, simple, nutritious diet, and refused the luxuries of the king's table. The desserts which take so much time to prepare, are, many of them, detrimental to health. Solid foods requiring mastication will be far better than mush or liquid foods... (SpTEd 187.1).

If our appetites are not under the control of a sanctified mind, if we are not temperate in all our eating and drinking, we shall not be in a state of mental and physical soundness to study the word with a purpose to learn what saith the Scripture... The diet has much to do with the disposition to enter into temptation and commit sin (CD 52.2).

Jesus authorized Peter, "Whatsoever thou shalt bind on earth shall be bound in heaven: and whatsoever thou shalt loose on earth shall be loosed in heaven" (Matthew 16:19), Then Peter refused to obey the command, "kill, and eat." Saying, "Not so, Lord; for I have never eaten anything that is common or unclean... This was done thrice: and the vessel was received up again into heaven" (Acts 10:13-16). Peter did not unbind unclean animals for food They went back to heaven bound. There is no reason for Christians to eat pigs.

Rather than to clean pigs for food, Jesus cast the devils into them. Paul taught that we, "cannot drink the cup of the Lord, and the cup of devils: ye cannot be partakers of the Lord's table, and of the table of devils" (1 Corinthians 10:21).

The devils besought Him, saying, If Thou cast us out, suffer us to go away into the herd of swine. And He said unto them, Go. And when they were come out, they went into the herd of swine (Mat 8:31-32; cf Mark 5:11-13; Luke 8:32-33).

The Reign of Cyrus

Jeremiah had prophesied, "After seventy years be accomplished at Babylon I will visit you...to return to this place" (Jeremiah 29:10).

Daniel was taken captive to Babylon in 605 BC. "Cyrus succeeded to the throne, and the beginning of his reign marked the completion of the seventy years" (PK 556.4). Though the 70 years of captivity prophesied by Jeremiah had ended in 535 BC when Cyrus' reign started, the Temple was in ruins, and the Jews had not returned to their homeland. The Lord had also said thru Jeremiah; "*I will bring them again into their land... first I will recompense their iniquity and their sin double"* (Jeremiah 16:15, 18). Thus, from 605, the 70 years ended in 535 BC and the seventy years doubled (140 years) ended in 465, King Artaxerxes ascension year.

Cyrus was a type of Christ. As he dried the Euphrates, conquered Babylon, and prepared the way for the kings from the East (Persian kings) to reign; Christ is prophesied to dry the Euphrates, to prepare the way for the kings of the east, and topple endtime spiritual Babylon (cf Revelation 16:12-19). In Daniel 2, Nebuchadnezzar was the *head of gold* that partially fulfilled the prophecy when his dynasty fell to Cyrus. This foreshadows Christ's eternal reign: The complete endtime final fulfillment of the vision in Daniel 2.

God's word is sure! Our understanding of it will increase, as the Holy Spirit continues to impress Present Truth upon our hearts. Bible prophecies confirm that God is all-knowing. Our increased understanding of the mysteries that have been hidden in plain sight for centuries will strengthen our faith and trust in our Omniscient all-loving Creator. The apostle Paul refers to "the ministers of Christ" as "stewards of the mysteries of God," and of their work he declares: "It is required in stewards, that a man be found faithful" (cf 1 Corinthians 4:1-5). Jesus promises His faithful followers:

> Unto you it is given to know the mysteries of the kingdom of God: but to others in parables; that seeing they might not see, and hearing they might not understand (Luke 8:10).

Daniel 2

¹And in the second year of the reign of Nebuchadnezzar, Nebuchadnezzar dreamed dreams, wherewith his spirit was troubled, and his sleep brake from him. ²Then the king commanded to call the magicians, and the astrologers, and the sorcerers, and the Chaldeans, for to show the king his dreams. So, they came and stood before the king. ³And the king said unto them, I have dreamed a dream, and my spirit was troubled to know the dream.

⁴Then spake the Chaldeans to the king in Syriack, O king, live forever: tell thy servants the dream, and we will show the interpretation. ⁵The king answered and said to the Chaldeans, The thing is gone from me: if ye will not make known unto me the dream, with the interpretation thereof, ye shall be cut in pieces, and your houses shall be made a dunghill. ⁶But if ye show the dream, and the interpretation thereof, ye shall receive of me gifts and rewards and great honour: therefore, show me the dream, and the interpretation thereof.

⁷They answered again and said, Let the king tell his servants the dream, and we will show the interpretation of it. ⁸The king answered and said, I know of certainty that ye would gain the time, because ye see the thing is gone from me. ⁹But if ye will not make known unto me the dream, [there is but] one decree for you: for ye have prepared lying and corrupt words to speak before me, till the time be changed: therefore tell me the dream, and I shall know that ye can show me the interpretation thereof.

¹⁰The Chaldeans answered before the king, and said, There is not a man upon the earth that can show the king's matter: therefore [there is] no king, lord, nor ruler, [that] asked such things at any magician, or astrologer,

or Chaldean. [11]And [it is] a rare thing that the king requires, and there is none other that can show it before the king, except the gods, whose dwelling is not with flesh. [12]For this cause the king was angry and very furious, and commanded to destroy all the wise [men] of Babylon. [13]And the decree went forth that the wise [men] should be slain; and they sought Daniel and his fellows to be slain.

[14]Then Daniel answered with counsel and wisdom to Arioch the captain of the king's guard, which was gone forth to slay the wise [men] of Babylon: [15]He answered and said to Arioch the king's captain, Why [is] the decree [so] hasty from the king? Then Arioch made the thing known to Daniel. [16]Then Daniel went in, and desired of the king that he would give him time, and that he would show the king the interpretation.

[17]Then Daniel went to his house, and made the thing known to Hananiah, Mishael, and Azariah, his companions: [18]That they would desire mercies of the God of heaven concerning this secret; that Daniel and his fellows should not perish with the rest of the wise [men] of Babylon.

[19]Then was the secret revealed unto Daniel in a night vision. Then Daniel blessed the God of heaven. [20]Daniel answered and said, Blessed be the name of God for ever and ever: for wisdom and might are His: [21]And He changeth the times and the seasons: He removeth kings, and setteth up kings: He giveth wisdom unto the wise, and knowledge to them that know understanding: [22]He revealeth the deep and secret things: He knoweth what [is] in the darkness, and the light dwelleth with Him.

[23]I thank Thee, and praise Thee, O Thou God of my fathers, who hast given me wisdom and might, and hast made known unto me now what we desired of Thee: for Thou hast [now] made known unto us the king's matter.

²⁴Therefore Daniel went in unto Arioch, whom the king had ordained to destroy the wise [men] of Babylon: he went and said thus unto him; Destroy not the wise [men] of Babylon: bring me in before the king, and I will show unto the king the interpretation. ²⁵Then Arioch brought in Daniel before the king in haste, and said thus unto him, I have found a man of the captives of Judah, that will make known unto the king the interpretation.

²⁶The king answered and said to Daniel, whose name [was] Belteshazzar, Art thou able to make known unto me the dream which I have seen, and the interpretation thereof? ²⁷Daniel answered in the presence of the king, and said, The secret which the king hath demanded cannot the wise [men], the astrologers, the magicians, the soothsayers, show unto the king; ²⁸But there is a God in heaven that revealeth secrets, and maketh known to the king Nebuchadnezzar what shall be in the latter days. Thy dream, and the visions of thy head upon thy bed, are these; ²⁹As for thee, O king, thy thoughts came [into thy mind] upon thy bed, what should come to pass hereafter: and He that revealeth secrets maketh known to thee what shall come to pass. ³⁰But as for me, this secret is not revealed to me for [any] wisdom that I have more than any living, but for [their] sakes that shall make known the interpretation to the king, and that thou mightest know the thoughts of thy heart.

³¹Thou, O king, sawest, and behold a great image. This great image, whose brightness [was] excellent, stood before thee; and the form thereof [was] terrible. ³²This image's head [was] of fine gold, his breast and his arms of silver, his belly and his thighs of brass, ³³His legs of iron, his feet part of iron and part of clay. ³⁴Thou sawest till that a stone was cut out without hands, which smote the image upon his feet [that were] of iron and clay, and brake them to pieces. ³⁵Then was the iron, the clay, the brass, the silver, and the gold, broken to pieces together, and became like the chaff of the summer threshingfloors;

and the wind carried them away, that no place was found for them: and the stone that smote the image became a great mountain, and filled the whole earth. 36This [is] the dream; and we will tell the interpretation thereof before the king.

37Thou, O king, [art] a king of kings: for the God of heaven hath given thee a kingdom, power, and strength, and glory. 38And wheresoever the children of men dwell, the beasts of the field and the fowls of the heaven hath He given into thine hand, and hath made thee ruler over them all. Thou [art] this head of gold. 39And after thee shall arise another kingdom inferior to thee, and another third kingdom of brass, which shall bear rule over all the earth. 40And the fourth kingdom shall be strong as iron: forasmuch as iron breaketh in pieces and subdueth all [things]: and as iron that breaketh all these, shall it break in pieces and bruise. 41And whereas thou sawest the feet and toes, part of potters' clay, and part of iron, the kingdom shall be divided; but there shall be in it of the strength of the iron, forasmuch as thou sawest the iron mixed with miry clay. 42And [as] the toes of the feet [were] part of iron, and part of clay, [so] the kingdom shall be partly strong, and partly broken. 43And whereas thou sawest iron mixed with miry clay, they shall mingle themselves with the seed of men: but they shall not cleave one to another, even as iron is not mixed with clay.

44And in the days of these kings shall the God of heaven set up a kingdom, which shall never be destroyed: and the kingdom shall not be left to other people, [but] it shall break in pieces and consume all these kingdoms, and it shall stand for ever. 45Forasmuch as thou sawest that the stone was cut out of the mountain without hands, and that it brake in pieces the iron, the brass, the clay, the silver, and the gold; the great God hath made known to the king what shall come to pass hereafter: and the dream [is] certain, and the interpretation thereof sure.

46Then the king Nebuchadnezzar fell upon his face, and worshipped Daniel, and commanded that they should offer an oblation and sweet odors unto him. 47The king answered unto Daniel, and said, Of a truth [it is], that your God [is] a God of gods, and a Lord of kings, and a revealer of secrets, seeing thou couldest reveal this secret. 48Then the king made Daniel a great man, and gave him many great gifts, and made him ruler over the whole province of Babylon, and chief of the governors over all the wise [men] of Babylon. 49Then Daniel requested of the king, and he set Shadrach, Meshach, and Abednego, over the affairs of the province of Babylon: but Daniel [sat] in the gate of the king.

Points to Ponder

1. God inspired the king's dream
2. Only the God who inspired the dream could reveal it
3. God revealed to Daniel the dream and its interpretation
4. The dream related to King Nebuchadnezzar personally
5. The interpretation is significant for future generations
6. The meaning of the dream was sealed until the last days
7. Earth's wisest men cannot understand the dream

Inspired Dreams

The secret [things belong] unto the LORD our God: but those [things which are] revealed [belong] unto us and to our children forever, that [we] may do all the words of this law (Deuteronomy 29:29).

God inspired King Nebuchadnezzar's dream to give him instruction. God had worked that way previously as well.

The dream of Pharaoh [is] one: God hath showed Pharaoh what He [is] about to do (cf Genesis 41).

1If there arise among you a prophet, or a dreamer of dreams, and giveth thee a sign or a wonder, 2And the sign or the wonder come to pass, whereof he spake unto thee, saying, Let us go after other gods, which thou hast not known, and let us serve them; ³Thou shalt not hearken unto the words of that prophet, or that dreamer of dreams: for the LORD your God proveth you, to know whether ye love the LORD your God with all your heart and with all your soul. ⁴Ye shall walk after the LORD your God, and fear Him, and keep His commandments, and obey His voice, and ye shall serve Him, and cleave unto Him. ⁵And that prophet, or that dreamer of dreams, shall be put to death; because he hath spoken to turn [you] away from the LORD your God, which…redeemed you…to thrust thee out of the way which the LORD thy God commanded thee to walk in (Deuteronomy 13:1-5).

There will be counterfeit messages coming from persons in all directions. One after another will rise up, appearing to be inspired, when they have not the inspiration of heaven, but are under the deception of the enemy. All who receive their messages will be led astray. Then let us walk carefully, and not open wide the door for the enemy to enter through impressions, dreams, and visions. God help us to look in faith to Jesus, and *be guided by the words He has spoken* (3SM 404.4).

There are also false dreams, as well as false visions, which are inspired by the spirit of Satan. But dreams from the Lord are classed in the word of God with visions and are as truly the fruits of the spirit of prophecy as visions. Such dreams, taking into the account the persons who have them, and *the circumstances under which they are given, contain their own proofs of their genuineness* (1T 569.2).

False dreams and false visions, which have some truth, but lead away from the original faith. The Lord has given men a rule by which to detect them: "To the law and to the testimony: if they speak not according to this word, it is because there is no light in them" (Isaiah 8:20). If they belittle the law of God, if they pay no heed to His will as revealed in the testimonies of His Spirit, they are deceivers. They are controlled by impulse and impressions, which they believe to be from the Holy Spirit, and consider more reliable than the Inspired Word. They claim that every thought and feeling is an impression of the Spirit; and when they are reasoned with out of the Scriptures, they declare that they have something more reliable. But while they think that they are led by the Spirit of God, they are in reality following an imagination wrought upon by Satan (2SM 98.3).

The spurious must be a close imitation of the genuine, else it would not be a counterfeit (14MR 190.3).

Truth

Daniel was a devoted servant of the Most High. His long life was filled up with noble deeds of service for his Master. His purity of character, and unwavering fidelity, are equaled only by his humility of heart and his contrition before God... The life of Daniel is an inspired illustration of true sanctification (RH, February 8, 1881 par. 33).

The agencies which will unite against truth and righteousness in this contest are now actively at work. God's holy Word, which has been handed down to us at such a cost of suffering and blood, is but little valued. The Bible is within the reach of all, but there are few who really accept it as the guide of life. Infidelity prevails to an alarming extent, not in the world merely, but in the church. Many have come to deny doctrines which are the very pillars of the Christian faith. The great facts of creation as presented by the inspired writers, the fall of man, the atonement, and the perpetuity of the law of God, are practically rejected, either wholly or in part, by a large share of the professedly Christian world. Thousands who pride themselves upon their wisdom and independence regard it an evidence of weakness to place implicit confidence in the Bible; they think it a proof of superior talent and learning to cavil at the Scriptures, and to spiritualize and explain away their most important truths. Many ministers...professors and teachers are instructing... that the law of God has been changed or abrogated; and those who regard its requirements as still valid, to be literally obeyed, are thought to be deserving only of ridicule or contempt (GC88 582.3).

It is the nobler work to build up; to present the truth in its force and power, and let it cut its way through prejudice, and reveal error in contrast with truth (20MR 136.3).

In every place God is working to bring men to a knowledge of Christ and His righteousness. He speaks to them in His Word. The Bible is the key that unlocks the mysteries which it is essential for human beings to understand in order to know what they must do to gain eternal life. The Bible is its own expositor. Its bright beams are to shine into all parts of the world, that sin may be revealed. The Bible is a chart, pointing out the waymarks of truth. Those who are acquainted with this chart will be enabled to tread with certainty the path of duty, wherever they may be called to go (7MR 236.2).

Daniel Interprets

The prophetic events related in Nebuchadnezzar's dream [Daniel 2] were of consequence to him, but the dream was taken from him in order that the wise men should not place upon it a false interpretation. *The lessons taught by the dream were given by God for those who live in our day. The inability of the wise men to tell the dream is a representation of the limitations of the wise men of the present day, who, not having wisdom and discernment from the Most High, are unable to understand the prophecies* (YI, Nov 24, 1903 par. 1).

The words, "Thou art this head of gold," had made a deep impression upon the ruler's mind (PK 504.1).

Jeremiah had prophesied of Nebuchadnezzar's dynasty that he, Evil-Merodach, and Belshazzar were to reign until God's judgment was to come upon Babylon. "All nations shall serve him, and his son, and his son's son, until the very time of his land come" (Jeremiah 27:7, cf 4-11). When Daniel told Nebuchadnezzar: *You are this head of gold*, this statement aligned him and his dynasty with Jeremiah. But since the translators rendered *malkuw* as kingdom in Daniel 2, the link to his dynasty is not clear: "After thee shall arise another *kingdom* [*malkuw* H4437] *inferior* [*ara* H772] to thee, and another third [*malkuw*] of brass, which shall bear rule over all the *ara*" (Daniel 2:39). Nebuchadnezzar's dynasty would have been obvious had *malkuw* been rendered *kingly throne* (as in 5:20), *realm* (6:3), or *reign* (6:28). But because the translators had the four kingdoms interpretation in mind based on their common understanding, they translated chapter 2 in accordance with that view that had been established in the 1500's before Daniel 2 and 7 were unsealed: "Everyone agrees on this view and interpretation. Subsequent events and the histories, prove it conclusively." (http://www.historicism.net/readingmaterials/loiatp.pdf).

Of course, their interpretation is not wrong, but it hides the truth that God had placed in His word in favor of another truth. The concealing of the application to Nebuchadnezzar's dynasty was ordained of God for He had commanded: "O Daniel, shut up the words, and seal the book, *even* to the time of the end: many shall run to and fro, and knowledge shall be increased... Go thy way, Daniel: for the words *are* closed up and sealed till the time of the end" (Da 12:4, 9).

God's command to seal Daniel was fulfilled by the translators' word choices. As Truth seals a statement's validity, a meaning can be sealed/hidden until a later date. Long *before the book of Daniel was opened and unsealed, the meaning that was understood, sealed its authenticity*. Daniel 2 was partially understood. The prophecy was expanded in

Daniel 7. When Daniel was opened and is unsealed in the endtime, knowledge increased!

> After thee shall arise another *reign* of your *land*, and another third *reign* of brass, which shall bear rule over all your *land* (Daniel 2:39, alternate).

While Daniel was sealed (before knowledge increased), the truth about Nebuchadnezzar's dynasty was hidden. This truth is for the endtime when Daniel is opened.

> As we near the close of this world's history, the prophecies recorded by Daniel demand our special attention, *as they relate to the very time in which we are living.* With them should be linked the teachings of the last book of the New Testament Scriptures. Satan has led many to believe that *the prophetic portions of the writings of Daniel and of John the revelator* cannot be understood. But the promise is plain that special blessing will accompany the study of these prophecies. "The wise shall understand" [Daniel 12:10], was spoken of the visions of Daniel that were to be unsealed in the latter days (PK 547.2).

"And in the days of these kings shall the God of heaven set up a kingdom [*reign*], which shall never be destroyed: and the kingdom [*reign*] shall not be left to other people, [but] it shall break in pieces and consume all these kingdoms [*reigns*], and it shall stand for ever" (2:44). The translators did not know that this statement about Cyrus foreshadowed endtime events because his kingdom was not an *eternal kingdom.* They naturally thought that the vision referred to the kings of the final kingdoms that exist at Christ's Advent. But earth's final kingdoms and Nebuchadnezzar's dynasty do not completely fulfill the conditions within Daniel 2. As King Nebuchadnezzar's dynasty was not replaced by an eternal kingdom when Cyrus toppled it; the four great kingdoms do not coexist to be: *broken to pieces together* (2:35) or *crushed all at the same time* (NASB). Thus, the primary focus on

Daniel 2 is another meaning that is to be revealed when knowledge increases in the endtime!

Those who will not accept the light in regard to the law of God will not understand the proclamation of the first, second, and third angel's messages. *The book of Daniel is unsealed in the revelation to John,* and carries us forward to the last scenes of this earth's history (TM 115.3).

Satan was leading very many to look far in the future for the great events connected with the judgment and the end of probation. It was necessary that the people be brought to seek earnestly for a present preparation (EW 246.2).

Daniel has been standing in his lot since the seal was removed and the light of truth has been shining upon his visions. He stands in his lot, bearing the testimony which was *to be understood at the end of the days* (1SAT 225.5).

Daniel 3

¹Nebuchadnezzar the king made an image of gold, whose height [was] threescore cubits, [and] the breadth thereof six cubits: he set it up in the plain of Dura, in the province of Babylon. ²Then Nebuchadnezzar the king sent to gather together the princes, the governors, and the captains, the judges, the treasurers, the counsellors, the sheriffs, and all the rulers of the provinces, to come to the dedication of the image which Nebuchadnezzar the king had set up. ³Then the princes, the governors, and captains, the judges, the treasurers, the counsellors, the sheriffs, and all the rulers of the provinces, were gathered together unto the dedication of the image that Nebuchadnezzar the king had set up; and they stood before the image that Nebuchadnezzar had set up.

⁴Then an herald cried aloud, To you it is commanded, O people, nations, and languages, ⁵[That] at what time ye hear the sound of the cornet, flute, harp, sackbut, psaltery, dulcimer, and all kinds of music, ye fall down and worship the golden image that Nebuchadnezzar the king hath set up: ⁶And whoso falleth not down and worshippeth shall the same hour be cast into the midst of a burning fiery furnace. ⁷Therefore at that time, when all the people heard the sound of the cornet, flute, harp, sackbut, psaltery, and all kinds of music, all the people, the nations, and the languages, fell down [and] worshipped the golden image that Nebuchadnezzar the king had set up.

⁸Wherefore at that time certain Chaldeans came near, and accused the Jews. ⁹They spake and said to the king Nebuchadnezzar, O king, live forever. ¹⁰Thou, O king, hast made a decree, that every man that shall hear the sound of the cornet, flute, harp, sackbut, psaltery, and dulcimer, and all kinds of music, shall fall down and worship the golden image: ¹¹And whoso falleth not down

and worshippeth, [that] he should be cast into the midst of a burning fiery furnace. 12There are certain Jews whom thou hast set over the affairs of the province of Babylon, Shadrach, Meshach, and Abednego; these men, O king, have not regarded thee: they serve not thy gods, nor worship the golden image which thou hast set up. 13Then Nebuchadnezzar in [his] rage and fury commanded to bring Shadrach, Meshach, and Abednego. Then they brought these men before the king.

14Nebuchadnezzar spake and said unto them, [Is it] true, O Shadrach, Meshach, and Abednego, do not ye serve my gods, nor worship the golden image which I have set up? 15Now if ye be ready that at what time ye hear the sound of the cornet, flute, harp, sackbut, psaltery, and dulcimer, and all kinds of music, ye fall down and worship the image which I have made; [well]: but if ye worship not, ye shall be cast the same hour into the midst of a burning fiery furnace; and who [is] that God that shall deliver you out of my hands?

16Shadrach, Meshach, and Abednego, answered and said to the king, O Nebuchadnezzar, we [are] not careful to answer thee in this matter. 17If it be [so], our God whom we serve is able to deliver us from the burning fiery furnace, and He will deliver [us] out of thine hand, O king. 18But if not, be it known unto thee, O king, that we will not serve thy gods, nor worship the golden image which thou hast set up.

19Then was Nebuchadnezzar full of fury, and the form of his visage was changed against Shadrach, Meshach, and Abednego: [therefore] he spake, and commanded that they should heat the furnace one seven times more than it was wont to be heated. 20And he commanded the most mighty men that [were] in his army to bind Shadrach, Meshach, and Abednego, [and] to cast [them] into the burning fiery furnace. 21Then these men were bound in their coats, their hosen, and their hats, and their [other] garments, and were cast into the midst of the burning fiery furnace. 22Therefore because the king's commandment was urgent, and the furnace exceeding hot, the flame of the fire slew those men that took up Shadrach, Meshach, and Abednego. 23And these three men, Shadrach, Meshach, and Abednego, fell down bound into the midst of the burning fiery furnace.

24Then Nebuchadnezzar the king was astonied, and rose up in haste, [and] spake, and said unto his counsellors, Did not we cast three men bound into the midst of the fire? They answered and said unto the king, True, O king. 25He answered and said, Lo, I see four men loose, walking in the midst of the fire, and they have no hurt; and the form of the fourth is like the Son of God. 26Then Nebuchadnezzar came near to the mouth of the burning fiery furnace, [and] spake, and said, Shadrach, Meshach, and Abednego, ye servants of the Most High God, come forth, and come [hither]. Then Shadrach, Meshach, and Abednego, came forth of the midst of the fire. 27And the princes, governors, and captains, and the king's counsellors, being gathered together, saw these men, upon whose bodies the fire had no power, nor was an hair of their head singed, neither were their coats changed, nor the smell of fire had passed on them.

28[Then] Nebuchadnezzar spake, and said, Blessed [be] the God of Shadrach, Meshach, and Abednego, who hath sent his angel, and delivered his servants that trusted in him, and have changed the king's word, and yielded their bodies, that they might not serve nor worship any god, except their own God. 29Therefore I make a decree, That every people, nation, and language, which speak anything amiss against the God of Shadrach, Meshach, and Abednego, shall be cut in pieces, and their houses shall be made a dunghill: because there is no other God that can deliver after this sort. 30Then the king promoted Shadrach, Meshach, and Abednego, in the province of Babylon.

Points to Ponder

1. The gold idol defied God's specific revelation in Daniel 2
2. By their faithfulness to God, they defied the king
3. God delivered His three faithful servants from death
4. Men died in their place when God' delivered His servants
5. King Nebuchadnezzar acknowledged God's supremacy

The Idol

Was the idol entirely of gold or merely clad in gold? It was an impressive priceless statue.

> From his rich store of treasure, Nebuchadnezzar caused to be made a great golden image, similar in its general features to that which had been seen in vision, save in the one particular of the material of which it was composed. Accustomed as they were to magnificent representations of their heathen deities, the Chaldeans had never before produced anything so imposing and majestic as this resplendent statue, threescore cubits in height and six cubits in breadth. And it is not surprising that in a land where idol worship was of universal prevalence, the beautiful and priceless image in the plain of Dura, representing the glory of Babylon and its magnificence and power, should be consecrated as an object of worship... A decree went forth that on the day of the dedication all should show their supreme loyalty to the Babylonian power by bowing before the image (PK 505.2).

Idolatry competes with God. The Lord wins.

> 2The LORD of hosts [is] His name. 3I have declared the former things from the beginning; and they went forth out of My mouth, and I showed them; I did [them] suddenly, and they came to pass...5I have even from the beginning declared [it] to thee; before it came to pass I showed [it] thee: lest thou shouldest say, Mine idol hath

done them, and my graven image, and my molten image, hath commanded them (Isaiah 48:2, 3, 5).

Manasseh...set a carved image, the idol which he had made, in the house of God, of which God had said to David and to Solomon his son, In this house, and in Jerusalem, which I have chosen before all the tribes of Israel, will I put my name for ever... Then Manasseh knew that the LORD He [was] God... And he took away the strange gods, and the idol out of the house of the LORD (cf 2 Chronicles 33:1, 7, 13, 15, 16).

The Holy Spirit transported Ezekiel to Jerusalem. He saw that an idol had been placed in the Temple "toward the north, and behold northward at the gate of the altar this image of jealousy in the entry (cf Ezekiel 8:3-5).

The Faithful Are Delivered

In ancient Israel and thru the generations that followed, God saved His people. He will do it until the end of time!

When they relied upon Him, not trusting to their own power, the mighty General of armies was faithful to Israel. He delivered them from many difficulties from which they could never have escaped, if left to themselves. God was able to manifest His great power through Moses because of his constant faith in the power and in the loving intentions of their Deliverer. It was this implicit faith in God that made Moses what he was. According to all that the Lord commanded him, so did he. All the learning of the wise men could not make him *a channel through which the Lord could labor, however, until he lost his self-confidence, realized his own helplessness, and put his trust in God; until he was willing to obey God's commands whether they seemed to his human reason to be proper or not* (FE 344.2).

By the deliverance of His faithful servants, the Lord declared that He takes His stand with the oppressed, and rebukes all earthly powers that rebel against the authority of Heaven. The three Hebrews declared to the whole nation of Babylon their faith in Him whom they worshiped. They relied on God. In the hour of their trial they remembered the promise, "When thou passest through the waters, I will be with thee; and through the rivers, they shall not overflow thee: when thou walkest through the fire, thou shalt not be burned; neither shall the flame kindle upon thee." Isaiah 43:2. And in a marvelous manner their faith in the living Word had been honored in the sight of all. The tidings of their wonderful deliverance were carried to many countries by the representatives of the different nations that had been invited by Nebuchadnezzar to the dedication. Through the faithfulness of His children, God was glorified in all the earth (PK 511.1).

The three worthies endured the fiery furnace, for Jesus walked with them in the fiery flame. If they had, of themselves, walked into the fire, they would have been consumed. Thus, will it be with you. If you do not walk deliberately into temptation, God will sustain you when the temptation comes (3T 47.2).

Falling back into idolatrous habits, he [the king] was again, by the miraculous deliverance of the three Hebrews from the fiery furnace, led to acknowledge that God's "kingdom is an everlasting kingdom, and His dominion is from generation to generation." (YI, Oct 11, 1904 par. 6).

If Christians would earnestly search the scriptures more hearts would burn with the vivid truths therein revealed. Their hopes would brighten with the precious promises strewn like pearls all along through the sacred writings. In contemplating the history of patriarchs and prophets, the men who loved and feared God and walked with Him, hearts will glow with the spirit that animated these worthies. *As the mind dwells on the virtue and piety of holy men of old, the spirit which inspired them will kindle a flame of love and holy fervor in the hearts of those who would be like them in character, and as they gather the golden truth from the word, the heavenly Instructor is close by their side* (WM Herald, October 26, 1904 par. 13).

Here is where the work of the Holy Ghost comes in, after your baptism. You are baptized in the name of the Father, of the Son, and of the Holy Ghost. You are raised up out of the water to live henceforth in newness of life--to live a new life. *You are born unto God, and you stand under the sanction and the power of the three holiest beings in heaven, who are able to keep you from falling.* You are to reveal that you are dead to sin; your life is hid with Christ in God. Hidden "with Christ in God,"-- wonderful transformation (7MR 267.2).

Noah had faithfully warned the inhabitants of the antediluvian world, while they had mocked and derided him. And as the waters descended upon the earth, and one after another was drowning, they beheld that ark, of which they had made so much sport, riding safely upon the waters, preserving the faithful Noah and His family. So, I saw that the people of God, who had faithfully warned the world of His coming wrath, would be delivered. God would not suffer the wicked to destroy those who were expecting translation and who would not bow to the decree of the beast or receive his mark... Those who have mocked at the idea of the saints' going up will witness the care of God for His people and behold their glorious deliverance (EW 284.1).

I heard the voice of God, which shook the heavens and the earth. There was a mighty earthquake. Buildings were shaken down on every side. I then heard a triumphant shout of victory, loud, musical, and clear. I looked upon the company, who, a short time before, were in such distress and bondage. Their captivity was turned. A glorious light shone upon them. How beautiful they then looked! All marks of care and weariness were gone, and health and beauty were seen in every countenance. Their enemies, the heathen around them, fell like dead men; they could not endure the light that shone upon the delivered, holy ones. This light and glory remained upon them, until Jesus was seen in the clouds of heaven, and the faithful, tried company were changed in a moment, in the twinkling of an eye, from glory to glory. And the graves were opened, and the saints came forth, clothed with immortality, crying, "Victory over death and the grave"; and together with the living saints they were caught up to meet their Lord in the air, while rich, musical shouts of glory and victory were upon every immortal tongue (EW 272.3).

Daniel 4

¹Nebuchadnezzar the king, unto all people, nations, and languages, that dwell in all the earth; Peace be multiplied unto you. ²I thought it good to show the signs and wonders that the high God hath wrought toward me. ³How great [are] His signs! and how mighty [are] His wonders! His kingdom [is] an everlasting kingdom, and His dominion [is] from generation to generation.

⁴I Nebuchadnezzar was at rest in mine house, and flourishing in my palace: ⁵I saw a dream which made me afraid, and the thoughts upon my bed and the visions of my head troubled me. ⁶Therefore made I a decree to bring in all the wise [men] of Babylon before me, that they might make known unto me the interpretation of the dream. ⁷Then came in the magicians, the astrologers, the Chaldeans, and the soothsayers: and I told the dream before them; but they did not make known unto me the interpretation thereof. ⁸But at the last Daniel came in before me, whose name [was] Belteshazzar, according to the name of my god, and in whom [is] the spirit of the holy gods: and before him I told the dream, [saying], ⁹O Belteshazzar, master of the magicians, because I know that the spirit of the holy gods [is] in thee, and no secret troubleth thee, tell me the visions of my dream that I have seen, and the interpretation thereof.

¹⁰Thus [were] the visions of mine head in my bed; I saw, and behold, a tree in the midst of the earth, and the height thereof [was] great. ¹¹The tree grew, and was strong, and the height thereof reached unto heaven, and the sight thereof to the end of all the earth: ¹²The leaves thereof [were] fair, and the fruit thereof much, and in it [was] meat for all: the beasts of the field had shadow under it, and the fowls of the heaven dwelt in the boughs thereof, and all flesh was fed of it. ¹³I saw in the visions of my head upon my bed, and, behold, a watcher and an

holy one came down from heaven; 14He cried aloud, and said thus, Hew down the tree, and cut off his branches, shake off his leaves, and scatter his fruit: let the beasts get away from under it, and the fowls from his branches: 15Nevertheless leave the stump of his roots in the earth, even with a band of iron and brass, in the tender grass of the field; and let it be wet with the dew of heaven, and [let] his portion [be] with the beasts in the grass of the earth: 16Let his heart be changed from man's, and let a beast's heart be given unto him: and let seven times pass over him. 17This matter [is] by the decree of the watchers, and the demand by the word of the holy ones: to the intent that the living may know that the Most High ruleth in the kingdom of men, and giveth it to whomsoever he will, and setteth up over it the basest of men.

18This dream I king Nebuchadnezzar have seen. Now thou, O Belteshazzar, declare the interpretation thereof, forasmuch as all the wise [men] of my kingdom are not able to make known unto me the interpretation: but thou [art] able; for the spirit of the holy gods [is] in thee. 19Then Daniel, whose name [was] Belteshazzar, was astonied for one hour, and his thoughts troubled him. The king spake, and said, Belteshazzar, let not the dream, or the interpretation thereof, trouble thee. Belteshazzar answered and said, My lord, the dream [be] to them that hate thee, and the interpretation thereof to thine enemies.

20The tree that thou sawest, which grew, and was strong, whose height reached unto the heaven, and the sight thereof to all the earth; 21Whose leaves [were] fair, and the fruit thereof much, and in it [was] meat for all; under which the beasts of the field dwelt, and upon whose branches the fowls of the heaven had their habitation: 22It [is] thou, O king, that art grown and become strong: for thy greatness is grown, and reacheth unto heaven, and thy dominion to the end of the earth. 23And whereas the king saw a watcher and an holy one coming down from heaven, and saying, Hew the tree down, and destroy it; yet leave the stump of the roots thereof in the earth, even with a band of iron and brass, in the tender grass of the field; and let it be wet with the dew of heaven, and [let] his portion [be] with the beasts of the field, till seven times pass over him.

24This [is] the interpretation, O king, and this [is] the decree of the Most High, which is come upon my lord the king: 25That they shall drive thee from men, and thy dwelling shall be with the beasts of the field, and they shall make thee to eat grass as oxen, and they shall wet thee with the dew of heaven, and seven times shall pass over thee, till thou know that the Most High ruleth in the kingdom of men, and giveth it to whomsoever He will. 26And whereas they commanded to leave the stump of the tree roots; thy kingdom shall be sure unto thee, after that thou shalt have known that the heavens do rule.

27Wherefore, O king, let my counsel be acceptable unto thee, and break off thy sins by righteousness, and thine iniquities by showing mercy to the poor; if it may be a lengthening of thy tranquility.

28All this came upon the king Nebuchadnezzar. 29At the end of twelve months he walked in the palace of the kingdom of Babylon. 30The king spake, and said, Is not this great Babylon, that I have built for the house of the kingdom by the might of my power, and for the honour of my majesty? 31While the word [was] in the king's mouth, there fell a voice from heaven, [saying], O king Nebuchadnezzar, to thee it is spoken; The kingdom is departed from thee. 32And they shall drive thee from men, and thy dwelling [shall be] with the beasts of the field: they shall make thee to eat grass as oxen, and seven times shall pass over thee, until thou know that the Most High ruleth in the kingdom of men, and giveth it to whomsoever He will.

33The same hour was the thing fulfilled upon Nebuchadnezzar: and he was driven from men, and did eat grass as oxen, and his body was wet with the dew of heaven, till his hairs were grown like eagles' [feathers], and his nails like birds' [claws]. 34And at the end of the days I Nebuchadnezzar lifted up mine eyes unto heaven, and mine understanding returned unto me, and I blessed the Most High, and I praised and honored Him that liveth forever, whose dominion [is] an everlasting dominion, and His kingdom [is] from generation to generation: 35And all the inhabitants of the earth [are] reputed as nothing: and He doeth according to His will in the army of heaven, and [among] the inhabitants of the earth: and none can stay His hand, or say unto Him, What doest thou?

36At the same time my reason returned unto me; and for the glory of my kingdom, mine honour and brightness returned unto me; and my counsellors and my lords sought unto me; and I was established in my kingdom, and excellent majesty was added unto me. 37Now I Nebuchadnezzar praise and extol and honour the King of heaven, all whose works [are] truth, and His ways judgment: and those that walk in pride He is able to abase.

Points to Ponder

1. The second dream God gave the king enhances the first
2. It was only partially fulfilled in Nebuchadnezzar's life
3. Daniel 2 & 4 apply both to Nebuchadnezzar & to Babylon
4. Dreams in the book of Daniel were sealed for the endtime
5. The 7 years are applicable to the entire book of Daniel
6. Nebuchadnezzar had a deadly wound that was healed
7. The healed deadly wound scenario repeats in Scripture

Comparing Daniel 2 & 4

Metal Idol (Daniel 2)	**Great Tree** (Daniel 4)
Thou art this head (2:38)	The tree is you (4:20-22)
A great image (2:31)	Height to heaven (4:11 & 20)
This head (2:38) [man's thought center]	Tree's heart (4:16) [cf Proverbs 23:7]
The beasts (2:38) given into thine hand	The beasts (4:12 & 21) had shadow under it
You are a king (2:21 & 37) for the God of heaven hath given thee a kingdom	Most High rules (4:17 & 22) the Kingdom of men, and giveth it to whomsoever He will
belly and thighs (2:32-33 & 39-40) of brass and iron	Leave the stump (4:15) of iron and brass
Stone destroyed it (2:34, 45)	Hew down the tree (4:13-14, 23)
The great God (2:45) has made known to the king what shall come...hereafter: and the dream is certain and the interpretation thereof sure	The interpretation (4:24) O king, and this *is* the decree of the Most High which is come upon my lord the king
The God of heaven will (2:44) set up a kingdom the kingdom shall stand for ever	Thy kingdom (4:26) is sure unto thee, the heavens do rule

The King of Babylon

In Daniel 2, the king of Babylon was interpreted to be his kingdom. He was virtually ignored.

Who was the king of Babylon identified in the king's dreams in Daniel 2 and 4? It is Nebuchadnezzar and his kingdom, Babylon! *The prophetic events related in Nebuchadnezzar's dream were of consequence to him* (White). As it was true in Daniel 2, it is true in Daniel 4.

In Daniel 2, the translators ignored Nebuchadnezzar and focused solely on his kingdom, Babylon. In Daniel 4, they did the opposite; they totally ignored his kingdom. In spite of the fact that both Daniel 2 & 4 use the same terminology: *You are the head of gold,* and *You are the Great Tree,* the translators tweaked God's word to convey, not the meaning that Daniel expressed, but the one that they assumed. Their inconsistencies skewed the meanings of Daniel's prophecies.

They were not wrong about the prophetic meaning of Daniel 2, but they prematurely shifted the focus of the dream from Nebuchadnezzar to his kingdom, and concealed the kingdom of Babylon meaning in Daniel 4. Thus, they shut up meanings that could have been understood about the king and his dynasty that correlated with Jeremiah's prophecy. But that was ordained of God. He closed, shut up and sealed them until the time of the end (cf Daniel 12:4 & 9). Now that Daniel is unsealed and opened and knowledge is increasing in the endtime, the significance of the translators' premature application of Daniel 2 to the great kingdoms will be better understood along with a more complete meaning of Daniel 4.

Some simple rules will avoid inconsistency in prophetic understanding as they help us to understand prophecy:

"1. Every word must have its proper bearing on the subject presented in the Bible; 2. All Scripture is necessary, and may be understood by diligent application and study; 3. Nothing revealed in Scripture can or will be hid from those who ask in faith, not wavering; 4. To understand doctrine, bring all the scriptures together on the subject you wish to know, then *let every word have its proper influence*; and if you can form your theory without a contradiction, you cannot be in error; 5. Scripture must be its own expositor, since it is a rule of itself. If I depend on a teacher to expound to me, and he should guess at its meaning, or desire to have it so on account of his sectarian creed, or to be thought wise, then his guessing, desire, creed, or wisdom is my rule, and not the Bible."

The above is a portion of these rules; and in our study of the Bible we shall all do well to heed the principles set forth (RH, Nov 25, 1884 par. 24, 25).

By the interpretation of Nebuchadnezzar's dream, Jehovah was exalted as more powerful *than earthly rulers* (7T 161.1).

Thou art the head of gold. THOU in its proper place is Nebuchadnezzar and the meaning that applies to his dynasty is revealed in Daniel 2 before more light is to come. His dynasty confirms Jeremiah's prophecy: "All nations shall serve him, and his son, and his son's son" (cf Jeremiah 27:4-11). When Daniel 7 expands and explains Daniel 2, the meaning about the kingdom of Babylon will be established. But before the prophecies were unsealed, the translators' skewed the meaning of Daniel 2 and 4. *The head of gold is the king* as is *the Great Tree.* As *the king of Babylon* depicts his kingdom, there is more to that symbol in Bible prophecy.

It is not wise to needlessly limit man's understanding of prophecy without examining all of the Scriptural evidence. To dogmatically say that the kingdom of Babylon is only the head of gold in Daniel 2 is to ignore all other meanings that are presented in Scripture in favor of the obvious. When considering all the Scriptures, the prophet Isaiah clearly states that the king of Babylon is Lucifer, Satan: "Take up this proverb against the king of Babylon, and say... How art thou fallen from heaven, O Lucifer" (Isaiah 14:4, 12).

Daniel 4 has also been limited by the translators to King Nebuchadnezzar: The king is the obvious meaning, but it is not the only meaning, because as noted: Scripture must be its own expositor!

In Daniel 2 and 4, both readings (the king and his kingdom, Babylon) foreshadow events relating to endtime spiritual Babylon and its endtime king, and there are insights revealed in these prophecies that must not be ignored to have a complete understanding of the prophecies. With Lucifer prophetically being the king of Babylon, the prophecy in Daniel 4 reveals that Lucifer is only allowed 7 times for his insane rebellion against God. This expands and explains Daniel 2 by specifying its duration.

> *We certainly need to be wise as serpents and harmless as doves. We might be very zealous, but it might be an unwise zeal, and serve to hedge up our way. Then there is danger of being so circumscribed in our work as to do very little good* (PC 28.3).

It is not a new thing for a man to be deluded by the arch-deceiver and array himself against God. Consider your course critically before you venture to go any further in the path you are traveling. The Jews were self-deceived. They rejected the teachings of Christ because He exposed the secrets of their hearts and reproved their sins. They would not come to the light, fearing that their deeds would be reproved. They chose darkness rather than light. "This is the condemnation," said Christ, "that light is come into the world, and men loved darkness rather than light, because their deeds were evil." The Jews pursued their course of rejecting Christ until, in their self-deceived, deluded state, they thought that in crucifying Him they were doing God service. This was the result of their refusing light. *You are in danger of similar deception. It will be profitable for your soul...to consider where the path which you are now traveling will end. God can do without you, but you cannot afford to do without God. He does not compel any man to believe.* He sets light before men, and Satan presents his darkness. While the deceiver is constantly crying, "Light is here; truth is here," Jesus is saying: "I am the truth; I have the words of eternal life. If any man follow Me, he shall not walk in darkness." *God gives to us all evidence sufficient to balance our faith on the side of truth. If we surrender to*

*God, we shall choose the light and reject the darkness. If we desire to maintain the independence of the natural heart, and refuse the correction of God, we shall, as did the Jews, stubbornly carry out our purposes and our ideas in the face of the plainest evidence, and shall be in danger of as great deception as came upon them; and **in our blind infatuation we may go to as great lengths as they did, and yet flatter ourselves that we are doing work for God*** (4T 230.1).

When Christ came into the world to exemplify true religion, and to exalt the principles that should govern the hearts and actions of men, falsehood had taken so deep a hold upon those who had had so great light, that they no longer comprehended the light, and had no inclination to yield up tradition for truth. They rejected the heavenly Teacher, they crucified the Lord of glory, that they might retain their own customs and inventions. *The very same spirit is manifested in the world today. Men are averse to investigating truth, lest their traditions should be disturbed, and a new order of things should be brought in. There is with humanity a constant liability to err, and men are naturally inclined to highly exalt human ideas and knowledge, while the divine and eternal is not discerned or appreciated.* To those who were unprejudiced, the words of Christ were as the light from heaven. "He spake as never man spake." As the great Teacher presented the absorbing realities of the eternal future, the things of this perishing world were eclipsed. How eagerly did those who had been praying for light receive the truth. But the proud and self-righteous refused His message (TSS 38.1).

Babylon

Babylon refers to the ancient kingdom and "The term Babylon, derived from Babel, and signifying confusion, is applied in Scripture to the various forms of false or apostate religion" (4SP 232.2). All false and apostate religions are Babylon. It is vital to understand Babylon in the endtime!

> [14:8]Babylon is fallen, is fallen, that great city, because she made all nations drink of the wine of the wrath of *her fornication...*[18:2]Babylon the great is fallen, is fallen, and is become the habitation of devils, and the hold of every foul spirit, and a cage of every unclean and hateful bird. [3]For all nations have drunk of the wine of the wrath of *her fornication, and the kings of the earth have committed fornication with her,* and the merchants of the earth are waxed rich through the abundance of her delicacies... [4]*Come out of her, My people, that ye be not partakers of her sins, and that ye receive not of her plagues* (Revelation 14:8; 18:2-4).

With Bible prophecy fast fulfilling, the identity of Babylon is clear! But billions of people may not yet know that God is talking about the apostate religions that they may love; Religions that may once have served Him. The blatant fornication scandals clearly identify Babylon by the depraved actions of the Roman Catholic priests, the Southern Baptist ministers, the Methodist, and the other Protestant denominations that have turned from Christ to fornication, along with Islam and Judaism!

Babylon's fornications clearly proclaim her identity. The command to flee Babylon cannot be clearer. God's people must flee Babylon or they endanger their very lives.

> In this scripture the announcement of the fall of Babylon, as made by the second angel, [Revelation 14:8.] is repeated, with the additional mention of the corruptions which have been entering the churches since 1844. (4SP 421.2).

> Romanism is now regarded by Protestants with far greater favor than in former years. In those countries where Catholicism is not in the ascendency, and the papists are taking a conciliatory course in order to gain

influence, there is an increasing indifference concerning the doctrines that separate the reformed churches from the papal hierarchy; the opinion is gaining ground, that, after all, we do not differ so widely upon vital points as has been supposed, and that a little concession on our part will bring us into a better understanding with Rome. The time was when Protestants placed a high value upon the liberty of conscience which has been so dearly purchased. They taught their children to abhor popery, and held that to seek harmony with Rome would be disloyalty to God. But how widely different are the sentiments now expressed (GC88 563.1).

Before the coming of Christ, important developments in the religious world, foretold in prophecy, were to take place. The apostle declared: "Be not soon shaken in mind, or be troubled, neither by spirit, nor by word, nor by letter as from us, as that the day of Christ is at hand. Let no man deceive you by any means: for that day shall not come, except there come a falling away first, and that man of sin be revealed, the son of perdition; who opposeth and exalteth himself above all that is called God, or that is worshiped; so that he as God sitteth in the temple of God, showing himself that he is God" (AA 265.1).

The fornication scandals in the churches are *important developments in the religious world!* They are happening! The falling away prophesied is here! Much of Christendom is turning away from sound doctrines to reunite with the fornicating mother Church. The man of sin is revealed!

Obedience to the word of God is a matter of life or death. It is not optional! When the last plagues fall, they will fall upon Babylon and the people who remain in Babylon. But God's faithful people will be saved when the seven final plagues fall. Our eternal life depends upon our hearing and obeying God's call to flee Babylon. It is written: "You shall know the truth and the truth shall set you free."

The negative consequences of denying the truth or trying to hide the identity of Babylon is the needless death of those who do not see Babylon as she is. Failing to warn those who are about to perish may be socially convenient, but such failure is an immoral act that lacks the love of Christ, who came to seek and to save the lost.

Who is fooling who? To be silent when life and death hang in the balance is hatred concealing itself behind false love. Who loves others so much that they will choose to be so cautious as to not say anything to those who are perishing for fear that it might hurt their feelings, when saying a word in season could possibly save their lives? Those who love others as Christ loves us cannot sit by in their comfort zone and let others die for the sake of a false peace.

When the warning is faithfully given, who will hear it if it does not fit their ideology? Prior to Pope Benedict's resignation, I wrote books and tweeted eight times from September 2011 to September 2012 that he was going to leave office in fulfillment of Bible prophecy. These tweets are time-stamped in Twitter's archives:

Pope Benedict XVI has but *a very short time left* (9/3/11)

#Pope Benedict XVI marks *his last year* with a Latin America trip that includes a visit to #Cuba (23 March 2012)

With Benedict XVI in his last year,
Who's going to be the new pope? ... (3 April 2012)

Is Pope Benedict going to be pope in 2013? (29 April 2012)

Months ago, I tweeted that pope *Benedict XVI is a short timer.* Now Vatican power play is news! *Y u b last 2 know?* (28 May 2012)

If Pope Benedict's 8th year is really his 7th, *his time ends before May 2013* (7 July 2012)

Pope Benedict's 8th year is really his 7th, because his ascension year was John-Paul II's last year. *Will Benedict XVI's 7th year B his last* (8 August 2012)

Pope #Benedict XVI As I read Daniel's prophecy, 7's number of completeness. His ascension year (zero) 2005. *He might last till spring 2013?* (30 September 2012)

Pope Benedict announced this morning (Monday February 11, 2013) that he is resigning as of 28 February 2013.

With each tweet, my understanding increased. Though I understood that the prophecy identified the short duration of Benedict's reign, there was much that I did not fully understand until the prophecy was fulfilled. But few would look at the study until all the evidence was presented in a perfect package as if Bible students are supposed to be infallible: Only God is all knowing and infallible! Bible students "Study to show" themselves "approved unto God, a workman that needeth not to be ashamed, rightly dividing the word of truth" (2 Timothy 2:15).

I was unaware that Steve Quayle and Tom Horn also said that Pope Benedict XVI would leave office before the fact. We came to the same conclusion quite differently: I studied Daniel and Revelation, while they used the Malachy list, "by a Benedictine monk Arnold Wion in 1595" (https://en. wikipedia.org/wiki/Prophecy_of_the_Popes).

Wion was a contemporary of Nostradamus (1503-1566). Note White's comment and the timing of Wion's publication:

> Satan was not idle. He now attempted what he has attempted in every other reformatory movement, —*to deceive and destroy the people by palming off upon them a counterfeit in place of the true* work. *As there were false christs in the first century of the Christian church, so there arose false prophets in the sixteenth century* (GC88 186.1).

Were you expecting Benedict XVI to leave office before it happened in 2013? Satan was! He knew it in the 16th century (1595). When the truth about Benedict was understood in 2011-2012 from Daniel and Revelation, some Christians assumed that the message linked to the *Malachy list* and refused to look at the biblical evidence.

Though White's 1888 statement implicated Nostradamus and Wion as false prophets, she does not warn against studying the Bible when knowledge increases! The Truth that God sent in White's Day was not the Present Truth for today! Present Truth is Truth for today!

Was your pastor or tv guru teaching Present Truth to prepare you for what is ahead? Are they prayerfully studying Bible prophecy to learn what is coming? Or are they relying on prophetic notions that are outdated?

Without some understanding of Bible prophecy, it would have been impossible to accurately tweet, before Benedict resigned, that he *has a short time left*; that 2012 is *his last year*; that *his time ends before May 2013*; and *he might last till spring 2013* The more prayerfully prophecy was studied, the more it was understood before it was fulfilled. Benedict was a short timer. His last year to head the papacy was 2012. He resigned before May, and he did not last in office until the spring 2013! My partial understanding of Bible prophecy became more complete as prophecy was fulfilled.

But before it happened, a friend rejected the study that identified Pope Benedict XVI without looking at the data that led to those statements. She dogmatically stated: "Popes are not in Bible prophecy!" If that were true, it would not be written: "Behold, in this horn [were] eyes like the eyes of man, and a mouth speaking great things" (Daniel 7:8).

Another friend advised: "Prophecy isn't so much about us seeing the future, but when it comes to pass, we can know God is in charge and believe." How can the fulfillment of prophecy confirm our belief *that God is in charge* if we do not at least partially grasp the meaning of Bible prophecy before it happens? Though God revealed that Pope Benedict XVI would only continue for a short space, centuries before he reigned, who could know that he fulfilled prophecy if they did not have a clue that the prophecy was about a pope? With Satan's counterfeit prophecy being so close to Bible prophecy, how are we to discern what really is TRUTH?

Both friends were explaining away something that they did not understand rather than to look a little closer. Their traditional views were skewing Bible study. All would do well to guard our influence for God's cause or our influence will not be "in union with the Spirit and work of God." Those who fail on this point "are not going forward but backward. The opinions of unbelievers are having too great an influence" upon our mind (cf UL 300.3).

Everything of a character to cause our brethren to be diverted from the very points now essential for this time should be kept in the background (15MR 21.2).

The great crisis is just before us. To meet its trials and temptations, and to perform its duties, will require persevering faith. But we may triumph gloriously; *not one watching, praying, believing soul will be ensnared by the enemy* (GCB, July 1, 1902 par. 13).

The precious, saving truth has been repeated over and over again to our church-members, while right in the cities where our churches are organized, there are souls perishing for the want of knowledge that the members of our churches could impart. Aggressive warfare is scarcely known. If believers were wide awake, were watching for opportunities to diffuse light, they would find plenty of work to do. The earnestness, the sobriety, the revelation of the sense of solemn responsibility which rests upon the followers of Christ, would count strongly in favor of the truth (RH, June 11, 1895).

To fail to worship God is to choose by default to worship another. Whoever gets our attention gets our service and our worship. God is not going to settle for second place. He expects His people to warn others: "If you do not speak to warn the wicked from his way, that wicked [man] shall die in his iniquity; but his blood will I require at your hand (Ezekiel 33:8). "Prepare to meet thy God" (Amos 4:12).

The Roman Church Transitions to Babylon

The rise of the papacy counterfeited Christ's anointing. After King Alaric I led the Visigoths' invasion of the Roman Empire, the Arian Heruli under King Odoacer deposed the Western Roman Emperor, Romulus Augustulus, in 476 AD. When King Odoacer advanced toward the Eastern Roman Empire, its Emperor, Zeno, appointed the Arian king of the Ostrogoths, Theodoric the Great to be king of Italy. To secure Italy, Theodoric killed Odoacer in a turf battle. The Arian Frank, King Clovis, became a Catholic in 506. The Saxons in England embraced Catholicism in 508. Of the ten Germanic tribes invading the Western Roman Empire, the first three that embraced the Arian Christian faith were the last three that held on to it.

> The *Visigoths* first embraced the gospel as a nation; they were followed by the *Ostrogoths*; with these the *Vandals*... (*Triumph of Christianity 1*, Advent Review, and Sabbath Herald. Sept 21, 1886, Periodical Issue).

After King Alaric I died, King Clovis attacked Spain thus, beginning the war upon which "the prevalence of the Catholic or the Arian creed in Western Europe depended" (https:// openlibrary.org/books/OL23435375M). Alaric II died during the war. His illicit son, Gesalic, became king of the Visigoths. In the meantime, King Theodoric, Alaric II's father-in-law and grandfather of Prince Amalaric, Alaric's younger son, sent an army from Rome in 508 to help the Visigoths defeat the Franks (http://www.historyofwar.org/articles/siege_arles _507.html). Theodoric's army deposed Gesalic, who fled to North Africa to seek the Vandals help to regain his kingdom.

Thus, in 508, Theodoric (an ally of the Eastern Roman Emperor) plucked up the first of the last three Arian kings, to secure the Visigoth throne for his grandson. The 508 AD victory over King Gesalic began the 30-year countdown to the rise of the papacy that counterfeited the 30 years that Jesus lived on earth before He was anointed the Christ.

Then 7 April 529, Emperor Justinian, issued the draft of *Codex Justiniani* that mingled Church and state. "The provisions... influenced the Canon Law of the church since... the church lives under Roman law" (https://en.wiki pedia.org/wiki/Portal:Byzantine_Empire/Selected_article).

In North Africa, King Hilderic, the Vandal became a Catholic. His Arian cousin, Gelimer, deposed him. Then the Eastern Roman Army invaded to reestablish Catholicism:

> In June, 533...Belisarius, invaded North Africa, and victory came fast. Belisarius defeated the Vandals by December 533... Churches confiscated by the Vandals were to be returned to Catholic worship, and anyone guilty of having been an Arian Christian was to be excluded from public office (http://www.fsmitha.com/h3/h01const.htm).

Gelimer was the 2nd of the last three Arian kings to be plucked up by the pope's allies. Of the initial ten, the king of the Goths was the only Arian horn left.

Theodoric the Great died. His daughter, Amalasuntha (Justinian's ally) merged the Goths into Roman society. The Gothic nobility opposed her. Then her husband and son died. She was compelled to appoint a male figurehead as king. The elderly relative that she appointed, King Theodahad, seized power and banished her. Meanwhile, Emperor Justinian finalized *Codex Justiniani* (534). It made the pope, John II (533-535), the head of all the churches.

> Paying honor to the Apostolic See and to your holiness, as always has been and is our desire, and honoring your blessedness as a father, we hasten to bring to the knowledge of Your Holiness all that pertains to the condition of the churches, since it has always been our great aim to safeguard the unity of your Apostolic See and the position of the holy churches of God which now prevails and abides securely without any disturbing trouble. Therefore, we have been sedulous to subject and unite all the priests of the orient throughout its whole

extent to the See of Your Holiness. Whatever questions happen to be mooted at present, we have thought necessary to be brought to Your Holiness's knowledge, however clear and unquestionable they may be, and though firmly held and taught by all the clergy in accordance with the doctrine of your Apostolic See; for we do not suffer that anything which is mooted, however clear and unquestionable, pertaining to the state of the churches, should fail to be made known to Your Holiness, as being the head of all the churches. For, as we have said before, we are zealous for the increase of the honor and authority of your See in all respects (Codex Justiniani, lib. 1, tit. 1; translation given by R. F. Littledale, The Petrine Claims, p. 293).

The title *Augustus* signified that Justinian was claiming to be Pontifex Maximus/High Priest Emperor, the head of church and state. Justinian, as *ever Augustus* was making it clear that the Roman Catholic Church was under his authority and that the Bishop of Rome/Pope John II was his subordinate. Justinian clearly intended that the pope: 1) Receive honor, 2) Take charge of all the churches, 3) Extend his influence to the orient, 4) Institute doctrines for the entire church, and 5) To have his authority to be increased.

After Justinian had put all of the churches under Pope John II and had given him authority as his subordinate, John II died. Agapetus became pope. Queen Amalasuntha was assassinated. And King Theodahad pleaded with Pope Agapetus to go to Constantinople to pacify Justinian (https://en.wikipedia.org/wiki/Pope_Agapetus_I#cite_ref-6).

Agapetus died in Constantinople. Silverius was "made pope through the influence of the King of the Goths" (http://www.newadvent.org/cathen/15427b.htm). After Theodahad had meddled with the selection of Pope Silverius, Justinian reasserted his authority over the Roman Catholic Church: The Court at Constantinople gave Vigilius 700 pounds of gold and sent him to Rome to be pope (https://www.catholic.org/encyclopedia/view.php?id =12068).

Justinian's Army returned to Italy from the war with the Vandals in North Africa. King Theodahad was killed. The Ostrogoths selected Witigis to be their king.

King Witigis left Rome to marry Matasuntha, Theodoric's granddaughter. When he returned, Justinian's army was camped outside of Rome: Witigis attacked it. Pope Silverius let the Roman army into the city. General Belisarius turned on Pope Silverius and installed Pope Vigilius. Belisarius then broke the siege of Rome in 538 and pursued King Witigis, who was captured and sent to Constantinople where he died.

Pope Vigilius (the head of the Roman Catholic Church) was enabled to execute Roman law: *Codex Justiniani.* The Roman Church had become a political state church.

> The vast empire of Rome crumbled to pieces, and from its ruins rose that mighty power, the Roman Catholic Church (YI, September 22, 1903 par. 6).

> Whenever and wherever the Lord works in giving a genuine blessing, a counterfeit is also revealed, in order to make of none effect the true work of God. Therefore, we need to be exceedingly careful, and walk humbly before God, that we may have spiritual eyesalve that we may distinguish the working of the Holy Spirit of God from the working of that spirit that would bring in wild license and fanaticism (RH, February 6, 1894 par. 8).

The Counterfeit Christ

As much as God would allow, the papacy counterfeited Christ's life and ministry. Jesus lived for 30 years before being anointed: The papacy gradually increased in favor with men for 30 years from 508-538. As Jesus had victory over three temptations before beginning His ministry, the papacy's allies plucked up three Arian kings to enable the pope to be anointed as a subordinate of the state. As Christ's ministry continued for 3.5 years/1260 days, the papacy reigned 1260 years from 538 to 1798. As Christ was crucified and arose, the papacy counterfeited this when it received its deadly wound that was later healed.

A friend betrayed Jesus, and the French, who befriended the pope and advanced his supremacy: Betrayed Pope Pius VI when they imprisoned him in France. As Jesus was jailed on Thursday, Pius VI was jailed in 1798. Jesus died Friday. Pope Pius VI died in 1799. Jesus rested in His tomb on Sabbath. The papacy rested: There was no pope for the balance of 1799. Jesus rose Sunday, the first day of the new week: Pope Pius VII was installed in 1800. Thus, the papacy was resurrected in the first year of the new century, but it did not have the power that it had previously.

As much as God would allow, from 508-1800, the papacy counterfeited Christ's life, ministry, death, and resurrection. It was not until the Vatican kingdom was restored to Pope Pius XI in 1929 that the papacy more fully counterfeited Christ's resurrection (the healing of the deadly wound). Even then, the *whole world* did not yet follow after the papacy.

Deadly wounds

When Nebuchadnezzar went insane for seven times, i.e., seven years, his insanity foreshadowed spiritual Babylon's deadly wound and Satan's 1000-year imprisonment. God's message of hope to King Nebuchadnezzar was that he would eventually be restored as the king of Babylon.

> The promise was made that whosoever looked upon the brazen serpent should live; and to those who looked the promise was verified. But if anyone said: "What good will it do to look? I shall certainly die under the serpent's deadly sting;" if he continued to talk of his deadly wound, and declared that his case was hopeless, and would not perform the simple act of obedience, he would die. But everyone who looked, lived (ST, April 2, 1894 par. 4).

As foreshadowed by the king of Babylon's deadly wound in Daniel 4, papal Babylon received its deadly wound in

1798. The endtime healing of the deadly wound was from February to June 1929. As prophesied:

> "Power was given unto him to continue forty and two months." And, says the prophet, "I saw one of his heads as it were wounded to death." And again, "He that leadeth into captivity shall go into captivity; he that killeth with the sword must be killed with the sword." The forty and two months are the same as the "time and times and the dividing of time," three years and a half, or 1260 days, of Daniel 7, —the time during which the papal power was to oppress God's people. This period... began with the establishment of the papacy, A. D. 538, and terminated in 1798. At that time, when the papacy was abolished and the pope made captive by the French army, the papal power received its deadly wound, and the prediction was fulfilled, "He that leadeth into captivity shall go into captivity" (GC88 439.2).

> Pius VI...the pope specified in prophecy, which received the deadly wound (5MR 318.1).

This is true! Revelation 13 specifies that the first beast's wounded head depicted a pope, Pius VI; "I saw one of his heads as it were wounded to death; and his deadly wound was healed" (13:3). A head depicts a pope: "*Wast* thou not [made] the head of the tribes of Israel, and the LORD anointed thee king over Israel?" (1 Samuel 15:17.) Mussolini restored the secular kingdom to a pope named Pius (IV) in 1929. The prophetic focus (*his deadly wound healed*) is not the 1798 Pius VI wounded head, but the post-1929 healed papacy that began with Pius XI. Only seven popes have ruled it as solo kings since 1929: Pius XI & XII, John XXIII, Paul VI, John-Paul I & II, and Benedict XVI.

As Mussolini had restored a kingdom to Pius XI, President Ronald Reagan recognized Pope John-Paul II as a head of state on America's behalf. Subsequently, President George Bush I recognized Pope John-Paul II as *The World's Moral Leader*, i.e., the *head* of all the churches.

As Nebuchadnezzar, *the head of gold* and *the tree*, was substituted for Babylon; the papal beast is symbolically interchangeable with its head. And like Nebuchadnezzar, the papacy had a healed wound as did Pope John-Paul II: An attempted assassination did not kill him. As the papacy had ruled for 42 months symbolizing 1260 prophetic years from 538 to 1798, Pope John-Paul II lived for 42 months from 9/11/01 until he died 4/2/05.

And the beast which I saw...the dragon gave him his power, and his seat, and great authority. And I saw one of his heads as it were wounded to death; and his deadly wound was healed: and all the world wondered after the beast. And they worshipped the dragon which gave power unto the beast: and they worshipped the beast, saying, Who [is] like unto the beast? Who is able to make war with him? (Revelation 13:2-3).

After one of the papacy's heads, John-Paul II, survived; the world wondered after the papacy. Who could resist Pope John-Paul II? His charisma awed Presidents Reagan, Bush I, and Clinton. Who could make war with him? "Communism fell as a result of the activities of the Apostolic See and John-Paul II" (http://www.miszlivetzferenc.com/wp-content/up loads/2012/01/Michnik_The-Rebirth-of-Civil-Society_.pdf).

Satan will receive his deadly wound: "The dragon, that old serpent, which is the Devil and Satan" is bound "a thousand years;" the earth rests from his temptations. His wound is then healed for a *little season*, but after that he is cast into the lake of fire (cf Revelation 20:2-3).

Seven Times

"Let seven times pass over him" (cf Daniel 4:16, 23). When the *seven times* were fulfilled, Daniel called them *days*: "At the end of the days" (4:34). Thus, according to Daniel, times and days are interchangeable. In Bible prophecy, a day can symbolize a year: "each day for a year" (Ezekiel 4:6). A year can also be called a time. And "A thousand years in Thy sight are but as yesterday" (Psalms 90:4). Peter confirms that the calculation goes in both directions: "Be not ignorant of this one thing, that one day is with the Lord as a thousand years, and a thousand years as one day" (2 Peter 3:8).

In Daniel 4, Nebuchadnezzar, King of Babylon, partially fulfilled the prophecy when he went insane for seven years/prophetically seven days. In the endtime, at the end of the prophetic seven days/seven thousand years allotted for the king of Babylon, Satan's insane rebellion ends.

Crosier put it this way: "The last act of deliverance will be at the end of the 1000 years" which is at the end of "the great Sabbath, *the seventh millennium*; Hebrews 4:3" (http://www.sdadefend.com/Our%20Firm%20Foundation/ Crosier-sanctuary.pdf). White affirmed his observation: "Brother *Crosier had the true light*...in the Day-Star, Extra, February 7, 1846. *I feel fully authorized by the Lord, to recommend that Extra, to every saint*" (WLF 12.8). White also stated, "The great controversy between Christ and Satan that has been carried forward for nearly six thousand years is soon to close" (GC88 518.1). And from the perspective of the redeemed in heaven, White wrote: "Satan's work of ruin is forever ended. *For six thousand years he has wrought his will*... The whole earth is at rest..." (GC88 673.2).

Sin's duration is limited to six thousand years and its destruction comes at the end of the seventh thousand-year sabbath. Before the idol in Daniel 2 is crushed, papal Babylon receives its deadly wound that is healed. It is impossible to know exactly when the 6,000 years end. Ussher's chronology has the earth older than 6000 years. The Hebrew Calendar puts August 2019 in the year 5779.

> And he laid hold on the dragon, that old serpent, which is the Devil, and Satan, and bound him a thousand years... And when the thousand years are expired, Satan shall be loosed out of his prison (cf Revelation 20:3, 6-7).

> The word of God covers a period of history reaching from the creation to the coming of the Son of man in the

clouds of heaven... Through all these centuries the truth of God has remained the same. That which was truth in the beginning is truth now. Although new and important truths appropriate for succeeding generations have been opened to the understanding, *the present revealings do not contradict those of the past. Every new truth understood only makes more significant the old* (RH, March 2, 1886 par. 6).

All that God has in prophetic history specified to be fulfilled in the past has been, and all that is yet to come in its order will be. Daniel, God's prophet, stands in his place. John stands in his place. In the Revelation, *the Lion of the tribe of Judah has opened to the students of prophecy the book of Daniel,* and thus is Daniel standing in his place. *He bears his testimony, that which the Lord revealed to him in vision of the great and solemn events which we must know as we stand on the very threshold of their fulfillment* (17MR 10.2).

Historical events, showing the direct fulfillment of prophecy, were set before the people, and the prophecy was seen to be a figurative delineation of events leading down to the close of this earth's history... The people now have a special message to give to the world... (17MR 1.3).

The testing time is right upon us. We must build upon the Rock that will stand the storm of test and trial. As we see the fulfillment of prophecy, we know that the end of all things is at hand. Present the eternal principles of truth. Show what the Word of God declares is to take place on this earth. The God who gave Daniel instruction regarding the closing scenes of this earth's history will certainly confirm the testimony of His servants as at the appointed time they give the loud cry (21MR 436.6).

Light comes from the very throne of God. When some familiar truth presents itself to your mind in a new aspect, when a text of Scripture suddenly bursts upon you with new meaning like a flash of light that scatters the mist, and you see the relation of other truths to some part of the plan of redemption, God is leading you, and a divine Teacher is at your side. Will you not then open the door of your heart to receive more and more of the heavenly illumination? (ST, August 27, 1894 par. 3)

Except your righteousness exceeds that of the scribes and Pharisees, you shall not enter into the kingdom of heaven. They sit in Moses' seat. Woe to those hypocrites! For they shut up the kingdom of heaven against men: while they do not go in themselves (cf Matthew 5:20; 23:2, 13).

Daniel 5

¹Belshazzar the king made a great feast to a thousand of his lords, and drank wine before the thousand. ²Belshazzar, whiles he tasted the wine, commanded to bring the golden and silver vessels which his father Nebuchadnezzar had taken out of the temple which [was] in Jerusalem; that the king, and his princes, his wives, and his concubines, might drink therein. ³Then they brought the golden vessels that were taken out of the temple of the house of God which [was] at Jerusalem; and the king, and his princes, his wives, and his concubines, drank in them. ⁴They drank wine, and praised the gods of gold, and of silver, of brass, of iron, of wood, and of stone.

⁵In the same hour came forth fingers of a man's hand, and wrote over against the candlestick upon the plaster of the wall of the king's palace: and the king saw the part of the hand that wrote. ⁶Then the king's countenance was changed, and his thoughts troubled him, so that the joints of his loins were loosed, and his knees smote one against another. ⁷The king cried aloud to bring in the astrologers, the Chaldeans, and the soothsayers. [And] the king spake, and said to the wise [men] of Babylon, Whosoever shall read this writing, and show me the interpretation thereof, shall be clothed with scarlet, and [have] a chain of gold about his neck, and shall be the third ruler in the kingdom. ⁸Then came in all the king's wise [men]: but they could not read the writing, nor make known to the king the interpretation thereof. ⁹Then was king Belshazzar greatly troubled, and his countenance was changed in him, and his lords were astonied.

¹⁰[Now] the queen by reason of the words of the king and his lords came into the banquet house: [and] the queen spake and said, O king, live forever: let not thy thoughts trouble thee, nor let thy countenance be

changed: ¹¹There is a man in thy kingdom, in whom [is] the spirit of the holy gods; and in the days of thy father light and understanding and wisdom, like the wisdom of the gods, was found in him; whom the king Nebuchadnezzar thy father, the king, [I say], thy father, made master of the magicians, astrologers, Chaldeans, [and] soothsayers; ¹²Forasmuch as an excellent spirit, and knowledge, and understanding, interpreting of dreams, and showing of hard sentences, and dissolving of doubts, were found in the same Daniel, whom the king named Belteshazzar: now let Daniel be called, and he will show the interpretation. ¹³Then was Daniel brought in before the king.

[And] the king spake and said unto Daniel, [Art] thou that Daniel, which [art] of the children of the captivity of Judah, whom the king my father brought out of Jewry? ¹⁴I have even heard of thee, that the spirit of the gods [is] in thee, and [that] light and understanding and excellent wisdom is found in thee. ¹⁵And now the wise [men], the astrologers, have been brought in before me, that they should read this writing, and make known unto me the interpretation thereof: but they could not show the interpretation of the thing: ¹⁶And I have heard of thee, that thou canst make interpretations, and dissolve doubts: now if thou canst read the writing, and make known to me the interpretation thereof, thou shalt be clothed with scarlet, and [have] a chain of gold about thy neck, and shalt be the third ruler in the kingdom.

¹⁷Then Daniel answered and said before the king, Let thy gifts be to thyself, and give thy rewards to another; yet I will read the writing unto the king, and make known to him the interpretation. ¹⁸O thou king, the most high God gave Nebuchadnezzar thy father a kingdom, and majesty, and glory, and honour: ¹⁹And for the majesty that He gave him, all people, nations, and languages, trembled and feared before him: whom he would he slew; and whom he would he kept alive; and whom he would

he set up; and whom he would he put down. 20But when his heart was lifted up, and his mind hardened in pride, he was deposed from his kingly throne, and they took his glory from him: 21And he was driven from the sons of men; and his heart was made like the beasts, and his dwelling [was] with the wild asses: they fed him with grass like oxen, and his body was wet with the dew of heaven; till he knew that the most high God ruled in the kingdom of men, and [that] he appoints over it whomsoever He will.

22And thou his son, O Belshazzar, hast not humbled thine heart, though thou knew all this; 23But hast lifted up thyself against the Lord of heaven; and they have brought the vessels of His house before thee, and thou, and thy lords, thy wives, and thy concubines, have drunk wine in them; and thou hast praised the gods of silver, and gold, of brass, iron, wood, and stone, which see not, nor hear, nor know: and the God in whose hand thy breath [is], and whose [are] all thy ways, hast thou not glorified: 24Then was the part of the hand sent from Him; and this writing was written.

25And this [is] the writing that was written, MENE, MENE, TEKEL, UPHARSIN. 26This [is] the interpretation of the thing: MENE; God hath numbered thy kingdom, and finished it. 27TEKEL; Thou art weighed in the balances, and art found wanting. 28PERES; Thy kingdom is divided, and given to the Medes and Persians.

29Then commanded Belshazzar, and they clothed Daniel with scarlet, and [put] a chain of gold about his neck, and made a proclamation concerning him, that he should be the third ruler in the kingdom. 30In that night was Belshazzar the king of the Chaldeans slain. 31And Darius the Median took the kingdom, [being] about threescore and two years old.

Points to Ponder

1. God reveals His intentions before He acts
 A. In Nebuchadnezzar's early years
 B. Before Babylon fell
2. When Babylon arose and fell, food was a "test"
3. Rebellion against God has consequences: Judgment
4. Judgment comes when least expected
5. Babylon's *wise men* did not discern God's messages
6. Babylon's fall foreshadows the fall of spiritual Babylon
7. Babylon had three rulers (kings) when it fell
8. King Belshazzar was slain: King Belteshazzar lived

God Reveals Secrets

"The Lord God will do nothing, but He revealeth His secret unto His servants the prophets." "The secret things belong unto the Lord our God, but those things which are revealed belong unto us and to our children forever" (Amos 3:7; Deuteronomy 29:29).

Each period of the fulfillment of prophetic history is a preparation for the advanced light which will succeed each period. As the prophecy comes to an end, there is to be a perfect whole (13MR 15.3).

Why, then, this widespread ignorance concerning an important part of Holy Writ? Why this general reluctance to investigate its teachings? It is the result of a studied effort of the prince of darkness to conceal from men that which reveals his deceptions. For this reason, Christ the Revelator, foreseeing the warfare that would be waged against the study of the Revelation, pronounced a blessing upon all who should read, hear, and observe the words of the prophecy (GC88 342.1).

Great truths that have lain unheeded and unseen... are to shine from God's word in their native purity. To those who truly love God the Holy Spirit will reveal truths that have faded from the mind, and will also reveal truths that are entirely new. **Those who eat the flesh and drink the blood of the Son of God will bring from the books of Daniel and Revelation truth that is inspired by the Holy Spirit.** *They will start into action forces that cannot be repressed* (RH, August 17, 1897 par. 19).

In your study of the word of God, penetrate deeper and still deeper beneath the surface. Lay hold by faith on divine power and sound the depths of inspiration (9T 151.1).

Every child of God should be intelligent in the Scriptures, and able, by tracing the fulfillment of prophecy, to show our position in this world's history (RH January 27, 1885, par. 7).

If the Bible student learns from the great Teacher who inspired Bible history, he will know the truth... History and prophecy testify that the God of the whole earth revealeth secrets through His chosen light-bearers to the world (3MR 186.2).

These predictions of the Infinite One, recorded on the prophetic page and traced on the pages of history, were given to demonstrate that God is the ruling power in the affairs of this world. He changes the times and the seasons, He removes kings and sets up kings, to fulfill His own purpose (YI, September 29, 1903 par.3).

We who are living in this age have greater light and privileges than were given to Abraham, Joseph, Moses, Daniel, Ezra, Nehemiah, and other ancient worthies, and we are under correspondingly greater obligation to let our light shine to the world. God has made us the depositaries of His law. We have been redeemed by the precious blood of Christ, and we are to follow in His footsteps, to represent Him before the world. But are we faithful depositaries of the truth, correctly representing it amid the spiritual declension and moral corruption that now exist? Are we doing all that we might and should do to diffuse the precious light of truth? Brethren, you see the truth, you understand the claims of God's law; you know that no willful transgressor will enter into life, and yet you see that law made void in the world. What is your duty? You are not to ask, "What is convenient for me? What is agreeable?" but, "What can I do to save souls?" (GW92 434.1).

Even the prophets who were favored with the special illumination of the Spirit did not fully comprehend the import of the revelations committed to them. The meaning was to be unfolded from age to age, as the people of God should need the instruction therein contained (GC88 344.1).

The Revelation is the supplement of Daniel... *These messages were given, not for those that uttered the prophecies, but for us who are living amid the scenes of their fulfillment* (17MR 19.1).

Study Revelation in connection with Daniel; for history will be repeated (1888 1491.1).

God designed that the discovery of these things... establish the faith of men in inspired history (1SP 90.1).

History has been and will be repeated. [But] There will always be those who, though apparently conscientious, will grasp at the shadow, preferring it to the substance. They take error in the place of truth... (RH February 5, 1901, par. 5).

I saw the necessity of the messengers, especially, watching and checking all fanaticism wherever they might see it rise. Satan is pressing in on every side, and unless we watch for him, and have our eyes open to his devices and snares, and have on the whole armor of God, the fiery darts of the wicked will hit us. *There are many precious truths contained in the Word of God, but **it is "present truth" that the flock needs now**. I have seen the danger of the messengers running off from the important points of present truth, to dwell upon subjects that are not calculated to unite the flock and sanctify the soul. Satan will here take every possible advantage to injure the cause* (EW 63.1).

Such subjects as the sanctuary, in connection with the 2300 days, the commandments of God and the faith of Jesus, are perfectly calculated to explain the past Advent movement and show what our present position is, establish the faith of the doubting, and give certainty to the glorious future. These, I have frequently seen, were the principal subjects on which the messengers should dwell (EW 63.2).

Food Test Repeats

Daniel's first test in Babylon was that of appetite: To obey God's dietary laws or to eat whatever was set before him at the king's whim. Diet was Adam and Eve's first test as well. Such a simple test determined the fate of the human race! By failing, Adam and Eve lost paradise and their heirs inherited untold misery. By passing the test: Daniel, who loved God fully, acquired heaven's wisdom, good health, worldly success, and honor, as well as living to an old age.

Obeying God in such a small matter as eating a healthy diet prepared Daniel and his three friends to serve God. On the other hand, the other Jewish captives that conformed to the king's diet are never mentioned again in Scripture.

Notably, diet also attended Babylon's downfall. When eternal matters should have preoccupied the mind, the king was feasting, yielding to passion, pride, and self-exaltation.

In his pride and arrogancy, with a reckless feeling of security Belshazzar "made *a great feast* to a thousand of his lords, and drank wine before the thousand." All the attractions that wealth and power could command, added splendor to the scene. Beautiful women with their enchantments were among the guests in attendance at the royal banquet. Men of genius and education were there. Princes and statesmen drank wine like water and reveled under its maddening influence (PK 523.2).

With reason dethroned through shameless intoxication, and with lower impulses and passions now in the ascendancy, the king himself took the lead in the riotous orgy. As the feast progressed, he "commanded to bring the golden and silver vessels which... Nebuchadnezzar had taken out of the temple which was in Jerusalem; that the king, and his princes, his wives, and his concubines, might drink therein." The king would prove that nothing was too sacred for his hands to handle. "They brought the golden vessels...and the king, and his princes, his wives, and his concubines, drank in them. They drank wine, and praised the gods of gold, and of silver, of brass, of iron, of wood, and of stone" (PK 523.3).

God has permitted the light of health reform to shine upon us in these last days, that by walking in the light we may escape many of the dangers to which we shall be exposed. Satan is working with great power to lead men to indulge appetite, gratify inclination, and spend their days in heedless folly. He presents attractions in a life of selfish enjoyment and of sensual indulgence. Intemperance saps the energies of both mind and body. He who is thus overcome has placed himself upon Satan's ground, where he will be tempted and annoyed, and finally controlled at pleasure by the enemy of all righteousness. Parents need to be impressed with their obligation to give to the world children having well-developed characters, --children who will have moral power to resist temptation, and whose life will be an honor to God and a blessing to their fellowmen. Those who enter upon active life with firm principles, will be prepared to stand unsullied amid the moral pollutions of this corrupt age. Let mothers improve every opportunity to educate their children for usefulness (CE 175.3).

Consequences

The prophet first reminded Belshazzar of matters with which he was familiar, but which had not taught him the lesson of humility that might have saved him. He spoke of Nebuchadnezzar's sin and fall, and of the Lord's dealings with him--the dominion and glory bestowed upon him, the divine judgment for his pride, and his subsequent-t acknowledgment of the power and mercy of the God of Israel; and then in bold and emphatic words he rebuked Belshazzar for his great wickedness. He held the king's sin up before him, showing him the lessons, he might have learned but did not. Belshazzar had not read aright the experience of his grandfather, nor heeded the warning of events so significant to himself. The opportunity of knowing and obeying the true God had been given him, but had not been taken to heart, and he was about to reap the consequence of his rebellion (PK 529.2).

In the history of Nebuchadnezzar and Belshazzar, God speaks to the people of today. *The condemnation that will fall upon the inhabitants of the earth in this day will be because of their rejection of light. Our condemnation in the judgment will not result from the fact that we have lived in error, but from the fact that we have neglected Heaven-sent opportunities for discovering truth.* The means of becoming conversant with the truth are within the reach of all; but, like the indulgent, selfish king, we give more attention to the things that charm the ear, and please the eye, and gratify the palate, than to the things that enrich the mind, the divine treasures of truth. It is through the truth that we may answer the great question, "What must I do to be saved?" (BEcho, September 17, 1894 par. 5)

"As it was in the days of Noe, so shall it be also in the days of the Son of man" (Luke 17:26).

The days before the Flood steal silently on as a thief in the night. Noah is now making his last effort in warnings, entreaty, and appeal to the rejecters of God's message. With tearful eye, trembling lip, and quivering voice he makes his last entreaty for them to believe and secure a refuge in the ark. But they turn from him with impatience and contempt that he should be so egotistical as to suppose his family are the only ones right in the vast population of the earth. They have no patience with his warnings, with his strange work of building an immense boat on dry ground. Noah, they said, was insane (10MR 374.1).

Reason, science, and philosophy assured them Noah was a fanatic. None of the wise men and honored of the earth believed the testimony of Noah. If these great men were at ease and had no fears, why should they be troubled? (10MR 374.2)

The Spirit of God is departing from many among His people. Many have entered into dark, secret paths, and some will never return. They will continue to stumble to their ruin. They have tempted God; they have rejected light. All the evidence that will ever be given them they have received, and have not heeded. They have chosen darkness rather than light, and have defiled their souls... The world is polluted, corrupted, as was the world in the days of Noah. The only remedy is belief in the truth, acceptance of the light. Yet many have listened to the truth spoken in demonstration of the Spirit, and they have not only refused to accept the message, but they have hated the light. These men are parties to the ruin of souls. They have interposed themselves between the heaven-sent light and the people (PH154 34.2).

The righteous and the wicked will still be living upon the earth in their mortal state—men will be planting and building, eating and drinking, all unconscious that the final, irrevocable decision has been pronounced in the sanctuary above. Before the flood, after Noah entered the ark, God shut him in, and shut the ungodly out; but for seven days the people, knowing not that their doom was fixed, continued their careless, pleasure-loving life, and mocked the warnings of impending judgment. "So," says the Saviour, "shall also the coming of the Son of man be." [Matthew 24:39.] Silently, unnoticed as the midnight thief, will come the decisive hour which marks the fixing of every man's destiny, the final withdrawal of mercy's offer to guilty men. (GC88 491.2).

Where Are the Wise Men?

The return of Christ to our world will not be long delayed. Let this be the keynote of every message.

The blessed hope of the second appearing of Christ, with its solemn realities, needs to be often presented to the people. Looking for the soon appearing of our Lord will lead us to regard earthly things as emptiness and nothingness (6T 406.1 & 2).

The battle of Armageddon is soon to be fought. He on whose vesture is written the name, King of kings, and Lord of lords, is soon to lead forth the armies of heaven.

It cannot now be said by the Lord's servants, as it was by the prophet Daniel: "The time appointed was long." Daniel 10:1. It is now but a short time till the witnesses for God will have done their work in preparing the way of the Lord (6T 406.3 & 4).

We are to throw aside our narrow, selfish plans, remembering that we have a work of the largest magnitude and highest importance. In doing this work we are sounding the first, second, and third angel's messages, and are thus being prepared for the coming of that other angel from heaven who is to lighten the earth with his glory (6T 406.5).

The day of the Lord is approaching with stealthy tread; but the supposed great and wise men know not the signs of Christ's coming or of the end of the world. Iniquity abounds, and the love of many has waxed cold.

There are thousands upon thousands, millions upon millions, who are now making their decision for eternal life or eternal death. The man who is wholly absorbed in his counting room, the man who finds pleasure at the gaming table, the man who loves to indulge perverted appetite, the amusement lover, the frequenters of the theater [TV] and the ballroom, put eternity out of their reckoning. The whole burden of their life is: What shall we eat? what shall we drink? And wherewithal shall we be clothed? They are not in the procession that is moving heavenward. They are led by the great apostate, and with him will be destroyed (6T 406.6 & 7).

Unless we understand the importance of the moments that are swiftly passing into eternity, and make ready to stand in the great day of God, we shall be unfaithful stewards. *The watchman is to know the time of night.* Everything is now clothed with a solemnity that all who believe the truth for this time should realize. They should act in reference to the day of God. The judgments of God are about to fall upon the world, and we need to be preparing for that great day (6T 407.1).

Our time is precious. We have but few, very few days of probation in which to make ready for the future, immortal life. We have no time to spend in haphazard movements. We should fear to skim the surface of the word of God (6T 407.2).

It is as true now as when Christ was upon the earth, that every inroad made by the gospel upon the enemy's dominion is met by fierce opposition from his vast armies. The conflict that is right upon us will be the most terrible ever witnessed. But though Satan is represented as being as strong as the strong man armed, his overthrow will be complete, and everyone who unites with him in choosing apostasy rather than loyalty will perish with him (6T 407.3).

The restraining Spirit of God is even now being withdrawn from the world. Hurricanes, storms, tempests, fire and flood, disasters by sea and land, follow each other in quick succession. Science seeks to explain all these. The signs thickening around us, telling of the near approach of the Son of God, are attributed to any other than the true cause. Men cannot discern the sentinel angels restraining the four winds that they shall not blow until the servants of God are sealed; but when God shall bid His angels loose the winds, there will be such a scene of strife as no pen can picture (6T 408.1).

To those who are indifferent at this time Christ's warning is: "Because thou art lukewarm, and neither cold nor hot, I will spew thee out of My mouth." Revelation 3:16. The figure of spewing out of His mouth means that He cannot offer up your prayers or your expressions of love to God. He cannot endorse your teaching of His word or your spiritual work in anywise. He cannot present your religious exercises with the request that grace be given you (6T 408.2).

Could the curtain be rolled back, could you discern the purposes of God and the judgments that are about to fall upon a doomed world, could you see your own attitude, you would fear and tremble for your own souls and for the souls of your fellow men. Earnest prayers of heart-rending anguish would go up to heaven. You would weep between the porch and the altar, confessing your spiritual blindness and backsliding (6T 408.3).

"Blow the trumpet in Zion, sanctify a fast, call a solemn assembly: gather the people, sanctify the congregation, assemble the elders, gather the children... let the bridegroom go forth of his chamber, and the bride out of her closet. Let the priests, the ministers of the Lord, weep between the porch and the altar, and let them say, Spare Thy people, O Lord, and give not Thine heritage to reproach" Joel 2:15-17 (6T 408.4).

"Turn ye even to Me with all your heart, and with fasting, and with weeping, and with mourning: and rend your heart, and not your garments, and turn unto the Lord your God: for He is gracious and merciful, slow to anger, and of great kindness, and repenteth Him of the evil. Who knoweth if He will return and repent, and leave a blessing behind Him?" Verses 12-14 (6T 409.1).

Many, very many, will be terribly surprised when the Lord shall come suddenly as a thief in the night. Let us watch and pray, lest coming suddenly He find us sleeping. My soul is deeply stirred as I consider how much we ought to do for perishing souls. The prediction of Daniel, "Many shall run to and fro, and knowledge shall be increased," is to be fulfilled in our giving of the warning message; many are to be enlightened regarding the sure word of prophecy (https://egwwritings.org/Lt12-1907.4-5).

Transgression has almost reached its limit. Confusion fills the world, and a great terror is soon to come upon human beings. The end is very near. We who know the truth should be preparing for what is soon to break upon the world as an overwhelming surprise (https://egwwritings.org/Lt141-1902.18-21).

Spiritual Babylon Falls

The Spirit of God is gradually but surely being withdrawn from the earth. Plagues and judgments are already falling upon the despisers of the grace of God. The calamities by land and sea, the unsettled state of society, the alarms of war, are portentous. They forecast approaching events of the greatest magnitude. The agencies of evil are combining their forces, and consolidating. They are strengthening for the last great crisis. *Great changes are soon to take place in our world, and the final movements will be rapid ones* (9T 11.1-2).

Belshazzar made Daniel the third ruler of Babylon (cf Daniel 5:29). In the endtime, spiritual Babylon (the papacy) will have three rulers when it falls as per Revelation 16 while the seven last plagues are falling upon the earth.

After Benedict resigned, papal Babylon transitioned from having one solo living pope to having two popes. Ancient Babylon's history repeats in the endtime: The Euphrates is dried up and the papacy briefly has three *rulers.*

12And the sixth angel poured out his vial upon the great river Euphrates; and the water thereof was dried up, that the way of the kings of the east might be prepared. 13And I saw three unclean spirits like frogs [come] out of the mouth of the dragon, and out of the mouth of the beast, and out of the mouth of the false prophet. 14For they are the spirits of devils, working miracles, [which] go forth unto the kings of the earth and of the whole world, to gather them to the battle of that great day of God Almighty (Revelation 16:12-14).

Prophecy is meeting history. Prophetically, ISIS has almost dried up the Euphrates, i.e., waters "are peoples, and multitudes, and nations, and tongues" (Revelation 17:15). People have evacuated the area around the Euphrates basin to save their lives. And the flow of people into endtime papal Babylon is drying up. Thus, the drying of the Euphrates is also ending the flow of people into Babylon (Apostate Christendom). The priests' pedophile scandal has begun causing decent people to flee from the apostate Churches. To *bring people back into his fold,* Pope Benedict XVI proclaimed a Year of Faith (11 October 2012 to 24 November 2013). It did not stop the exodus from the Catholic Church. And the Protestant churches that embrace gay marriage are splitting. *Babylon is fallen because of her fornication!*

Some people teach that the dragon is Spiritualism, the beast is Catholicism, and the false prophet is Apostate American Protestantism rather than linking the three frog spirits in Revelation 16 to three endtime rulers of papal Babylon. That may be partially correct, but the Bible is its own best interpreter.

Satan is the dragon (Revelation 12:9). The beast depicts a king (beasts, which are four, [are] four kings, Daniel 7:17), i.e., Pope Francis I. The false prophet is Benedict Emeritus.

Is Pope Benedict Emeritus really the false prophet in Revelation 16:13? He links to the fornication scandal and lasciviousness. Or is the false prophet the United States?

The Lord said, "The prophets prophesy lies in My name: I sent them not, neither have I commanded them, neither spake unto them: they prophesy unto you a false vision...and the deceit of their heart" (Jeremiah 14:14). False prophets "deceive many" by their "great signs and wonders; insomuch that, if it were possible, they shall deceive the very elect" (Matthew 24:11, 24). And "false prophets...false teachers among you, who privily shall bring in damnable heresies, even denying the Lord that bought them, and bring upon themselves swift destruction" (2 Peter 2:1). Regarding popes:

> *Are not such teachers the pretenders to whom Christ referred when He said, "Beware of false prophets,* which come to you..." in opposition to the requirements of God, he measures himself and others by his own finite, fallible standard...*the pope of Rome...* he claims great spiritual riches...and boasts of the grace of Christ, which he has turned into *lasciviousness...*and by smooth words and deceptive speeches will deceive the unwary and those

who do not try the professions of men by the great Tester of character (RH, July 24, 1888 par. 11).

Satan had tried to eclipse from human minds the knowledge of God, and to eradicate from their hearts the attributes of God. Man was seeking out many inventions, which he supposed that he himself had originated, and he thought himself wiser than God. That which God had revealed was misconstrued, misapplied, and mingled with satanic delusions. Satan will quote Scripture in order to deceive. He tried to deceive Christ in this way. So, he still tries to deceive men. *He will lead them to misconstrue the Scriptures, and make them testify to falsehood* (17MR 21.3).

Christ came to adjust truths that had been misplaced and made to serve the cause of error. He recalled them, repeated them, placed them in their proper position in the framework of truth, and bade them stand fast forever. *Thus, it was with the law of God, with the Sabbath, and with the marriage institution.* We are to study His example. Satan seeks to obliterate everything that would keep the true God in remembrance; but the followers of Christ are to treasure up what God has revealed. *No truth of His Word, opened to them by His Spirit, is to be set aside* (17MR 21.4).

Theories will be continually agitated to divert the mind, to unsettle the faith. *Those who have had the actual experience in the unfolding of the prophecies, have been made what they are today, Seventh-day Adventists, by these prophecies.* They are to stand with their loins girt about with truth, and with the whole armor on. Those who have not had this experience are privileged to hold the message of truth with the same confidence. *The light that God has been pleased to give His people will not weaken their confidence in the path in which He has led them in the past, but will strengthen them to hold fast the faith. We must hold the beginning of our confidence firm unto the end* (17MR 22.1).

"Here is the patience of the saints: here are they that keep the commandments of God, and the faith of Jesus" (Revelation 14:12). Here we stand, under the third angel's message. "And after these things I saw another angel come down from heaven, having great power; and the earth was lightened with his glory. And he cried mightily with a strong voice, saying, *Babylon the great is fallen, is fallen, and is become the habitation of devils, and the hold of every foul spirit, and a cage of every unclean and hateful bird. For all nations have drunk of the wine of the wrath of her fornication, and the kings of the earth have committed fornication with her, and the merchants of the earth are waxed rich through the abundance of her delicacies. And I heard another voice from heaven, saying, Come out of her, My people, that ye be not partakers of her sins, and that ye receive not of her plagues. For her sins have reached unto heaven, and God hath remembered her iniquities*" [Revelation 18:1-5] (17MR 22.2).

The Third Angel's Message in Revelation 18 aligns with recent history: 1) Babylon is fallen (18:2) Benedict resigned amidst the priests' fornication scandal (18:3) that was drying up the flow of decent people into papal Babylon. 2) Pope Francis' light show (9 December 2015) demonstrated that St. Peter's Basilica is a cage of unclean birds (18:2, https://www.youtube.com/watch?v=WtI6P9R3x4E). 3) The US Supreme Court ruled that the priests' gay sex acts now constitute marriage (26 June 2015). 4) President Obama, an earth-king (18:3), hailed homosexual *marriage* as a *victory.* 5) God warns: Her sins have reached Heaven (judgment), flee Babylon, reject her sins, and avoid her plagues, (18:4-5), and *another angel has come down from heaven, having great power; and the earth was lightened with his glory* (18:1).

Satan's Final Deceptions

As the second appearing of our Lord Jesus Christ draws near, satanic agencies are moved from beneath. *Satan will not only appear as a human being,* but *he will personate Jesus Christ*; and the world who has rejected the truth will receive him as the Lord of lords and King of kings. He will exercise his power, and work upon the human imagination. *He will corrupt both the minds and the bodies of men,* and will work through the children of disobedience, fascinating and charming, as does a serpent. What a spectacle for God, the Creator of the world, to behold! *The form Satan assumed in Eden when leading our first parents to transgress was of a character to bewilder and confuse the mind. He will work in as subtle a manner as we near the end of earth's history. All his deceiving power will be brought to bear upon human subjects, to complete the work of deluding the human family.* So deceptive will be his working, that men will do as they did in the days of Christ... Christ will be represented in the person of those who accept the truth, and who identify their interest with that of their Lord (RH, April 14, 1896 par. 6).

Before personating Christ, *Satan personates a human being, Babylon's 3rd endtime ruler,* as it was when ancient Babylon fell (it had three kings): Nabonidus, Belshazzar and Daniel. In the endtime the rulers of spiritual Babylon are: the dragon (Satan appearing as Pope John-Paul II, this is revealed in Revelation 17:9-14), Pope Francis I (the beast), and Pope Benedict (the false prophet)! *John-Paul II* also links *to* an *immortal soul* and *Sunday sacredness*!

9And here [is] the mind which hath wisdom. The seven heads are seven mountains, on which the woman sitteth. 10And there are seven kings: five are fallen, and one is, [and] the other is not yet come; and when he cometh, he must continue a short space. 11And the beast that was, and is not, even he is the eighth, and is of the seven, and goeth into perdition. [12]And the ten horns which thou sawest are ten kings, which have received no kingdom as yet; but receive power as kings one hour with the beast. [13]These have one mind, and shall give their power and strength unto the beast. [14]These shall make war with the Lamb, and the Lamb shall overcome them: for he is Lord of lords, and King of kings: and they that are with him [are] called, and chosen, and faithful.

This beast has seven heads (17:9). It is the same beast as the first beast with seven heads (in Revelation 13), the papal beast. As noted, a head can depict a pope as in the case of Pius VI, the head that received the deadly wound. Thus, in 1929, the Pius head received its healing when Pius XI had the kingdom restored by Mussolini thru the Lateran Treaty. The seven heads are seven kings (popes after the kingdom was restored, i.e., post-1929 popes; 17:10).

Five of the restored popes were fallen or dead ("their lord [was] *fallen* down *dead*" Judges 3:25) when the prophecy met history: Popes Pius XI & XII, John XXIII, Paul VI, and John-Paul I were dead. John-Paul II is the *one that is*. The one that is to reign for a short space (Revelation 17:10) was Benedict XVI. A short space is not defined, but seven is the number of completeness. By Babylonian reckoning, it will be seen that Benedict ruled less than seven years, i.e., *for a short space.*

The eighth is of the seven (17:11). Thus, it cannot be Pope Francis I because he is not of the seven. The eighth has to be one of the dead popes, or Benedict XVI. The prophecy states that *the beast that was, and is not, even he is the eighth* and he goes *into perdition.* Benedict was pope and then he was not. Likewise, the dead popes were pope before they died and then they were not. Who is identified in Bible prophecy as one that goes into perdition, which is utter destruction?

[3]Let no man deceive you by any means: for *that day shall not come*, except there come a falling away first, and that man of sin be revealed, the son of perdition; [4]Who opposeth and exalteth himself above all that is called God, or that is worshipped; so that he as God sitteth in

the temple of God, shewing himself that he is God (2 Thessalonians 2:3-4).

The falling away has come. Babylon has fallen because of her fornication. In a sense, Satan has already pretended to be Jesus, but he is to do it again on earth. And Satan has given Pope John-Paul II his power, seat, and authority.

I turned to look at the company who were still bowed before the throne; *they did not know that Jesus had left it.*--Satan appeared to be by the throne, trying to carry on the work of God; I saw them look up to the throne and pray, my Father give us Thy Spirit; then *Satan would breathe upon them an unholy influence; in it there was light and much power, but no sweet love, joy and peace.* Satan's object was to keep them deceived, and to draw back and deceive God's children. I saw one after another leave the company who were praying to Jesus in the Holiest, and go and join those before the throne, and they at once received the unholy influence of Satan (Broadside1, April 6, 1846 par. 7).

And the beast which I saw was like unto a leopard, and his feet were as *[the feet]* of a bear, and his mouth as the mouth of a lion: and *the dragon gave him his power, and his seat, and great authority* (Revelation 13:2).

As the second appearing of our Lord Jesus Christ draws near...Satan will not only appear as a human being... Why will Satan appear as *a human being*, the dead John-Paul II?

Through the two great errors, the immortality of the soul, and Sunday sacredness, Satan will bring the people under his deceptions. While the former lays the foundation of Spiritualism, the latter creates a bond of sympathy with Rome. The Protestants of the United States will be foremost in stretching their hands across the gulf to grasp the hand of Spiritualism; they will reach over the abyss to clasp hands with the Roman power;

and under the influence of this threefold union, this country will follow in the steps of Rome in trampling on the rights of conscience (GC88 588.1).

Pope John-Paul II is dead and buried in his Vatican crypt. And he famously declared that God changed Sabbath to Sunday in *Dies Domini*. Regarding the immortality of the soul and Sunday sacredness, imagine Satan appearing as the dead Pope John-Paul II and saying something like: *Touch me and feel me; this is my spiritual body* and *when I was your pope, did I not tell you that Sabbath was changed to Sunday? Or I will go to the Father and send Christ to comfort you?* Then Satan as the *human being*, John-Paul II ascends into the sky. Soon afterwards Satan personating Jesus comes down to earth. A scenario along that line would align with Revelation 17 (*the beast that was, and is not, even he is the eighth, and is of the seven, and goeth into perdition*). It will deceive those who do not know that the dead are dead. "The soul that sinneth, it shall die" (Ezekiel 18:20). "For the living know that they shall die: but the dead know not anything" (Ecclesiastes 9:5). "[As] the cloud is consumed and vanisheth away: so, he that goeth down to the grave shall come up no [more]. He shall return no more to his house, neither shall his place know him anymore" (Job 7:9-10).

The things of this world are about to close... See the waymarks that are all along the way. When we are traveling...and see a guide board; *if we can read, we know that we are at such a place; so it is if our minds are active and so consecrated to God that we can understand His workings, we can know just where we are in this world's history...* The powers of darkness are working with an intensity from within, but God has been working for us, and He will work for us that Christ shall not have died in vain, that we may have of the life that runs parallel with the life of Jehovah. It is this little, little atom of a world that is absorbing all our force (2SAT 48.5).

The substance of the second angel's message is again given to the world by that other angel who lightens the earth with his glory. These messages all blend in one, to come before the people in the closing days of this earth's history. All the world will be tested, and all that have been in the darkness of error in regard to the Sabbath of the fourth commandment will understand the last message of mercy that is to be given to men (17MR 23.1).

Our work is to proclaim the commandments of God and the testimony of Jesus Christ. "Prepare to meet thy God" [Amos 4:12], is the warning given to the world. It is a warning to us individually. We are called upon to lay aside every weight, and the sin which doth so easily beset us. There is a work for you, my brother, to do, to yoke up with Christ. Make sure that your building is on the rock. Do not risk eternity on a probability. You may not live to participate in the perilous scenes on which we are now entering. The life of no one of us is assured for any given time. Should you not watch every moment? Should you not closely examine your own self, and inquire, What will eternity be to me? (17MR 23.2).

A crisis has arrived in the government of God in which something great and decisive must be done. The delay will not be prolonged long. The wrath of God will not be long withheld. Justice has only to speak the word and in a moment what confusion there will be. Voices and thunderings, and lightnings and earthquakes, and universal desolation. Now is our time to be good and to do good, while with wideawake senses we watch every movement in the government of God with apprehension. But if our life and character is after the divine model, we shall be hid with Christ in God (Ms10-1889).

Daniel 6

¹It pleased Darius to set over the kingdom a hundred and twenty princes, which should be over the whole kingdom; ²And over these three presidents; of whom Daniel [was] first: that the princes might give accounts unto them, and the king should have no damage. ³Then this Daniel was preferred above the presidents and princes, because an excellent spirit [was] in him; and the king thought to set him over the whole realm.

⁴Then the presidents and princes sought to find occasion against Daniel concerning the kingdom; but they could find none occasion nor fault; forasmuch as he [was] faithful, neither was there any error or fault found in him. ⁵Then said these men, We shall not find any occasion against this Daniel, except we find [it] against him concerning the law of his God.

⁶Then these presidents and princes assembled together to the king, and said thus unto him, King Darius, live forever. ⁷All the presidents of the kingdom, the governors, and the princes, the counsellors, and the captains, have consulted together to establish a royal statute, and to make a firm decree, that whosoever shall ask a petition of any God or man for thirty days, save of you, O king, he shall be cast into the den of lions. ⁸Now, O king, establish the decree, and sign the writing, that it be not changed, according to the law of the Medes and Persians, which alters not. ⁹Wherefore king Darius signed the writing and the decree.

¹⁰Now when Daniel knew that the writing was signed, he went into his house; and his windows being open in his chamber toward Jerusalem, he kneeled upon his knees three times a day, and prayed, and gave thanks before his God, as he did aforetime. ¹¹Then these men assembled, and found Daniel praying and making

supplication before his God. 12Then they came near, and spake before the king concerning the king's decree;

Have you not signed a decree, that every man that shall ask [a petition] of any God or man within thirty days, save of you, O king, shall be cast into the den of lions? The king answered and said, The thing [is] true, according to the law of the Medes and Persians, which alters not. 13Then answered they and said before the king, That Daniel, which [is] of the children of the captivity of Judah, regards you not, O king, nor the decree that you have signed, but makes his petition three times a day. 14Then the king, when he heard [these] words, was sore displeased with himself, and set [his] heart on Daniel to deliver him: and he labored till the going down of the sun to deliver him.

15Then these men assembled unto the king, and said unto the king, Know, O king, that the law of the Medes and Persians [is], That no decree nor statute which the king establishes may be changed. 16Then the king commanded, and they brought Daniel, and cast [him] into the den of lions. [Now] the king spake and said unto Daniel, Your God whom you serve continually, He will deliver you. 17And a stone was brought, and laid upon the mouth of the den; and the king sealed it with his own signet, and with the signet of his lords; that the purpose might not be changed concerning Daniel. 18Then the king went to his palace, and passed the night fasting: neither were instruments of music brought before him: and his sleep went from him.

19Then the king arose very early in the morning, and went in haste unto the den of lions. 20And when he came to the den, he cried with a lamentable voice unto Daniel: [and] the king spake and said to Daniel, O Daniel, servant of the living God, is your God, whom you serve continually, able to deliver thee from the lions?

²¹Then said Daniel unto the king, O king, live forever. ²²My God has sent his angel, and has shut the lions' mouths, that they have not hurt me: forasmuch as before him innocence was found in me; and also, before thee, O king, have I done no hurt. ²³Then was the king exceeding glad for him, and commanded that they should take Daniel up out of the den.

So, Daniel was taken up out of the den, and no manner of hurt was found upon him, because he believed in his God. ²⁴And the king commanded, and they brought those men which had accused Daniel, and they cast [them] into the den of lions, them, their children, and their wives; and the lions had the mastery of them, and brake all their bones in pieces or ever they came at the bottom of the den.

²⁵Then king Darius wrote unto all people, nations, and languages, that dwell in all the earth; Peace be multiplied unto you. ²⁶I make a decree, That in every dominion of my kingdom men tremble and fear before the God of Daniel: for He [is] the living God, and steadfast forever, and His kingdom [that] which shall not be destroyed, and His dominion [shall be even] unto the end. ²⁷He delivers and rescues, and He works signs and wonders in heaven and in earth, who hath delivered Daniel from the power of the lions.

²⁸So, this Daniel prospered in the reign of Darius, and in the reign of Cyrus the Persian. [text updated]

Points to Ponder

1. The lion's den law was based on a deception
2. Daniel broke a law that restricted liberty of conscience
3. Daniel was saved...his accusers were slain
4. God's vindication: The Temple's restoration
5. Prophetic history foreshadows Mark of the Beast
6. The power of prayer

Daniel's Preservation

As it was with Daniel's companions in Babylon, so it was with Daniel in Medo-Persia. These two instances foreshadow how it will be when the 666 Mark of the Beast is implemented.

Daniel and his companions had a conscience void of offense toward God. But this is not preserved without a struggle. What a test was brought...when they were required to worship the great image set up by King Nebuchadnezzar in the plains of Dura! Their principles forbade them to pay homage to the idol; for it was a rival to the God of heaven. They knew that they owed to God every faculty they possessed, and while their hearts were full of generous sympathy toward all men, they had a lofty aspiration to prove themselves entirely loyal to their God. To meet the appeals of the king and his counselors that they should comply with the royal edict, they had a store of arguments set forth most eloquently. The demand appeared contemptible to them. With Daniel as their companion, they had prayed and fasted, that they might understand the dream which God gave the king. The Lord had heard their cries, and had given to Daniel wisdom to interpret the dream; thus, their own lives and the lives of the astrologers and soothsayers had been saved. Now the very men who had escaped death through the mercy of God to His servants, were led by envy and jealousy to secure the decree in regard to the worshiping of the golden image (SpTEd 208.2).

"Satan sought to make Daniel's faithfulness to God the cause of his destruction" (ST, November 4, 1886 par. 2). But "Did Daniel cease to pray because this decree was to go into force? —No, that was just the time when he needed to pray" (Review and Herald, May 3, 1892 par. 11).

The decree goes forth from the king. Daniel is acquainted with the purpose of his enemies to ruin him.

But he does not change his course in a single particular. With calmness he performs his accustomed duties, and at the hour of prayer he goes to his chamber, and with his windows open toward Jerusalem, he offers his petitions to the God of heaven. By his course of action, he fearlessly declares that no earthly power has the right to come between him and his God and tell him to whom he should or should not pray. Noble man of principle! He stands before the world today a praiseworthy example of Christian boldness and fidelity. He turns to God with all his heart, although he knows that death is the penalty for his devotion (SL 43.3).

Daniel was a man of prayer; and God gave him wisdom and firmness to resist every influence that conspired to draw him into the snare of intemperance. Even in his youth he was a moral giant in the strength of the Mighty One. Afterward, when a decree was made that if for thirty days any one should ask a petition of God or man, save of the king, he should be cast into a den of lions, Daniel, with firm, undaunted step, made his way to his chamber, and with his windows open prayed aloud three times a day, as he had done before. He was cast into the lions' den; but God sent holy angels to guard His servant (ST, Aug 14, 1884 par. 6).

Daniel's history is a remarkable one. He carried out his faith and principles against great opposition. He was condemned to death because he would not abate one jot of his allegiance to God even in the face of the king's decree. It might, at this day, be called overrighteousness to go, as was his wont, three times a day and kneel before the open window for prayer while he knew that prying eyes were observing him and that his enemies were ready to accuse him of disloyalty to the king; but Daniel would allow no earthly power to come in between him and his God, even with the prospect of death in the den of lions. Although God did not prevent Daniel from being cast into a den of lions, an angel went in with him and closed their mouths, so that no harm befell him; and in the morning, when the king called him...He was a noble, steadfast servant of God (5T 527.1).

Through the moral courage of this one man who chose, even in the face of death, to take a right course rather than a politic one, Satan was defeated, and God honored. For the deliverance of Daniel from the power of the lions was a striking evidence that the Being whom he worshiped was the true and living God. And the king wrote unto "all people, nations, and languages, that dwell in all the earth:" "I make a decree, That in every dominion of my kingdom men tremble and fear before the God of Daniel; for He is the living God, and steadfast forever, and His kingdom that which shall not be destroyed, and His dominion shall be even unto the end" (ST, November 4, 1886 par. 7).

By prayer man is braced for duty and prepared for trial. Morning and evening our earnest prayers should ascend to God... and is as acceptable to God as if offered in the sanctuary (ST, Jan. 29, 1902 par. 2).

Repercussions

Because of Daniel's faithfulness, Darius' later decree recognized God in the laws (that could not be altered) of the Medo-Persians. "The deliverance of Daniel from the den of lions had been used of God to create a favorable impression upon the mind of Cyrus the Great" (PK 557.1). When it was time for God's Temple to be rebuilt in Jerusalem, Cyrus decreed that it was to be rebuilt.

As Satan attempted to kill Daniel when the Medo-Persian Empire arose; before it ended history repeated. During the reign of King Ahasuerus, who was also deceived to issue a death decree, Satan again attempted to kill God's faithful people. The Bible says that Satan will do it again.

The decree that will finally go forth against the remnant people of God will be very similar to that issued by Ahasuerus against the Jews. Today the enemies of the true church see in the little company keeping the Sabbath commandment, a Mordecai at the gate. The reverence of God's people for His law is a constant rebuke to those who have cast off the fear of the Lord and are trampling on His Sabbath (PK 605.2).

Satan will arouse indignation against the minority who refuse to accept popular customs and traditions. Men of position and reputation will join with the lawless and the vile to take counsel against the people of God. Wealth, genius, education, will combine to cover them with contempt. Persecuting rulers, ministers, and church members will conspire against them. With voice and pen, by boasts, threats, and ridicule, they will seek to overthrow their faith. By false representations and angry appeals, men will stir up the passions of the people. Not having a "Thus saith the Scriptures" to bring against the advocates of the Bible Sabbath, they will resort to oppressive enactments to supply the lack. To secure popularity and patronage, legislators will yield to the demand for Sunday laws. But those who fear God, cannot accept an institution that violates a precept of the Decalogue. On this battlefield will be fought the last great conflict in the controversy between truth and error. And we are not left in doubt as to the issue. Today, as in the days of Esther and Mordecai, the Lord will vindicate His truth and His people (PK 605.3).

Daniel 7

¹In the first year of Belshazzar king of Babylon Daniel, had a dream and visions of his head upon his bed: then he wrote the dream, [and] told the sum of the matters. ²Daniel spake and said, I saw in my vision by night, and, behold, the four winds of the heaven strove upon the great sea. ³And four great beasts came up from the sea, diverse one from another.

⁴The first [was] like a lion, and had eagle's wings: I beheld till the wings thereof were plucked, and it was lifted up from the earth, and made stand upon the feet as a man, and a man's heart was given to it.

⁵And behold another beast, a second, like to a bear, and it raised up itself on one side, and [it had] three ribs in the mouth of it between the teeth of it: and they said thus unto it, Arise, devour much flesh.

⁶After this I beheld, and lo another, like a leopard, which had upon the back of it four wings of a fowl; the beast had also four heads; and dominion was given to it.

⁷After this I saw in the night visions, and behold a fourth beast, dreadful and terrible, and strong exceedingly; and it had great iron teeth: it devoured and brake in pieces, and stamped the residue with the feet of it: and it [was] diverse from all the beasts that [were] before it; and it had ten horns. ⁸I considered the horns, and, behold, there came up among them another little horn, before whom there were three of the first horns plucked up by the roots: and, behold, in this horn [were] eyes like the eyes of man, and a mouth speaking great things.

⁹I beheld till the thrones were cast down, and the Ancient of days did sit, whose garment [was] white as snow, and the hair of His head like the pure wool: His

throne [was like] the fiery flame, [and] His wheels [as] burning fire. ¹⁰A fiery stream issued and came forth from before Him: thousand thousands ministered unto Him, and ten thousand times ten thousand stood before Him: the judgment was set, and the books were opened.

¹¹I beheld then because of the voice of the great words which the horn spake: I beheld [even] till the beast was slain, and his body destroyed, and given to the burning flame. ¹²As concerning the rest of the beasts, they had their dominion taken away: yet their lives were prolonged for a season and time.

¹³I saw in the night visions, and, behold, [one] like the Son of man came with the clouds of heaven, and came to the Ancient of days, and they brought Him near before Him. ¹⁴And there was given Him dominion, and glory, and a kingdom, that all people, nations, and languages, should serve Him: His dominion [is] an everlasting dominion, which shall not pass away, and His kingdom [that] which shall not be destroyed.

¹⁵I Daniel was grieved in my spirit in the midst of [my] body, and the visions of my head troubled me. ¹⁶I came near unto one of them that stood by, and asked him the truth of all this. So, he told me, and made me know the interpretation of the things.

¹⁷These great beasts, which are four, [are] four kings, [which] shall arise out of the earth. ¹⁸But the saints of the Most High shall take the kingdom, and possess the kingdom forever, even for ever and ever.

¹⁹Then I would know the truth of the fourth beast, which was diverse from all the others, exceeding dreadful, whose teeth [were of] iron, and his nails [of] brass; [which] devoured, brake in pieces, and stamped the residue with his feet; ²⁰And of the ten horns that [were] in his head, and [of] the other which came up, and

before whom three fell; even [of] that horn that had eyes, and a mouth that spake very great things, whose look [was] more stout than his fellows. 21I beheld, and the same horn made war with the saints, and prevailed against them; 22Until the Ancient of days came, and judgment was given to the saints of the Most High; and the time came that the saints possessed the kingdom.

23Thus, he said, The fourth beast shall be the fourth kingdom upon earth, which shall be diverse from all kingdoms, and shall devour the whole earth, and shall tread it down, and break it in pieces. 24And the ten horns out of this kingdom [are] ten kings [that] shall arise: and another shall rise after them; and he shall be diverse from the first, and he shall subdue three kings. 25And he shall speak [great] words against the Most High, and shall wear out the saints of the Most High, and think to change times and laws: and they shall be given into his hand until a time and times and the dividing of time.

26But the judgment shall sit, and they shall take away his dominion, to consume and to destroy [it] unto the end. 27And the kingdom and dominion, and the greatness of the kingdom under the whole heaven, shall be given to the people of the saints of the Most High, whose kingdom [is] an everlasting kingdom, and all dominions shall serve and obey Him. 28Hitherto [is] the end of the matter. As for me Daniel, my cogitations much troubled me, and my countenance changed in me: but I kept the matter in my heart.

Points to Ponder

1. This vision does not come chronologically
2. Daniel saw sea-beasts
3. Heaven explains earth-beasts as kings
4. Daniel 7 expands and explains Daniel 2 & 4
5. Knowledge has increased in the endtime
6. Bible prophecy: Past, Present, and Future

Daniel was taken captive to Babylon in 605 BC. Thus, the dream in Daniel 2 was inspired in 603 BC, which aligns with King Nebuchadnezzar's ascension year and the two years that followed. Daniel narrates chronologically for seventy years until the reign of Cyrus. After Babylon fell to Persia, Daniel interjects this vision that he had at the start of Belshazzar's reign.

The historical study of Daniel 7 is true. Now that the book of Daniel is unsealed and opened, the historical partial understanding must not skew the final endtime meaning that is to prepare us for Christ's Second Advent.

It is not enough to have an intellectual knowledge of the truth. This alone cannot give the light and understanding essential to salvation. *There must be an entrance of the word into the heart. It must be set home by the power of the Holy Spirit.* The will must be brought into harmony with its requirements. Not only the intellect but the heart and conscience must concur in the acceptance of the truth (RH, Sept 25, 1883 par. 7).

Daniel 7 describes a winged-lion, a fierce bear with three ribs in its mouth, a four-headed four-winged leopard, and an indescribable beast with iron teeth. The Bible explains itself. "Winds...strove upon the great sea" (Daniel 7:2). The gathered waters are *seas* (cf Genesis 1:10). "The great sea over against Lebanon" (Joshua 9:1) is the Mediterranean. Waters depict "peoples, and multitudes, and nations and tongues" (Revelation 17:15). Thus, "The great kingdoms that have ruled the world obtained their dominion by conquest and revolution, and they were presented to the prophet Daniel as beasts of prey, rising when the 'four winds of the heaven strove upon the great sea'" (4SP 276.2). These prophetic beasts arising from the sea depict four kingdoms that ruled the area adjacent to the Mediterranean.

[God] employed pictures and symbols to represent to His prophets lessons which He would have them give to the people...through the sense of sight. Prophetic history was presented to Daniel and John in symbols... that he who *reads* might understand (HS 212.2).

"The Holy Spirit represents worldly kingdoms under the symbol of fierce beasts of prey" (COL 77.1). These historical kingdoms that ruled adjacent to the Mediterranean Sea have sealed the validity of the vision in Daniel 7:1-14.

Daniel had his first vision while he was in Babylon. The head of gold (Daniel 2) like the winged-lion depicts Babylon.

The bear rising up on one side with ribs in its mouth was Medo-Persia, the Persian Empire. When it *devoured much flesh,* this symbolized: Lydia, Babylon, and Egypt. Though the Bible does not identify ribs as nations, it compares like to like. For example, "the rib, which the LORD God had taken from man, made He a woman" (Genesis 2:21-22). As the Lord formed a new person from Adam's rib, Medo-Persia formed a new kingdom from the *ribs* that it engulfed. The assimilation of these kingdoms into the Persian Empire is only a partial fulfillment of Daniel's prophecy because the directions of Persia's expansion do not align with the prophecy.

The leopard with four heads and four wings depicted Greece. History confirms that the four heads symbolize the generals (rulers) that divided the kingdom after Alexander's death. Thus, a head depicts a ruler in Bible prophecy. "*Wast thou not made* the head of the tribes of Israel, and the LORD anointed thee king over Israel?" (1 Samuel 15:17) The wings depict speed. "They that wait upon the LORD...shall mount up with wings as eagles; they shall run, and not be weary" (Isaiah 40:29). "As the eagle that hasteth to the prey," "the LORD shall bring a nation against thee from far, from the end of the earth, *as swift as the eagle flieth*" (Job 9:26; Deuteronomy 28:49). "He shall come as an eagle against the house of the LORD, because they have transgressed My covenant, and trespassed against My law" (Hosea 8:1).

The fourth indescribable beast, Imperial Rome, morphed into papal Rome: two different world powers that had their seat of authority in Rome. "The fourth kingdom shall be strong as iron: forasmuch as iron breaketh in pieces and subdueth all things: and as iron that breaketh all these, shall it break in pieces and bruise" (Daniel 2:40).

Long before Daniel was unsealed in the endtime: In the 4th century AD in TREATISE ON CHRIST AND ANTICHRIST, HIPPOLYTUS OF ROME explained the four kingdoms. In the 1500's Luther said: "Everyone agrees on this view and interpretation." In 1733, Sir Isaac Newton reaffirmed it in his book: *Observations Upon The Apocalypse Of St. John*.

> After this I saw in the night visions, and behold a fourth beast, dreadful and terrible, and strong exceedingly; and it had great iron teeth: it devoured and brake in pieces, and stamped the residue with the feet of it: and it [was] diverse from all the beasts that [were] before it; and it had ten horns. I considered the horns, and, behold, there came up among them another little horn, before whom there were three of the first horns plucked up by the roots: and, behold, in this horn [were] eyes like the eyes of man, and a mouth speaking great things. I beheld till the thrones were cast down, and the Ancient of days did sit, whose garment [was] white as snow, and the hair of His head like the pure wool: His throne [was like] the fiery flame, [and] His wheels [as] burning fire. (Daniel 7:7-9).

The fourth beast, Rome, conquered Greece. Then 1) Pagan Rome's Western flank was divided by ten Germanic Arian tribes. 2) Seven of the Arian kings became Catholic. 3) The three remaining Arian kings were plucked up during the 30 years allotted for the rise of papal Rome from 508-538. 4) After 538, papal Rome grew into a religio-political power. 5) It received its deadly wound in 1798 at which time the powerful religio-political papacy died. 6) France sold the Louisiana Territory to the USA in 1803. 7) The Investigative Judgment began in Heaven in 1844 (cf study of Daniel 8).

Daniel saw the thrones from Babylon to the ten tribes *cast down* and new thrones set up or *placed* by succeeding kings and kingdoms before the Judgment in Heaven convened. The Catholic Douay-Rheims Bible translates the phrase *thrones cast down* as *thrones were placed* (Daniel 7:9). Thus, Daniel's vision is describing the Judgment scene that occurs in Heaven after thrones were both *cast down* and *put in place* and that was done on earth as it was in Heaven, Daniel is not making statements that *must be read as either this or that*, but *he is saying both this and that* (both *cast down* and *placed*; both *on earth* and *in Heaven*). Daniel 7's usage of terms with dual meanings is significant.

Satan's throne was also cast down from Heaven. "How art thou fallen *from heaven*, O Lucifer... How art thou *cut down*...For thou hast said in thine heart, I will ascend into heaven, *I will exalt my throne above the stars* [angels] of God ...I will ascend above the heights of the clouds [angels]; I will be like the most High" (Isaiah 14:12-14, margin). Conversely, "The LORD'S throne is in heaven" (Psalms 11:4). And thrones are placed or set up for "I saw thrones, and they sat upon them, and judgment was given unto them" (Revelation 20:4).

Christ had come, not to the earth, as [Adventists] they expected [in 1844], but, as foreshadowed in the type, to the most holy place of the temple of God in Heaven. He is represented by the prophet Daniel as coming at this time to the Ancient of days: "I saw in the night visions, and, behold, one like the Son of man came with the clouds of heaven, and came"—not to the earth, but—"to the Ancient of days, and they brought Him near before Him." [Daniel 7:13] (GC88 424.1).

This coming is foretold also by the prophet Malachi. "The Lord, whom ye seek, shall suddenly come to His temple, even the messenger of the covenant, whom ye delight in: behold, He shall come, saith the Lord of hosts." [Malachi 3:1.] The coming of the Lord to His temple [in 1844] was sudden, unexpected, to His people. They were not looking for Him there. They expected Him to come to earth, "in flaming fire taking vengeance on

them that know not God, and that obey not the gospel."
[2 Thessalonians 1:8] (GC88 424.2).

As Daniel 7 initially related to Christ going to the Father
in Heaven in 1844 to commence the Investigative Judgment,
the complete fulfillment of Daniel 7 relates to Christ Second
Coming to the earth after the Judgment is concluded. In
1844, Adventists were focused on Christ's Advent. That was
not the Present Truth, for that day. By focusing on Christ's
Second Advent, they entirely missed the fact that Jesus had
to go to the Father in Heaven first. Now that Christ has
fulfilled the prophecy in Daniel 7 by going to His Father and
He has begun the Investigative Judgment in Heaven, there is
a danger of missing the fact that Daniel 7 is also describing
Christ's glorious Advent that the Adventists had awaited in
1844. This is a dual prophecy about Christ going to the
Father in Heaven to begin the Investigative Judgment in
1844, and it is also a prophecy of Christ's Second Advent in
the endtime at the conclusion of the Investigative Judgment:
But we do not know when Jesus will Come!

I beheld till the thrones were cast down, and the
Ancient of days did sit, whose garment [was] white as
snow, and the hair of His head like the pure wool: His
throne [was like] the fiery flame, [and] His wheels [as]
burning fire. A fiery stream issued and came forth from
before Him: thousand thousands ministered unto Him,
and ten thousand times ten thousand stood before Him:
the judgment was set, and the books were opened. I
beheld then because of the voice of the great words which
the horn spake: I beheld [even] till the beast was slain,
and his body destroyed, and given to the burning flame.
As concerning the rest of the beasts, they had their
dominion taken away: yet their lives were prolonged for
a season and time (Dan 7:9-12).

After Daniel saw the post-1803 thrones *placed* in the
prophetic earth, he saw Heaven's 1844 Judgment; he saw
the fourth beast burned; and he wrote of a season and a time.

A season is 90 days (1/4th of a 360-day year) and a time is 360 days (a year), their sum is 450 years (cf Num 14:34; Eze 4:6). Did Babylon (605-539 BC), Medo-Persia (539-331), and Greece (331-168 BC) have *their lives prolonged for a season and time* (450 years) *after the crown removed from Israel passed successively to the kingdoms of Babylon, Medo-Persia, and Greece?* Yes.

From Jerusalem's fall to Babylon in 605 BC, the 450 years ended in 155 BC when Johnathan, Judah's High Priest, began ruling Church and State. For 450 years, the state ruled the church, which is like having the kingdoms' lives prolonged. But when Johnathan ended the war between Judah and the Greeks, he gained the: "Affirmation of all Jewish religious freedoms. In return, Jonathan promised to keep peace and accept the continued status of Judah as a Seleucid dependency. This took place in 155 BC" (http://www.angelfire.com/nt/theology/15-400sy.html).

For 450 years, the kings ruled state and church. When God's people achieved religious autonomy in 155 BC, the church was no longer under a pagan state in Judea. Later, the church began ruling the state. But the prophecy was not completely fulfilled: Rome had not burned. Eventually, Imperial Rome and the Roman Church both burned and they both reverted to the worship of men (*as another god on earth*): Emperors and popes. Eventually, the Roman state ruled the church; and then, the Roman Church ruled the state.

A season and time are also identified after the Judgment began in 1844. They are in literal time, not *long time*.

> I saw in the night visions, and, behold, [one] like the Son of man came with the clouds of heaven, and came to the Ancient of days, and they brought Him near before Him. And there was given Him dominion, and glory, and a kingdom, that all people, nations, and languages, should serve Him: His dominion [is] an everlasting dominion, which shall not pass away, and His kingdom [that] which shall not be destroyed (7:13-14).

Christ returning to the Father partially fulfilled prophetic history. But He is to do it again. And the events relating to the *season and time*: The fourth beast being burned and the Judgment in Heaven have not entirely fulfilled the prophecy.

The sorrow of Jesus over an unsaved world pressed His divine soul, and was a sorrow to end only with His death. Now *He presents every soul who repents and believes before the Father with exceeding joy.* He sees of the travail of His soul, and is satisfied. *In the mansions above finally will be the Shepherd and his sheep.* The work will be complete, and victory will crown the ransomed ones. *When the redeemed of the Lord return unto Zion, the ransomed throng will sing:* "Worthy is the Lamb that was slain to receive power, and riches, and wisdom, and strength, and honor, and glory, and blessing" (RH, March 17, 1896 par. 12).

Daniel did not understand it as much as we do. These activities are embodied in Daniel 7: (1) Jesus went to the Father to begin the Investigative Judgment in 1844; (2) after it ends, He comes to the earth to get His people; (3) the fourth beast is burned at Christ's Advent; (4) Jesus takes us to the Father to present us to Him; (5) the Judgment of the lost then takes place in Heaven; (6) and finally, the earth is made new.

¹⁵I Daniel was grieved in my spirit in the midst of [my] body, and the visions of my head troubled me. ¹⁶I came near unto one of them that stood by, and asked him the truth of all this. So, he told me, and made me know the interpretation of the things (Daniel 7:15-16).

Heaven's Interpretation

The sea beasts/kingdoms bordering the Mediterranean sealed the validity of Daniel's prophecies. Until knowledge increased, the prophecy and *the interpretation* were interchanged. Now it is known that they are different because the interpretation is expanding and explaining the vision.

Heaven's interpretation is revealing the endtime meaning. It is true and clear. It does not need reinterpreting.

In Heaven's interpretation, the bystander did not say anything about the four sea-beasts. *"These great beasts, which are four, [are] four kings, [which] shall arise out of the earth"* (7:17). Heaven's interpretation that was sealed until the time of the end, focused on *earth kings*.

Kings can be interchanged with their kingdoms as King Nebuchadnezzar depicted Babylon in Daniel 2 and vice versa. But applying Daniel's clear statement, *You are the head of gold,* to the kingdom without first applying it to the king himself was a reinterpretation of the prophecy that totally overlooked that the king is the king. When the king was ignored, his kingdom became the focus of the prophecy. The meaning that applied to the king was lost sight of, and the meaning that applied to his kingdom became *all important.* The opposite was true in Daniel 4 when the essence of the dream's rendition totally overlooked the kingdom of Babylon, it focused entirely on the king.

> *The prophecies present a succession of events leading down to the opening of the Judgment. This is especially true of the book of Daniel. But that part of his prophecy which related to the last days, Daniel was bidden to close up and seal "to the time of the end." Not till we reach this time could a message concerning the Judgment be proclaimed, based on a fulfillment of these prophecies. But at the time of the end, says the prophet, "many shall run to and fro, and knowledge shall be increased."* [Daniel 12:4.] (GC88 355.3).

> *The people were not yet ready to meet their Lord.* There was still a work of preparation to be accomplished for them. Light was to be given, directing their minds to the temple of God in Heaven; and as they should by faith follow their High Priest in His ministration there, new duties would be revealed. *Another message of warning and instruction was to be given to the church* (GC88 424.3).

In spite of man's best efforts to study the Bible, his methods are not always consistent. God used those inconsistencies to seal the book of Daniel until the last days. There is no justification to reinterpret the words in Heaven's interpretation: To change the kings in Daniel 7:17 that Heaven is explaining in the endtime into the kingdoms that ruled in the past before Daniel was unsealed. Though it is true that thorough Bible study has identified the sea-beasts as kingdoms in the meaning of the vision in Daniel 7, this truth sealed Daniel's authenticity. In the endtime, now that knowledge has increased, Daniel 7:17 is obeying Heaven's command to: *Prophesy again* (Revelation 10:11). "The Revelation of Jesus Christ, which God gave unto Him, to show unto His servants things which must shortly come to pass" (1:1) is being revealed while "the Lion of the tribe of Judah has opened to the students of prophecy the book of Daniel" (1MR 47.2). Revelation explains that the water and earth symbolism in Daniel is different: *The waters are peoples, multitudes, nations, and tongues* (Rev 17:15) *and I beheld another beast coming up out of the earth* (13:11).

At this point another symbol is introduced. Says the prophet, "I beheld *another beast coming up out of the earth*; and he had two horns like a lamb." [Revelation 13:11.] Both the appearance of this beast and the manner of its rise indicate that *the nation which it represents is unlike those presented under the preceding symbols.* The great kingdoms that have ruled the world were presented to the prophet Daniel as beasts of prey, rising when the "four winds of the heaven strove upon the great sea." [Daniel 7:2.] In Revelation 17, an angel explained that *waters represent "peoples, and multitudes, and nations, and tongues"* [Revelation 17:15] (GC88 440.1).

Light comes from the very throne of God. When some familiar truth presents itself to your mind in a new aspect, when a text of Scripture suddenly bursts upon you with new meaning like a flash of light that scatters the mist, and you see the relation of other truths to some part of the plan of redemption, God is leading you, and a divine Teacher is at your side. **Will you not then open the door of your heart to receive more and more of the heavenly illumination?** (ST, Aug 27, 1894 par. 3).

Heretofore those who presented the truths of the third angel's message have often been regarded as mere alarmists. Their predictions...have been pronounced groundless and absurd... But as...the event so long doubted and disbelieved is seen to be approaching, and the third message will produce an effect which it could not have had before (GC 605.3).

As we have followed down the chain of prophecy, revealed truth for our time has been clearly seen and explained. We are accountable for the privileges that we enjoy and for the light that shines upon our pathway. Those who lived in past generations were accountable for the light which was permitted to shine upon them. Their minds were exercised in regard to different points of Scripture which tested them. *But they did not understand the truths which we do. They were not responsible for the light which they did not have. They had the Bible, as we have;* <u>but the time for the unfolding of special truth in relation to the closing scenes of this earth's history is during the last generations that shall live upon the earth</u> (2T 692.2).

In the Scriptures are presented truths that relate especially to our own time. To the period just prior to the appearing of the Son of man, the prophecies of Scripture point, and here their warnings and threatenings preeminently apply. The prophetic periods of Daniel, extending to the very eve of the great consummation, throw a flood of light upon events then to transpire. The book of Revelation is also replete with warning and instruction for the last generation. The beloved John, under the inspiration of the Holy Spirit, portrays the fearful and thrilling scenes connected with the close of earth's history, and presents the duties and dangers of God's people. None need remain in ignorance, none need be unprepared for the coming of the day of God (RH, September 25, 1883 par. 6).

Those who have been in any measure blinded by the enemy, and who have not fully recovered themselves from the snare of Satan, will be in peril because they cannot discern light from heaven, and will be inclined to accept a falsehood. This will affect the whole tenor of their thoughts, their decisions, their propositions, their counsels. The evidences that God has given are no evidence to them, because they have blinded their own eyes by choosing darkness rather than light. Then they will originate something they call light, which the Lord calls sparks of their own kindling, by which they will direct their steps. The Lord declares, "Who is among you that feareth the Lord, that obeyeth the voice of His servant, that walketh in darkness, and hath no light? Let him trust in the name of the Lord, and stay upon his God. Behold, all ye that kindle a fire, that compass yourselves about with sparks: walk in the light of your fire, and in the sparks that ye have kindled. This shall ye have at Mine hand; ye shall lie down in sorrow." Jesus said, "For judgment I am come into this world, that they which see not might see; and that they which see might be made blind." "I am come a light into the world, that whosoever believeth on Me should not abide in darkness." "He that rejecteth Me, and receiveth not My words, hath one that judgeth him: the word that I have spoken, the same shall judge him in the last day" (4BC 1146.10).

The book that was sealed is...that portion of the prophecy of Daniel relating to the last days (AA 585.1).

Daniel was written in three *portions*: 1) Daniel 1:1-2:3 was in Hebrew—it explains how Daniel got to be in Babylon; 2) the so called *historical* portion from Nebuchadnezzar's first dream to King Cyrus' reign (Daniel 2:4 to 7:28) was written in Aramaic; and 3) the third portion (Daniel 8:1-12:13) was written in Hebrew (see William H. Shea, *The Abundant Life Bible Amplifier*, pp. 20-21). Daniel's bilingual writing style is significant because some Aramaic (A) and Hebrew (H) words are the same, but their meanings are not always the same.

From chapter 7 to 8, Daniel switched from Aramaic to Hebrew. An English rendition of Daniel's Aramaic text in 7:2 is: "Four winds of the heaven strove upon the great sea." Look at Daniel's Aramaic words from the vantage point of the Hebrew meanings: "Four winds of heaven *gûach* [(A) *strove*, (H) *brought forth*] *rab* [(A&H) *captains*] *yâm* [(A) *great sea*, (H) *from the west*]." Comparing the Hebrew rendition of the Aramaic text (7:2) ... "Four *living captains* came up *from out of the west*" to Daniel 7:17 ... "Four kings shall arise out of the earth." In this comparison, Daniel's vision and Heaven's interpretation are remarkably similar (4 captains = 4 kings).

Heaven's interpretation was sealed until the endtime. No matter how precisely the translators understood the meaning of the prophecies before they were unsealed, they could not explain what God had sealed until God ordained that it should be opened and understood.

"*The books of Daniel and the Revelation are one...* but *no further light was to be revealed before these messages had done their specific work*" (1MR 99.3). Daniel expands and explains this vision in later visions that he saw by the "Ulai and Hiddekel Rivers" (Tigris and Euphrates) that are "now in process of fulfillment, and *ALL the events foretold will soon come to pass*" (TM 112.3, 16MR 334.2).

In this book are depicted scenes that are now in the past, and some... that are taking place around us; *other of its prophecies will not receive their complete fulfillment until the close of time* (RH, August 31, 1897 par. 5).

Jesus identified Daniel as the prophet (cf Matthew 24:15; Mark 13:14). Daniel's prophecies are unsealed by John in the book of Revelation. John is the revelator. He revealed God's message: "The Revelation of Jesus Christ, which God gave unto Him, to shew unto His servants things which must shortly come to pass; and He sent and signified [it] by His angel unto His servant John" (Revelation 1:1).

> *The book of Daniel is unsealed in the revelation to John, and it carries us forward to the last scenes of this earth's history* (CTr 334.5).

Thou must prophesy again (Revelation 10:11).

In the Revelation, the Lion of the tribe of Judah has opened to the students of prophecy the book of Daniel, and thus is *Daniel* standing in his place. He *bears his testimony, that which the Lord revealed to him in vision, of the great and solemn events that we must know as we stand on the very threshold of their fulfillment* (17MR 10.2).

[Christ] opened the seal that closed the book of divine instruction. The world was permitted to gaze upon pure, unadulterated truth. Truth itself descended to roll back the darkness and counteract error...as a light shining in a dark place (SpM 58.5).

The 2300-day/year prophecy (Daniel 8:14 and chapter 11) was fulfilled when the prophecy in Revelation 10 met history in 1844. Thus, after 1844, the command is executed: *Thou must prophesy again* (Revelation 10:11). Who is being told to *prophesy again*? Daniel, the prophet.

In some Bible prophecies, a day depicts a year: That is *long-time.* "A thing was revealed unto Daniel...and the thing [was] true, but the time appointed [was] long (Daniel 10:1).

Daniel's 2300-day/year *long-time* prophecy (8:14) was fulfilled from 457 BC to 1844 AD. In 1844, Revelation 10 was fulfilled. The command to *prophesy again* (10:11) repeats the prophetic history in the 2300-day/year prophecy without repeating the *long-time: Time shall be no longer* (10:6). When the 2300-year prophecy that ended in 1844 repeats, the prophetic history repeats, but it is not linked to *long-time.*

John's opening of Daniel's 2300-day/year prophecy in Revelation was supplemented with examples of *long-time* like the 42 months (Rev 13:5) that depicted 1260 years. When Revelation obeys the command to *prophesy again*, the times that are repeated are *literal-time*.

Daniel 7 and Revelation 13 are time prophecies of the same events. Using similar and different symbols, Revelation 13 explains and enlarges some aspects of Daniel 7. They both obey the command to *prophesy again*. However, the *season and time* (Daniel 7:12) are not explained and enlarged in Rev. 13. When Daniel 7 has its final fulfillment, *the season and time* are explained in *long and literal time, as 91 years.*

A Time Prophecy Problem

Our position has been one of waiting and watching, with no time-proclamation to intervene between the close of the prophetic periods in 1844 and the time of our Lord's coming (10MR 270).

That truth needs to be understood and heeded! No is no! But what is *time-proclamation?* White contrasted the world's *time-proclamation* that means *all time prophecies* with her use of *time-proclamation* that explicitly identifies the day and hour of Christ's Advent. Thus, from White's perspective there will be: *No time-proclamation OF THE TIME OF CHRIST'S ADVENT to intervene between the close of the prophetic periods in 1844 and the time of our Lord's coming.* But from the world's standpoint there will be: *No proclamation of Time-Prophecies to intervene between the close of the prophetic periods in 1844 and the time of our Lord's coming.* With those opposing views in mind, read White's statement in context:

THE WORLD PLACED ALL TIME-PROCLAMATION ON THE SAME LEVEL and called it a delusion, fanaticism and heresy. Ever since 1844 I have borne my testimony that we were now in a period of time in which we are to take heed to ourselves lest our hearts be overcharged with surfeiting and drunkenness, and cares of this life, and so *that day* come upon us unawares. *Our position has been one of waiting and watching, with no time-proclamation to intervene between the close of the* *prophetic periods in 1844 and the time of our Lord's coming. We do not know the day nor the hour, or <u>when the definite time is</u>, and yet the prophetic reckoning shows us that Christ is at the door* (10MR 270.1).

White warns against messages of *definite time*. There will be no more *definite time messages*! About all time prophecy? Or about the *definite time* of Christ's Advent?

*I was a firm believer in **definite time in 1844**, but **this prophetic time** was not shown me in vision, for it was some months after the passing of **this period of time** before the first vision was given me. There were many proclaiming **a new time** after this, but I was shown that **we should not have another definite time** to proclaim to the people. All who are acquainted with me and my work will testify that I have borne but one testimony in regard to **the setting of the time*** (16MR 177.2).

This time, which the angel declares with a solemn oath, is not the end of this world's history, neither of probationary time, but of prophetic time, which should precede the advent of our Lord. That is, the people will not have another message upon definite time. After this period of time, reaching from 1842 to 1844, there can be no definite tracing of the prophetic time. The longest reckoning reaches to the autumn of 1844 (7BC 971.7).

The preaching of a definite time for the judgment, in the giving of the first message, was ordered by God. The computation of the prophetic periods on which that message was based, placing the close of the 2300 days in the autumn of 1844, stands without impeachment. The repeated efforts to find new dates for the beginning and close of the prophetic periods, and the unsound reasoning necessary to sustain these positions, not only lead minds away from the present truth, but throw contempt upon all efforts to explain the prophecies. The more frequently <u>a definite time is set for the second advent</u>, and the more widely it is taught, the better it suits the purposes of Satan. After the time has passed, he excites ridicule and contempt of its advocates, and thus casts reproach upon the great advent movement of 1843 and 1844. Those who persist in this error will at last fix upon a date too far in the future for the coming of Christ. Thus, they will be led to rest in a false security, and **many will not be undeceived until it is too late** (GC 457).

In spite of White's clarifications and warnings, there are many scholars, professors, and teachers that do not understand. They emphatically reinterpret White's clear statements about: *Definite time, prophetic-time, the prophetic periods*, etc., to align with the worlds view about *all time prophecy rather than the specific time of Christ's Advent.* Thus, they twist White's statements to say that there are *no time prophecies after 1844.* If their reasoning is true, the season and time in Daniel 7:12 cannot be a 91-year prophecy that applies to our day. Are White's statements about time prophecy being misinterpreted? If they are being misread, is that concealing truth or bringing light from God's throne?

Time Prophecies After 1844

Misreading White's writings makes her contradict herself. An example: According to White, the 42 months (Rev 13:5) were fulfilled during the 1260 years of papal supremacy from 538 to 1798. The pope that led God's people into captivity had gone into captivity: Prophecy Fulfilled! Thus, the fulfillment of the deadly wound was the captivity of the pope by the French: "Pius VI...*the pope specified in prophecy,* which received the deadly wound" (5MR 318.1).

After White clearly stated that Revelation 13:3, 5, 10 related to the papacy and that this prophecy had been fulfilled in the past, she also placed 13:5 (42 months), 13:10 (captivity, i.e., the deadly wound), and 13:3 (its healing) after 1844: "*In the last days...will take place the final fulfillment of the Revelator's prophecy.* [Revelation 13:4-18, quoted.]" (19MR 282.1). *This post-1844 statement is not saying that Revelation 13 will be repeated apart from the 42 months!*

White did not omit the 42 months in Revelation 13 when she personally wrote out in longhand the portion of prophecy that repeats! White's statement from 19MR 282.1 really says that the 42 months (13:5) will also be repeated!

The reference you asked about [19MR 282.1] is correct. When you see an item like this in the Manuscript Releases, enclosed in square brackets, it means that in Ellen White's material, she quoted the named passage, but for economy of space, we will not quote it here, but merely give the reference so that the reader can look it up and read it, if desired. So, it does indeed refer to these verses in Revelation 13, and this is the prophecy that she mentioned just before the reference. ...I confirmed it by going to the manuscript, where the verses were written out (Email response, William Fagal, Associate Director, Ellen G. White Estate, 12501 Old Columbia Pike, Silver Spring, MD 20904-6600 U.S.A).

But many allege that White taught that *all time prophecy* stopped *after 1844*. Yet after 1844, White wrote out in longhand the specific verse (Revelation 13:5) in 19MR 282.1 saying that the 42 months will have *their final fulfillment in the last days. After White had written that the 42 months (Revelation 13:5) had been fulfilled in the past, she also placed them in the future!* She did it again in another article: She wrote out the text word by word in longhand:

"And they worshipped the dragon which gave power unto the beast: and they worshipped the beast, saying, Who is like unto the beast? Who is able to make war with him? And there was given unto him a mouth speaking great things and blasphemies; and power was given unto him to continue forty and two months. And he opened his mouth in blasphemy against God, to blaspheme his name, and his tabernacle, and them that dwell in heaven. And it was given unto him to make war with the saints, and to overcome them: and power was given him over all kindreds, and tongues, and nations. And all that dwell upon the earth shall worship him, whose names are not written in the book of life of the Lamb slain from the foundation of the world. If any man have an ear, let him hear. He that leadeth into captivity shall go into captivity: he that killeth with the sword must be killed with the sword. Here is the patience and the faith of the saints." Revelation 13:4-10. _This entire chapter is a revelation of what will surely take place_ (7BC 979.10).

THIS ENTIRE CHAPTER is WHAT WILL SURELY TAKE PLACE! White wrote this after 1844. *This 42-month time prophecy will surely take place in literal time!* It will happen before Christ's Advent! Is White contradicting herself? No!

Turning Truth into Error

There have always been people that have not understood White's statements. She repeatedly rebuked individuals for misquoting her and misrepresenting her.

> With their distorted views of the matter they have discussed the question...until their spiritual vision has become so confused that they can only see men as trees walking. They have thought they could see a contradiction in my article... and that article on the same subject... I must contend that I am the best judge of the things which have been presented before me in vision; and none need fear that I shall by my life contradict my own testimony, or that I shall fail to notice any real contradiction in the views given me (1T 462.3).

> When the word of the Lord comes to churches and to individuals, there are always those who refuse to hear aright or to see aright. Their defective hearing and seeing puts them far out of the way... those who would misinterpret my words to mean what they want them to mean. Their eyes are so blinded that they cannot see; their ears are so dulled that they cannot hear. They circulate reports as being what Sister White has said, when I said no such thing (21MR 428.1).

My words are so wrested and misinterpreted... What I say is reported in such a perverted light that it is new and strange to me. It is mixed with words spoken by men to sustain their own theories (2MR 152.2).

Do not quote my works again as long as you live until you can obey the Bible. When you make the Bible your food, your meat and your drink, when you make its principles the elements of your character, you will know better how to receive counsel from God. I exalt the precious word before you today. Do not repeat what I have said, saying, "Sister White said this," and, "Sister White said that." Find out what the Lord God...says, and then do what He commands (5MR 141.1).

They put their own interpretation upon the Word and make it contradict what the Lord has revealed in the testimonies (10MR 311.2).

If we are the Lord's appointed messengers, we shall not spring up with new ideas and theories to contradict the message that God has given through His servants since 1844. At that time many sought the Lord with heart and soul and voice. *The men whom God raised up were diligent searchers of the Scriptures.* And those who today claim to have light, and who contradict the teaching of God's ordained messengers, who were working under the Holy Spirit's guidance, those who get up new theories, which remove the pillars of our faith, are not doing the will of God, but are bringing in fallacies of their own invention, which, if received, will cut the church away from the anchorage of truth, and set them drifting, drifting, to where they will receive any sophistries that may arise (4MR 247.2).

By changing the meaning of *prophetic time* from the *definite time* of Christ Coming as White used it, to mean *all time prophecy*, some have cut the church away from the anchorage of truth, and set it adrift, to where it has received many sophistries that have arisen. Those who have been deceived to reject all time prophecies after 1844 (a theory that contradicts the message that God has given through His servants) have removed the pillars of our faith. What pillars? Time prophecies! God has led His people with time prophecy. They do not do God's will. They are in darkness. They are casting their shadow upon the paths of others and blocking White's writings from doing their work.

We have nothing to fear for the future, *except as we shall forget the way the Lord has led us, and His teaching in our past history* (LS 196.2).

As I have imparted the light given me. I have very much more light on the Old and New Testament Scriptures, which I shall present to our people if my way is not blocked (9MR 23.2).

"There is nothing in the word of God to be thrown aside" (ST, June 3, 1886 par. 13). "The Bible must be your counselor. Study it and the testimonies God has given; for they never contradict His Word" (3SM 32.3). White's writings agree with the Bible! *There are no time prophecies that give the definite time of Christ's Advent,* but they still warn of pending trials and they testify of God's foreknowledge.

Time Prophecies Fulfilled After 1844!

After White wrote that the 42 months (Reve 13:5) had been fulfilled, she places its final fulfillment in the future. The 42 months (13:5) is the same as the *time and times and the dividing of time* (Dan 7:25) that is linked to the *changing of the law.* The 42 months/1260 day's (7:25) were fulfilled by the papacy. White applies a dual meaning to 7:25 by placing *changing of times and laws* in the endtime.

And now began the 1260 years [538-1798] of papal oppression foretold in the prophecies of Daniel and John. [Daniel 7:25; Revelation 13:5-7] (4SP 57.2).

After *the warning against the worship of the beast and his image, the prophecy declares,* "Here are they that keep the commandments of God, and the faith of Jesus." Since those who keep God's commandments are thus placed in contrast with *those that worship the beast and his image and receive his mark,* it follows that the keeping of God's law, on the one hand, and its violation, on the other, will make the distinction between the worshipers of God and the worshipers of the beast (GC88 445.3).

The special characteristic of the beast, and therefore of his image, is the breaking of God's commandments. Says Daniel, of the little horn, the papacy, "He shall think to change the times and the law." [Daniel 7:25, Revised Version.] And Paul styled the same power the "man of sin," who was to exalt himself above God. *One prophecy is a complement of the other.* Only by changing God's law could the papacy exalt itself above God; whoever should understandingly keep the law as thus changed would be giving supreme honor to that power by which the change was made. Such an act of obedience to papal laws would be a mark of allegiance to the pope in the place of God (GC88 446.1).

The vision in Daniel 7 corresponds with prophetic history fulfilled from Babylon to Rome (Imperial [pagan] and papal). For papal Rome to arise, Daniel prophesied that three horns must be plucked up. A horn prophetically depicts a king (cf Daniel 8: 21, 22). Traditionally, the three horns are said to be the Germanic tribes: Heruli, Vandals, and the Ostrogoths.

The Heruli do not align with the 30-years allotted for the forming of the papacy that counterfeited the life of Christ. The horns (kings that align with the 30-years (508-538) that parallel Christ's life until His anointing when He had victory over the three temptations) are kings: Gesalic (Visigoth, 508), Gelimer (Vandal, 533), and Witigis (Ostrogoth, 538).

It may seem insignificant, but to correctly understand prophecy fulfilled, it must align with historical facts. As knowledge increases, it is important to know the truth.

Some of us have had time to get the truth and to advance step by step, and every step we have taken has given us strength to take the next. But now time is almost finished, and what we have been years learning, they will have to learn in a few months. *They will also have much to unlearn and much to learn again* (EW 67.2).

Daniel asked Heaven's bystander the truth about the fourth earth-king linked to the ten horns and a little horn that plucks up three. And Daniel added a feature that had not been in the vision: "Nails [of] brass" (Daniel 7:19). Thus, the interpretation is expanding the vision while explaining it.

The vision was fulfilled all the way to Rome: The last *sea-kingdom*. Then Heaven's interpretation focuses on the *earth-kings*. The sea depicted the Mediterranean people groups. To learn about the earth-kings, first identify the prophetic earth.

The papacy was at last *deprived of its strength, and forced to desist from persecution.* [Revelation 13:3, 10.] *At that time the prophet beheld a new power coming up, represented by the beast with lamb-like horns. The appearance of this beast...is unlike those brought to view under the preceding symbols.* The great kingdoms... were presented to the prophet Daniel as beasts of prey, rising when the "four winds of the heaven strove upon the great sea." [Daniel 7:2.] *But the beast with horns like a lamb is seen "coming up out of the earth;"* [Revelation 13:11.] signifying that instead of overthrowing other powers to establish itself, *the nation thus represented arose in territory previously unoccupied* (4SP 276.2).

Here is a striking figure of the rise and growth of our own nation...the United States... (4SP 277.1).

France *forced* Rome to desist from persecution in 1798. *At that time,* in1803, *the prophet beheld a new power coming up*: France sold the Louisiana Territory, the *prophetic earth* to the USA, which almost doubled it. The Louisiana Territory was *unoccupied in comparison to the civilizations inhabiting the old world.* Thus, it fits the prophetic description. After the Louisiana Territory was added to America, did the USA continue to fulfill the prophecy in Revelation 13:11-18?

In Revelation 13 this subject is plainly presented: "I beheld **another beast coming up out of the earth**; and he had two *horns like a lamb,* and he *spake as a dragon.* And he exercised all the power of the first beast before him, and causeth the earth and them that dwell therein to worship the first beast, whose deadly wound was healed." *Then the miracle-working power is revealed:* *"And deceiveth them that dwell on the earth by the means of those miracles which he had power to do in the sight of the beast;* saying to them that dwell on the earth, that they should make an image to the beast, which had the wound by a sword, and did live. And he had power to give life unto the image of the beast, that the image of the beast should both speak, and cause that as many as would not worship the image of the beast should be killed. *And he causeth all, both small and great, rich and poor, free and bond, to receive a mark in their right hand, or in their foreheads and that no man might buy or sell, save he that had the mark, or the name of the beast, or the number of his name"* (1888 700.2).

Revelation is a sealed book, but it is also an open book, recording marvelous events that are to take place in the last days of this earth's history. *Its teachings are definite, not mystical and unintelligible, and God would have us understand it* (ST, January 11, 1899 par. 5).

It was *through putting a mystical meaning upon the plain words of God, that sacred and vital truths were made of little significance, while the theories of men were made prominent.* It was in this way that men were led to teach for doctrines the commandments of men, and that they rejected the commandment of God, that they might keep their own tradition (RH June 2, 1896).

After Monroe negotiated the Louisiana Purchase, he became President. *The Monroe Doctrine spoke like a dragon.* It warned the Europeans: *Stop colonizing the Americas or else!* After the 2300-year prophecy (cf Daniel 8) ended in 1844, Monroe put *thrones in place* in the prophetic earth, i.e., governors and legislators in the Louisiana Territory. After the 1929 healing of the papacy's wound, President Truman, who came from Missouri, a state in the heart of the *prophetic earth,* literally called fire down from heaven. As predicted, the USA has made fire come down from heaven *in the sight of eyewitnesses.* Hiroshima and Nagasaki partially fulfilled Revelation's prophecy and confirmed America's identity.

> Over the city of Hiroshima, the *Enola Gay* dropped an 8,900-pound atomic weapon... *Two thousand feet above the ground, the bomb...detonated* (http://www.factmonster.com/spot/hiroshima1.html).

> After the flash, she saw a brilliant orange orb, the color of the sun as it sets in the ocean, *erupt in the sky -* and she hit the ground. When she looked up, the buildings around her and much of the city were on fire... West was stunned by the hellish ruins of Hiroshima (http://www.nydailynews.com/archives/news/hiroshima-survivor-hell-n-y-er-tells-day-sky-turned-orange-article-1.580801).

Over Nagasaki when *Bockscar's bombardier,* Captain Kermit Beahan, visually sighted the target; the Fat Man was *exploded above the ground.* "The explosion generated heat estimated at 3,900 degrees Celsius (...7,050 F)" (http://en.wikipedia.org/wiki/Atomic_bombings_of_Hiroshima_and_Nagasaki#The_bombing_2).

More recently, As Revelation 13 nears its complete and final fulfillment, President Trump has threatened to rain "FIRE AND FURY" upon North Korea. Vice President Pence said "The time has come to establish the United States Space Force" (https://www.washingtonpost.com/business/economy/pence-details-plan-for-creation-of-space-force-

in-what-would-be-the-sixth-branch-of-the-military/2018
/08/09/0b40b8d0-9bdc-11e8-8d5e-c6c594024954_story
.html?utm_term=.8cdf66e7ec05) "The U.S. Space Command
officially starts Aug. 29, [2019] serving as the launching pad
for the Space Force, they said. Air Force Gen. John Raymond
has been tapped and confirmed by the Senate as its first
leader" (https://www.msn.com/en-us/news/ us/space-
command-will-launch-aug-29-vice-president-mike-pence-
says/ar-AAG 4FaV?ocid=spartanntp).

The earth-beast of Revelation 13 and Daniel 7: The USA
that partially fulfilled Bible prophecy in the past, is still
fulfilling Bible prophecy! But the USA has not yet given *life
unto the image of the beast.* It is getting closer day by day!

The Four Earth-Kings

"These great beasts, which are four, [are] four kings,
[which] shall arise out of the earth" (Dan 7:17). After the
papacy received its deadly wound, America became the focus
of Daniel 7 and Revelation 13. The kings arise from the USA,
but it does not have kings. The Bible explains: "Put the crown
upon him...they made him king" (2 Kings 11:12). "He shall
be king...I have appointed him to be ruler" (1 Kings 1:35).

White points out: "The crown removed from Israel passed
successively to the kingdoms of Babylon, Medo-Persia,
Greece, and Rome" (Ed 179.3). "Crowned heads, presidents,
rulers in high places" (RH, August 17, 1897 par. 14).

> Read the book of Daniel. Call up, point by point, the
> history of the kingdoms there represented. *Behold
> statesmen,* councils, powerful armies, and see how God
> wrought to abase the pride of men, and lay human glory
> in the dust. God alone is represented as great. *In the
> vision of the prophet He is seen casting down one mighty
> ruler, and setting up another* (4BC 1166.4).

Daniel 7's narration of the vision is sequential thru the
Judgment and the destruction of the fourth beast. *"The
Judgment was set, and the books were opened"* (7:10). After
the 1844 Judgement sat, then Daniel tells of "the voice of the

great words which the horn spake" (7:11). The 1844 Judgment began before the little horn speaks. Then Daniel "beheld [even] till the beast was slain, and his body destroyed, and given to the burning flame" (7:11). This 4th beast that is consumed by the flames is the earth king (7:17), an American President that heard the post-1844 horn speak. "As concerning the rest of the beasts" (7:12) the American Presidents that correspond to the lion, bear, and leopardlike beasts: "They had their dominion taken away: yet their lives were prolonged for a season and time" (Daniel 7:12). The *season and time*, which is 91 years, explain the time immediately before the 4th earth beast's destruction. *This is the endtime meaning that is needed now.*

In the context, after seeing the 1844 judgment, Daniel is asking: "The truth of the fourth beast, which was diverse from all the others, exceeding dreadful, whose teeth [were of] iron, and his nails [of] brass; [which] devoured, brake in pieces, and stamped the residue with his feet; And of the ten horns that [were] in his head..." (Dan 7:19-20). The brass feature was added to the vision in the interpretation. The 4th endtime earth king is the President that is consumed by Christ's glory at His Second Advent. He is synonymous with his kingdom, America, as evidenced by his having ten horns in his head. The kingdom (USA) can have ten rulers (7:20), but an American President cannot.

Daniel 7 is supplemented by Revelation 13. America's President that called fire from heaven that confirms the identity of the earth beast was Truman. He came from the prophetic earth that had been purchased in 1803. Thus, starting at Truman, the one that rained fire down, the ten American Presidents (horns) that bonded with the post-1929 popes are: Truman, Eisenhower, Kennedy, Johnson, Nixon, Ford, Carter, Reagan, Bush I, and Clinton.

Concerning the "ten horns that [were] in his head, and [of] the other which came up, and before whom three fell; even [of] that horn that had eyes, and a mouth that spake very great things, whose look [was] more stout than his fellows" (Dan 7:20), this little horn is a pope. What endtime pope interacted with three of these Presidents?

Pope Paul VI aligned with four Presidents: Kennedy, Johnson, Nixon, and Ford. John-Paul II interacted with Carter, Reagan, Bush I, Clinton and Bush II. Of these nine Presidents, which four are depicted as the earth-kings?

The sea-beasts are *like a lion, and had eagle's wings; a bear, and it raised up itself on one side, and [it had] three ribs in the mouth; and like a leopard, which had upon the back of it four wings of a fowl; the beast had also four heads* (cf 7:4-6). Reagan was the Great Orator (a lion's mouth); Bush I fought in Panama, Somalia, and Iraq to bring about a New World Order; and Clinton aligns with the leopardlike features (that correlate with the idol's brass midsection in Daniel 2...his midsection almost got him put out of office). John-Paul II bonded so thoroughly with Presidents: Reagan, Bush I, and Clinton that the post-1929 sea-beast in Revelation 13 was seen as a leopardlike-beast with a lion's mouth and bears feet.

President Reagan continued Mussolini's healing of the papacy's 1798 deadly religio-political wound on America's behalf by recognizing Pope John-Paul II as the head of the Vatican state while the pope headed the Catholic Church. In vision, John "saw one of his heads as it were wounded to death; and his deadly wound was healed: and all the world wondered after the beast" (Revelation 13:3). As the papacy had been wounded and healed, Pope John-Paul II literally received a deadly assassination wound that was healed.

Bush I continued the spiritual healing process, when he said that Pope John-Paul II was the world's *moral leader,* i.e., *the head of all the churches*: "I had an opportunity to express my profound gratitude to the Holy Father for the *spiritual and moral leadership...*" (https://bush41library.tamu.edu/archives/public-papers/3601).

President Clinton also sang the praises of Pope John-Paul II: "Whether I agree or disagree with him, this guy is on my side" (http://www.nbcnews.com/id/7423221/ns/nbc_nightly_news_with_brian_williams/t/bill-clinton-remembers-pope-john-paul-ii/).

The charismatic Pope John-Paul II plucked up three horns (American Presidents) that align with the sea-beasts' features: Reagan, Bush I, and Clinton. President Reagan turned 90 years old on 6 February 2001. He was in his 91st year when the 9/11 tragedy struck America, which aligns with the prophetic *season and time* (91 years of Daniel 7:12).

Endtime Prophecy Fulfilled

In Reagan's *91st* year, on 9/11/01, Presidents: Reagan, Bush I, and Clinton fulfilled the prophecy "concerning the rest of the beasts, *they had their dominion taken away: yet their lives were prolonged for a season and time*" (7:12). They were *out of office*, and *they were alive*. All of their political feats had taken place during Reagans 91 years.

These three-specific earth kings (American Presidents), precede the fourth earth king, President Bush II, which was not "the beast" who is "slain, and his body destroyed, and given to the burning flame" (7:11). Why not? Christ has not yet come in glory and thus, Bush II is still living.

By count, four earth-kings are prophetically identified. Reagan, Bush I, and Clinton aligned with the prophecy, but the fourth, Bush II has not yet completely aligned.

To understand that prophetic dilemma, remember how the sea-beasts fulfilled Daniel 7. Babylon, Medo-Persia, and Greece were political kingdoms. The fourth beast that was centered in Rome was a political kingdom (Imperial Rome). But the religious kingdom (papal Rome) that replaced it was a different kingdom that was still the 4th beast.

The fourth king from the prophetic earth, President Bush II is clearly identified in Daniel 9 as well as President Obama. And as this study continues, Presidents Trump and Pence will also be identified. But at this point in the study, Daniel 7 and Revelation 13 has clearly identified these endtime men that fulfill Bible prophecy: Pope John-Paul II, Presidents: Reagan, Bush I, Clinton, and Bush II.

"The fourth beast shall be the fourth *kingdom* upon earth, which shall be diverse from all kingdoms, and shall devour the whole earth, and shall tread it down, and break it in pieces" (Dan 7:23). The focus on the fourth earth-king (Bush II) changes from the individual to the kingdom (various presidents that come to power in America).

Until knowledge increases about the four earth kings, notice this regarding Pope John-Paul II: September 11, 2001 clearly links to the *season and time* (7:12). From 9/11, a time (360-day year) times (2 years or 720 days) and the dividing of times (1/2 of a year or 180 days), these 1260 days ended 22 February 2005; the day, Pope John-Paul II, who was in the dying process got out of the hospital. The following day he sat for a video. He was readmitted to the hospital (24 February 2005) where he remained until he died.

Feb. 22 Pope's newest book, *Memory and Identity*, is officially launched. Describes for first time moments after being shot in 1981, saying he was "almost on the other side" but thought he'd live.

Feb. 23: Holds longest audience — 30 minutes — since being hospitalized. It's broadcast by video instead of being held in person (http://www.usatoday.com/news/world/2005-04-02-pope-highlights_x.htm).

"There was given unto him a mouth speaking great things and blasphemies" in *Dies Domini* "and power was given unto him to continue forty [and] two months" (Revelation 13:5). From 9/11/01, 42 full months are: October, November, December; 12 months each in 2002, 2003, 2004; January, February, and March 2005: John-Paul II died 2 April 2005. Thus, by the Gregorian calendar, he died 42 full months after 9/11, which fulfills Bible prophecy. But in addition to the 42 full-months, there is some time remaining that has not been accounted for in September 2001 and April 2005. Thus, all the time is not accounted for in the prophecy!

The Bible writers did not use the Gregorian calendar, they used the Hebrew calendar that is a lunar calendar. To keep it in sync with the solar calendar, "A leap year occurs 7 times in the 19-year Metonic cycle. With years 3, 6, 8, 11, 14, 17, and 19 of the cycle being leap years, this corresponds to a frequency of every 2 to 3 years" (https://www.Timeanddate.com/date/jewish-leap-year.html). The month Adar I is added in these leap years. "The extra month is inserted before the regular month of Adar" (http://www.jew faq.Org/ calendar.htm). According to the Hebrew calendar — John-Paul II died *42 months* plus *two* months *to the day* from 9/11/01 to 4/2/05. 42 plus 2 is more than 42 months!

"To continue forty [and] two months" (Revelation 13:5). *Forty* in the phrase *40* [and] *2 months* is *40* every time it is in the Bible, but *duo* (two) is also translated as *both* and *twain*. In Luke 10:1, the word *ana* is used in conjunction with *duo*. Jesus sent them out *ana* (by) *duo* (twos) or translated: *ana* (by) *duo* (two and two). In Luke 10:1, *ana* is *by* and *duo* is *twos* or *2 and 2*. The *40* [and] *duo* in Revelation 13:5 is 42 full months from 9/11/01 to 4/2/05 on the Gregorian calendar: That fulfilled the prophecy! But on the Hebrew calendar (used by Bible writers), the *40 two and two* reading perfectly matches Pope John-Paul II's life to the prophecy as 42 & 2 months because there were 42 regular months and Adar I was added twice to end on the very day he died, 2 April 2005.

This exact match of prophecy to history that aligns with the Hebrew calendar confirms that the meaning of *duo* is *two and two* in Rev 13:5. *That is an extremely important prophetic fact*, because *duo* occurs a second time in chapter 13. "And I beheld another beast coming up out of the earth; and he had two (*duo*) horns like a lamb" (13:11). For the sake of prophetic consistency, the beast with the *duo* lamblike horns must have *two and two* lamblike horns.

Pope John-Paul II has fulfilled the 42 months (42 & 2) and he has fulfilled the complete final application of (13:5) that White said was to happen before Christ Comes and "he opened his mouth in blasphemy against God, to blaspheme His name" (Revelation 13:6). "And he shall speak [great] words against the Most High, and shall wear out the saints of the Most High, and think to change times and laws: and they shall be given into his hand until a time and times and the dividing of time" (Daniel 7:25).

Blasphemy is speaking evil against God. In his Apostolic Letter, *Dies Domini* (the Lord's Day), a teaching of peace, the little horn, Pope John-Paul II accused God of lying. *Dies Domini* links Sunday to *peace* in sections 1, 18, 26, 33, 44, 52, 67, & 73. It was issued on 31 May 1998, which was the

6th of Sivan on the Hebrew calendar that year. That is significant because according to Jewish Tradition, "On the 6th Sivan...after the Exodus, G-d revealed Himself on Mount Sinai" and God gave the *Ten Commandments* (www.Chabad .org/calendar/view/day_cdo/aid/282243/jewish/Torah-Given.htm).On the anniversary of the day that God gave Moses the Ten Commandments, John-Paul II issued *Dies Domini* that voids God's Sabbath Commandment.

God said, "Remember the Sabbath Day, to keep it holy" (Exodus 20:8). This was one of "The Ten Commandments, which the LORD spake" (Deut10:4). "For I *am* the LORD, I change not" (Mal 3:6). God does NOT change! But Pope John-Paul II contradicted God, and this man changed the word that came from God's mouth. "God [is] not a man, that He should lie; neither the son of man, that He should repent: hath He said, and shall He not do [it]? or hath He spoken, and shall He not make it good?" (Num 23:19)

God is not a liar. That is not true of man! "Add thou not unto His words, lest He reprove thee, and thou be found a liar" (Proverbs 30:6). The liar says that the Sabbath has changed. But the Bible, read aright, says no such thing.

It is written, "I have heard all thy blasphemies which thou hast spoken" (Ezekiel 35:12). "This sign shalt thou have of the LORD, that the LORD will do the thing that He hath spoken" (2 Kings 20:9). "But if ye refuse and rebel, ye shall be devoured with the sword: for the mouth of the LORD hath spoken it" (Isaiah 1:20).

God's unchangeable Commandment to keep Sabbath holy was changed to *keep Sunday holy* by the Catholic Church and John-Paul II. He blasphemed God by changing God's unchangeable Law. When John-Paul II substituted a common day in place of the Sabbath in God's word, he accused God of lying! When Peter changed Christ's words, Jesus "said to Peter, 'Out of My way, Satan! ... you stand right in My path, Peter, when you look at things from man's point of view and not from God's'" (Matthew 16:23, Philips).

Forming the Image Beast

What is the "image to the beast"? and how is it to be formed? The image is made by the two-horned beast, and is an image to the first beast. It is also called an image of the beast. Then to learn what the image is like, and how it is to be formed, we must study the characteristics of the beast itself, —the papacy (GC88 443.2).

The last sea-beast in Daniel 7 is the first beast in Revelation 13:1-10, the papacy. After its deadly wound was healed in 1929, it had seven heads. The heads are symbolic of the popes: Pius XI & XII, John XXIII, Paul VI, John-Paul I & II, and Benedict XVI. They bonded with ten horns, the American Presidents from Truman to Clinton. The last three: Reagan, Bush I, and Clinton, gave the beast its leopardlike appearance. Then Revelation 13 moves from the papal beast to the earth beast with lamblike horns.

The transition from the papal beast to the American beast will be studied more fully in Daniel 9. Revelation gives some insights: "And there are seven kings: five are fallen, and one is, [and] the other is not yet come; and when he cometh, he must continue a short space" (Rev 17:10).

When prophecy met history, the five popes that were fallen were: Pius XI & XII, John XXIII, Paul VI, and John-Paul I. The one that *is* was John-Paul II. And the pope that was to continue for a *short space* was Benedict XVI.

The Bible does not define *short space*. The papacy is spiritual Babylon. By Babylonian reckoning, a king began his reign on New Year's Day, which aligns with 29 March on today's Gregorian calendar. When the predecessor died, the new king finished the old king's reign in what was called an Ascension Year. The new king's Ascension Year was counted as the balance of the old king's last year. The new king's first year began when 29 March arrived. That is how Daniel and his three companions stood before Nebuchadnezzar in his third year when he had only officially been king for 2 years.

John-Paul II died 2 April 2005 (after 29 March 2005). By Babylonian reckoning, Benedict XVI's Ascension Year finished John-Paul II's last year, and 29 March 2006 began Pope Benedict XVI's first year. He resigned effective 28 February 2013, which according to Babylonian custom was one month and one day short of seven years.

> *The number 7 indicates completeness, and is symbolic of the fact that the messages extend to the end of time, while the symbols used reveal the condition of the church at different periods in the history of the world* (AA 585.3).

Benedict XVI reigned one month and one day short of completeness (7 years). Benedict is the pope identified in Revelation 17:10 that reigned for a *short space.*

To understand the formation of the Image-beast: Study the characteristics of the papacy. The head of the first beast in Revelation 13 is the pope. His traditional title is: VICARIUS FILII DEI. Some Roman letters double as numbers: I (1), V (5), [U is a form of V = 5], L (50), C (100), and D (500). With non-Roman Numerals removed: VICIU [VI (6) + C (100) + IV (4)] = 110; ILII [IL (49) + II (2)] = 51; DI [D (500) + I (1)] = 501. In this example, VICIU ILII DI adds up to 663. Because this is a title, the sequencing for VICIU ILII DI does not follow the rules for Roman Numerals.

VICARIUS FILII DEI
non-numerals removed: VICIU ILII DI

V=	5	I=	1	D=	500
I=	1	L=	50	I=	1
C=	100	I=	1		
I=	1	I=	1		
U [V]=	5				
	112		53	501	=666

In a real Roman numeral, an I would never be placed before the L. So, when the pope's title VICARIUS FILII DEI is counted, the Roman numerals are listed as a vertical column with one digit in each place. That eliminates the incorrect sequencing of IL. For the sake of consistency, it also changes the sequencing of IV that is 4 to a value of 6. When this papal title is evaluated that way, the number of his title is 666.

The second beast in Revelation 13:11-18 links to the prophetic earth, the USA with the Louisiana Territory added, which links to President Monroe. *For the 2nd-beast to be an image of the papal beast, it must also have the number 666.*

> I saw all that "would not receive the mark of the Beast, and of his Image, in their foreheads or in their hands," could not buy or sell. [Revelation 13:15-17.] *I saw that the number (666) of the Image Beast was made up*; [Revelation 13:18.] and that it was the Beast that changed the Sabbath, and *the Image Beast had followed on after, and kept the Pope's, and not God's Sabbath.* And all we were required to do, was to give up God's Sabbath, and keep the Pope's, and then we should have the mark of the Beast, and of his image (WLF 19.1).

"The number of a *man*" is 666 (Rev 13:18); the pope is a man, who links to the number 666 because of his title: VICARIUS FILII DEI that adds up to 666. Man is translated from the word *anthropos*. It has also been used in the Bible as *men*: "Fishers of *men* (*anthropos*)" (Matthew 4:19). "*His* (*autos*) number is 666." *Autos* is also translated as *their*. "All liars shall have *their* (*autos*) part in...the second death" (Rev 21:8). *The number of men, their number is 666* (13:18, alternate). In the formation of the image-beast (for it to be an image of the 666 papal-beast, the number that is made up of the Presidents has to be 666 as well): Their number 666 has been made up.

Because President Monroe was the first President to speak like a dragon, after the *prophetic earth* was added to America, he begins the count. President Bush II is literally the fourth earth-king in Daniel 7. As pagan Rome and papal Rome were like they were one, Presidents Bush II and Obama are also as though they were one.

James Monroe	11
John Quincy Adams	15
Andrew Jackson II	13
Martin Van Buren	14
William Henry Harrison	20
John Tyler II	11
James Knox Polk	13
Zachary Taylor	13
Millard Fillmore	15
Franklin Pierce	14
James Buchanan II	15
Abraham Lincoln	14
Andrew Johnson	13
Ulysses Simpson Grant	19
Rutherford Birchard Hayes	23
James Abram Garfield	18
Chester Alan Arthur	17
Stephen Grover Cleveland	22
Benjamin Harrison	16
William McKinley II	17
Theodore Roosevelt II	19
William Howard Taft	17
Woodrow Wilson	13
Warren Gamaliel Harding	21
Calvin Coolidge	14
Herbert Clark Hoover	18
Franklin Delano Roosevelt	23
Harry S Truman	12
Dwight David Eisenhower	21
John Fitzgerald Kennedy	21
Lyndon Baines Johnson	19
Richard Milhous Nixon	19
Gerald Rudolph Ford II	19
James Earl Carter II	17
Ronald Wilson Reagan	18
George Herbert Walker Bush	23
William Jefferson Clinton	23
George Walker Bush	16
Barack Hussein Obama II	<u>20</u>
	666

Counting the value of the letters in the pope's title VICARIUS FILII DEI gives him the number 666. Counting the number of the letters in the names of the Presidents from Monroe to Obama, gives the image-beast the beast's number (666) during President Obama's term. The Russian Scandal linked to President Trump's election implies that President Obama was America's last legitimately elected president.

This power, the last that is to wage war against the church and the law of God, is represented by a beast with lamblike horns. The beasts preceding it had risen from the sea; but this came up out of the earth, representing the peaceful rise of the nation which it symbolized—the United States (ST, Feb 8, 1910 par. 5).

The 666 number of the papacy has been made up in the formation of the Image-beast. The amalgamation of state and church in which the state directs the teachings of the church began, when under President Obama, the state redefined marriage. The US majority Catholic Supreme court has ruled that the union of two men or two women is the same as God's institution of marriage between a man and a woman.

The Eastern Roman Empire in the Endtime

What is the "image to the beast"? and how is it to be formed? The image is made by the two-horned beast, and is an image to the first beast. It is also called an image of the beast. Then *to learn what the image is like, and how it is to be formed, we must study the characteristics of the beast itself, —the papacy* (GC88 443.2).

An overview: The Western Emperor was deposed in 476. The Eastern Emperors then intruded in the affairs of the ten Germanic tribes that had split the Western Empire and taken Arianism to Rome. The Eastern Emperor, Zeno appointed the king of the Goths to be Italy's king. Eventually, the Goths cut their alliance with Emperor Justinian, who then appointed the Bishop of Rome to stabilize the western flank.

The 30 years (508-538) in which the papacy arose to power in the west counterfeited the 30 years before Christ's anointing. To counterfeit Christ's victory over the three temptations, the Eastern Emperor's army and allies plucked up three horns in the west: Kings Gesalic, Gelimer, and Witigis (who had become king of the Goths after Justinian's ally), Queen Amalasuntha was murdered. While Justinian, Pontifex Maximus/High Priest Emperor, the head of church was abolishing the Arian Christian faith in the west, he placed the Roman Catholic Church under his control.

A powerful influence, not under man's control, is working. Man may fancy that he is directing matters, but there are higher than human influences at work. The servants of God know that He is working to counteract Satan's plans. Those who know not God cannot comprehend His movements. There is at work a wheel within a wheel. Apparently, the complication of machinery is so intricate that man can see only a complete entanglement. But the divine hand, as seen by the prophet Ezekiel, is placed upon the wheels, and every part moves in complete harmony, each doing its specified work, yet with individual freedom of action (MS 13, 1898).

During the days of Daniel's fourth sea-beast, the Easter Roman Emperor worked behind the scenes in the ancient Western Roman Empire to change the papacy into a religio-political power. Likewise, the four earth-kings, beginning with President Reagan, have worked behind the scenes in the territory of the Eastern Empire that had also been carved up by ten tribes: Sassanids, Visigoths, Bulgars, Magyars, Seljuks, Normans, Serbians, Ottoman Turks, Franks, and Arabs (cf http://www.scaruffi.com/ politics/romans.html).

The Shah, an emperor of an area in the former Eastern Roman Empire, was deposed in 1979 as the Western Emperor had been centuries earlier. While President Reagan was being inaugurated, Iran released its American hostages.

The main branches of Islam are Sunni (the largest) and Shia. After the Shah was deposed, a Shiite Muslim,

Ayatollahh Ruhollah Khomeini, became Iran's Supreme leader. His rise to power was to Islam what the rise of Arian Christianity had been to Catholicism centuries ago. The two branches of Islam are vying to control Islam.

Prior to the formation of the papacy, the Eastern Roman Emperor appointed the king of the Ostrogoths to stabilize its western flank. After the fall of the Shah, the USA conscripted Pakistan to stabilize what had been Rome's eastern flank. In 1979, Russia invaded Afghanistan. While the image-beast was forming, the USA armed the Afghan resistance thru Pakistan. As it had happened in the pro-Eastern Roman Empire, the Queen was assassinated while the papacy was forming; Pakistan's President Zia was allegedly assassinated in 1988 by a pro-American Pakistani, General Beg.

Beg was accused of playing an internal role in the airplane crash that killed President Zia... due to his [Beg's] open-mindedness and his pro-democracy views (https://en.wikipedia.org/wiki/Mirza_Aslam_Beg).

Ayatollah Khomeini died in 1989. The 30 years allotted to pluck up three Islamic rulers in the eastern flank most likely began in 1989-1990. Reagan had influenced Iranian politics by secretly selling arms to Iran (Iran-Contra Affair) in spite of an American embargo. Khomeini's successor, Ali Khamenei, vowed to eradicate Iran's "American-influenced leftists" (https://en. wikipedia.org/wiki/Ali_Khamenei).

May 31, 1990 Our nation missed the best historical opportunities...kings sold Iran to...the interests of the regime and of the foreign corporations (https://english.khamenei.ir/Opinions/Pahlavi_crimes)

While Khamenei expressed anti-American views in Iran, US propaganda promoted the claim that America favored an Islamic clerical government in Afghanistan. The government that arose there was led by the Sunni Taliban: an "Islamic fundamentalist group that ruled Afghanistan from 1996 until 2001, when a U.S.-led invasion toppled the regime for providing refuge to al-Qaeda and Osama bin Laden" (https://www.cfr.org/backgrounder/taliban-afghanistan). General Beg was promoting *Afghanistan, Pakistan, and Iran to grow into the core of the Muslim world*.

In late 1989, Pakistan and U.S. propagated the message of departing of communist government in order to bring the clerical government instead. Authors and media reporters maintained that Beg controversially proposed an intelligence contingency plan between the agencies of *Afghanistan, Pakistan and Iran that would grow into the "core of the Muslim world"* (Wikipedia).

As the endtime 30 years (2019-2020) end, the USA has overthrown three prominent *Sunni Islamic leaders* in the former Eastern Roman Empire: Saddam Hussein (2006, Iraq), Osama bin Laden (2011, Afghanistan), and Abū Bakr al-Baghdadi (2019, Syria). When the papacy formed, the Arian tribes converted or their kings were deposed and then the tribes were assimilated into the Roman Church.

Feb 27, 2019 · Pope Francis and the grand imam of Egypt's Al-Azhar, the highest seat of learning in *Sunni Islam*, have signed a statement with their hopes for world peace and human understanding (https://www.snopes .com/ap/2019/02/27/pope-senior-muslim-cleric-pledge-hope-for-peace/).

Saudi Arabian *Sunnis* link to 9/11. America plucked up three *Sunni leaders* in the Mideast. America claims that it does not want war with *Shia Iran*, but it claims to be prepared if one should come. It has also abandoned its Kurd allies to the vengeance of the Sunni Turks.

As it happened in the Western Roman Empire that was manipulated by the Eastern Roman Empire to pluck up three Arian kings, the mirror image is happening today in the remnants of the Eastern Roman Empire. Three Islamic leaders have been killed by America, an ally of the papacy that reigns in the territory that was once part of the Western

Roman Empire. President Pence is now arising as a religio-political power allied with the papacy as Pope Vigilius arose to become a religio-political appointee of the Eastern Roman Emperor. The image-beast is forming. On 24 January 2020, Michael Pence had a long meeting with Pope Francis I.

> Pence, who had a strict Irish Catholic upbringing but later converted to evangelical Protestantism, chatted with the pontiff...for about an hour — roughly twice as long as President Trump's meeting...in May 2017 (https://nypost.com/2020/01/24/pence-tells-pope-francis-you-made-me-a-hero/)

If the 30 years prophesied for the formation of the image-beast have ended, tensions will increase between Iran and America. As prophecy is being fulfilled, more will soon be understood. A universal Sunday Law will soon be here. Daniel 11 tells about the pending war with Iran.

> The prophecies of Daniel and of John are to be understood; they interpret each other. They give to the world truths which everyone should understand. These prophecies are to be witnesses in the world. *By their fulfillment in these last days, they will explain themselves* (PH068 15.1).

Why did America target Iraq? The Bible answer may be in the study of Daniel 9. The American, Ambassador Wilson, gives his thoughts about it:

> The heart of the reason, Wilson believes, lies in a document called the Project for the New American Century. In it, a group that came to be known as the "Neo-Cons" postulate an American military presence around the world, rather like the great Roman Empire. "It says quite clearly that in order to make their grandiose imperialistic ambitions come to life, you were going to need a cataclysmic event along the lines of Pearl Harbor - 9/11 provided them that."

"...9/11 provided an excuse to push that global agenda?" – the response: "I am not sure it provided an excuse; it was certainly an opportunity they seized." (https://www.aljazeera.com/indepth/spotlight/the911 decade/2011/09/201197155513938336.html).

Creating an opportunity mindset foreshadows the Iranian crisis: American sanctions are making Iran desperate. The US alleges that Iran has attacked a Saudi oil refinery as if Iran is saying: *Stop our oil sales, and we'll stop yours!* The stopping of the oil flow from the Gulf could devastate the world's economy: Perhaps Iran is attempting to create a need for its oil in the market. (A big winner would be Russia.)

We are living in the time of the end. Thrones and churches have united to oppose God's purposes...It is the reign of Antichrist. God's law is set aside. The Scriptures are exchanged for the traditions of men. Satan has become the ruler of the world... (RH, December 15, 1904 par. 1-2).

When the early church became corrupted by departing from the simplicity of the gospel, and accepting heathen rites and customs, she lost the Spirit and power of God; and in order to control the consciences of the people she sought the support of the secular power. The result was the papacy, a church that controlled the power of the State, and employed it to further her own ends, especially for the punishment of "heresy." *In order for the United States to form an image of the beast, the religious power must so control the civil government that the authority of the State will also be employed by the church to accomplish her own ends* (GC88 443.2).

The Truth About the Fourth Beast

And of the ten horns that [were] in his head, and [of] the other which came up, and before whom three fell; even [of] that horn that had eyes, and a mouth that spake very great things, whose look [was] more stout than his fellows (Daniel 7:23).

The endtime little horn, Pope John-Paul II plucked up three American Presidents. The last one that is to come, President Pence, will completely form the image-beast now that the three Islamic horns in the former Eastern Roman Empire have been plucked up. He will also speak great words against the Sabbath and God's people.

Fallen angels upon earth form confederations with evil men. In this age antichrist will appear as the true Christ, and then the law of God will be fully made void in the nations of our world. Rebellion against God's holy law will be fully ripe. But the true leader of all this rebellion is Satan clothed as an angel of light. *Men will be deceived and will exalt him to the place of God, and deify him.* But Omnipotence will interpose, and to the apostate churches that unite in the exaltation of Satan, the sentence will go forth, "Therefore shall her plagues come in one day, death, and mourning, and famine; and she shall be utterly burned with fire: for strong is the Lord God who judgeth her" (RH, September 12, 1893 par. 21).

In the counsels of the synagogue of Satan it was determined to obliterate the sign of allegiance to God in the world. Antichrist, the man of sin, exalted himself as supreme in the earth, and through him Satan has worked in a masterly way to create rebellion against the law of God and against the memorial of His created works. Is this not sin and iniquity? What greater contempt could be cast upon the Lord God, the Creator of the heavens and the earth, than is cast upon Him by ignoring the Sabbath, which He instituted, sanctified, and blessed, that it might ever be a memorial of His power as Creator? How dare men change and profane the day which God has sanctified? How dare the Christian world accept the spurious sabbath, the child of the Papacy? The Christian world has nourished and cherished the spurious sabbath, as though it had a divine origin, when the fact is that it originated with the father of lies, and was introduced to the world by his human agent, the man of sin. The false sabbath has been upheld through superhuman agency in order that God might be dishonored. It is a sign of Satan's supremacy in the earth, for men are worshiping the god of this world (ST, March 12, 1894 par. 3).

John writes, "I have not written unto you because ye know not the truth, but because ye know it, and that no lie is of the truth. Who is a liar but he that denieth that Jesus is the Christ? He is antichrist, that denieth the Father and the Son." There are those who claim to have great light, who say that they have communication with the spirits of the dead, who deny the divinity of Christ, and in so doing deny the Father whom Christ represented on earth. "Whosoever denieth the Son, the same hath not the Father: [but] he that acknowledgeth the Son hath the Father also." *The classes who deny the Father and the Son are rapidly increasing in the world, and the name given to this class by the Bible is antichrist.* There are many who have their names upon the church records, who claim to possess superior piety; and yet should Christ appear among them, they would rebuke the Son of God. *There are men who profess to be ministers of the gospel who are teaching heresy, and deceiving many, and leading thousands in the way of apostasy* (YI, September 27, 1894 par. 4).

This power, the last that is to wage war against the church and the law of God, was ...the United States (ST, November 1, 1899 par. 4).

The same horn made war with the saints, and prevailed against them; Until the Ancient of days came, and judgment was given to the saints of the Most High (cf Daniel 7:21, 22, 28).

Daniel 8

¹In the third year of the reign of king Belshazzar a vision appeared unto me, [even unto] me Daniel, after that which appeared unto me at the first. ²And I saw in a vision; and it came to pass, when I saw, that I [was] at Shushan [in] the palace, which [is] in the province of Elam; and I saw in a vision, and I was by the river of Ulai.

³Then I lifted up mine eyes, and saw, and, behold, there stood before the river a ram which had [two] horns: and the [two] horns [were] high; but one [was] higher than the other, and the higher came up last. ⁴I saw the ram pushing westward, and northward, and southward; so that no beasts might stand before him, neither [was there any] that could deliver out of his hand; but he did according to his will, and became great.

⁵And as I was considering, behold, an he goat came from the west on the face of the whole earth, and touched not the ground: and the goat [had] a notable horn between his eyes. ⁶And he came to the ram that had [two] horns, which I had seen standing before the river, and ran unto him in the fury of his power. ⁷And I saw him come close unto the ram, and he was moved with choler against him, and smote the ram, and brake his two horns: and there was no power in the ram to stand before him, but he cast him down to the ground, and stamped upon him: and there was none that could deliver the ram out of his hand. ⁸Therefore the he goat waxed very great: and when he was strong, the great horn was broken; and for it came up four notable ones toward the four winds of heaven.

⁹And out of one of them came forth a little horn, which waxed exceeding great, toward the south, and toward the east, and toward the pleasant [land]. ¹⁰And it waxed great, [even] to the host of heaven; and it cast

down [some] of the host and of the stars to the ground, and stamped upon them. [11]Yea, he magnified [himself] even to the prince of the host, and by him the daily [sacrifice] was taken away, and the place of his sanctuary was cast down. [12]And an host was given [him] against the daily [sacrifice] by reason of transgression, and it cast down the truth to the ground; and it practiced, and prospered.

[13]Then I heard one saint speaking, and another saint said unto that certain [saint] which spake, How long [shall be] the vision [concerning] the daily [sacrifice], and the transgression of desolation, to give both the sanctuary and the host to be trodden under foot? [14]And he said unto me, Unto two thousand and three hundred days; then shall the sanctuary be cleansed.

[15]And it came to pass, when I, [even] I Daniel, had seen the vision, and sought for the meaning, then, behold, there stood before me as the appearance of a man. [16]And I heard a man's voice between [the banks of] Ulai, which called, and said, Gabriel, make this [man] to understand the vision. [17]So he came near where I stood: and when he came, I was afraid, and fell upon my face: but he said unto me, Understand, O son of man: for at the time of the end [shall be] the vision. [18]Now as he was speaking with me, I was in a deep sleep on my face toward the ground: but he touched me, and set me upright. [19]And he said, Behold, I will make thee know what shall be in the last end of the indignation: for at the time appointed the end [shall be].

[20]The ram which thou sawest having [two] horns [are] the kings of Media and Persia. [21]And the rough goat [is] the king of Grecia: and the great horn that [is] between his eyes [is] the first king. [22]Now that being broken, whereas four stood up for it, four kingdoms shall stand up out of the nation, but not in his power. [23]And in the latter time of their kingdom, when the

transgressors are come to the full, a king of fierce countenance, and understanding dark sentences, shall stand up. 24And his power shall be mighty, but not by his own power: and he shall destroy wonderfully, and shall prosper, and practice, and shall destroy the mighty and the holy people. 25And through his policy also he shall cause craft to prosper in his hand; and he shall magnify [himself] in his heart, and by peace shall destroy many: he shall also stand up against the Prince of princes; but he shall be broken without hand. 26And the vision of the evening and the morning which was told [is] true: wherefore shut thou up the vision; for it [shall be] for many days.

27And I Daniel fainted, and was sick [certain] days; afterward I rose up, and did the king's business; and I was astonished at the vision, but none understood [it].

Points to Ponder

1. This vision was in the reign of Belshazzar
2. This follow-up vision is written in a different language
3. Chapter 8 expands and explains earlier visions
4. Given to Daniel by the River Ulai, it is endtime specific
5. The sacrificial animals link this vision to churchcraft
6. Horns specifically denote kings
7. The war against the saints is endtime specific
8. Transgression of desolation: Sin that destroys sinners
9. The duration of the 2300 days is: Days and Years
10. Craft will prosper
11. Nobody understood the vision in Daniel's Day

Chronology

This vision was received while Daniel was at Shushan in the province of Elam to the east of Babylon; before the fall of Babylon; after the vision in Belshazzar's first year (chapter 7); and it is included in the third portion of Daniel, which adds insights that he omitted from his narration to the reign of Cyrus. It enlarges and explains Daniel 2, 4, & 7 and aspects relating to the sea-beasts and the four endtime earth-kings. It switches from Aramaic to Hebrew.

Especially to Daniel, God made known His mind and His will. *Light was given for future ages, for the very time in which we are now living. By the River Hiddekel, Daniel saw that which would transpire in the latter days* (https://egwwritings.org/, Lt60-1898.30)

The Vision

Daniel saw the ram *pushing* to the west, north, and south (Daniel 8:4). The expansion of the Medo-Persian Empire was North to Lydia, West to Babylon and South to Egypt. The directions in the vision are not a historical match.

"Behold, an he goat came from the west on the face of the whole earth, and touched not the ground: and the goat [had] a notable horn between his eyes" (8:5). "When the Son of man shall come in His glory, and all the holy angels with Him, then shall He sit upon the throne of His glory: and before Him shall be gathered all nations: and He shall separate...[His] *sheep from the goats*" (Mathew 25:31-32). Thus, the ram, a mountain sheep and the goat are endtime specific: They depict nations that exist in the endtime when Christ Comes. The ram's horns are broken by the goat.

In the Medo-Persian partial fulfillment, the first horn, King Darius, was a Mede. Under his successor, King Cyrus (the second horn), became the Persian Empire. Some scholars hypothesize that Darius and Cyrus co-ruled with Darius being a governor or king of the province of Babylon, while Cyrus was the real king. But that postulation overlooks the biblical record: "It pleased Darius to set over the kingdom an hundred and twenty princes, which should be *over the whole kingdom*" (Daniel 6:1), and "in the days of Ahasuerus, (this [is] Ahasuerus which reigned, from India even unto Ethiopia, [over] an hundred and seven and twenty provinces)" (Esther 1:1). Darius obviously ruled the *whole kingdom* that was enlarged after his death. When the kingdom was toppled, it had only one king, Darius III.

The goat from the west with a notable horn between his eyes attacked the ram and killed it and broke his horns. The ram was powerless to stand before him. When the goat cast him to the ground, and stamped upon him, there was no one that could deliver the ram out of his hands (cf Daniel 8:5-7). During the Greek (bronze-period), which is the four-winged four-headed leopard period as described in Daniel 2 & 7 respectively, the solo king, Darius III lost his Empire to Alexander the Great. Alexander died and his four generals divided his kingdom.

At this point in Bible study, *some folks would rather fight than switch*. Some assert that Antiochus IV Epiphanes is this little horn...prophecy fulfilled! Others emphatically assert that it is the papacy, the little horn in Daniel 7. Both have features that partially match the prophecy, but neither are a complete match. Rather than getting embroiled in a prophetic tug-of-war, study Heaven's interpretation.

Daniel 8 resumes from where chapter 7 ended. The sea beasts transitioned to Rome, but its meaning primarily foreshadows the endtime earth-kings, American Presidents.

When Will We Know?

13How long [shall be] the vision [*chazon* (entire vision)]...? 14Unto two thousand and three hundred days; then shall the sanctuary be cleansed...15I Daniel, had seen the vision [*chazon*], and sought for the meaning, then, behold, there stood before me as the appearance of a man. 16And I heard a man's voice between the banks of Ulai, which called, and said, Gabriel, make this man to understand the vision [*mareh* (what is seen)]. 17So, he came near where I stood: and...he said unto me, Understand, O son of man: for at the time of the end shall be the vision [*chazon*] (Daniel 8:13-17).

Mareh (what is seen) is in Daniel 8 three times in verses 16, 26, and 27. Otherwise, the word for *vision* is *chazon*.

Gabriel explained, "At the time of the end, shall be the vision [*chazon* (the entire vision)]" (8:17). Thus, the context is that *"the last end of the indignation"* (8:19) is not at its beginning when Medo-Persia or Greece ruled, nor in the midst of it, but at the *last end after the entire vision ends.*

It is a 2300-day vision. Is the *last end* of the vision after 2300 literal days? No, that could be its first end. A day can be a year in Bible prophecy, so the 2300 days can be 2300 years. The last end has to come after the 2300 years. Not before. This is the backstory of the 2300-day/year prophecy.

> It was Gabriel, the angel next in rank to the Son of God, who came with the divine message to Daniel... whom Christ sent to open the future (DA 234.2).

> When the angel Gabriel came to Daniel to give him skill and understanding, Daniel could not look upon him. The angel had to reveal himself as a man before he could speak with the prophet (YI, Feb 22, 1900 par. 6).

> The angel Gabriel, though commanded to make Daniel understand the vision, gave him only a partial explanation... He could endure no more, and the angel left him for the time (GC88 325.1).

> There was one important point in the vision of chapter 8 which had been left unexplained, namely, that relating to time--the period of the 2300 days; therefore, the angel, in resuming his explanation, dwells chiefly upon the subject of time: "Seventy weeks are determined ..." (GC 325.2-326.1).

In Daniel 9, the beginning point for the 2300 days is identified. "Know therefore and understand, that from the going forth of the commandment to restore and to build Jerusalem" (9:25). Before Cyrus' birth, he was ordained to command: Jerusalem "be built; and to the temple, Thy foundation shall be laid" (Isaiah 44:28). Prophecy fulfilled:

> I have raised him [Cyrus] up in righteousness, and I will direct all his ways: he shall build My city, and he

shall let go My captives, not for price nor reward, saith the Lord of hosts (Isaiah 45:13).

In the first year of Cyrus the king of Babylon the same king Cyrus made a decree to build this house of God (Ezra 5:13).

The Babylonians besieged Jerusalem in the 3rd year of Jehoiakim's reign (605 BC), when God gave Jerusalem to Nebuchadnezzar (cf Dan 1:1-2). Jeremiah prophesied, "*After seventy years be accomplished at Babylon, I will visit you...to return to this place*" (Jer 29:10). Thus, the 605 conquest of Jerusalem, would last for 70 years until 535.

Jerusalem fell	605 BC
Jeremiah prophesied	-70 years
Cyrus reigns--captivity ends	535 BC

In the first year of his reign [King Darius the Mede] I Daniel understood by books the number of the years, whereof the word of the LORD came to Jeremiah the prophet, that He would accomplish *seventy years* in the desolations of Jerusalem (Daniel 9:2).

The year that Cyrus succeeded Darius the Mede to the throne of Medo-Persia marked the completion of seventy years since the first company of Hebrews had been carried captive to Babylon by Nebuchadnezzar (RH, March 28, 1907 par. 5).

Jerusalem's Temple was not completely rebuilt when Cyrus issued his decree. There were Jews that had not returned. Not all of Jeremiah's book was available in Babylon for Daniel to study. There was more to discover and understand because the Lord had also said: "I will bring them again into their land...*first I will recompense their iniquity and their sin double* (Jeremiah 16:15, 18).

Jerusalem fell	605 BC
70 years	-70 years
Jeremiah's 70 years ended	535 BC
70 years doubled (140 years)	-70 years
Temple built/Captivity ends	465 BC

The 70 years of captivity prophesied by Jeremiah had ended in 535 during the reign of Cyrus as prophesied. But the years were doubled! Thus, the 140 years ended in 465 BC, which was King Artaxerxes' ascension year. "The vision is yet for an appointed time, but at the end it shall speak, and not lie: though it tarry, wait for it...it will surely come, it will not tarry (Habakkuk 2:3). After a brief tarrying time, Artaxerxes began his official First Year 464 BC.

After the 70 years were doubled, Jeremiah's prophecy was fulfilled. Artaxerxes issued the final decree regarding Jerusalem and the Temple in his 7th year, 457 BC. Notice that Ezra "came to Jerusalem in the fifth month, which [was] in the seventh year of the king...on the first [day] of the fifth month..." (Ezra 7:8-9). After Artaxerxes had ruled 6 years and 4 months, on the 1st day of the 5th month in his 7th year, Ezra arrived in Jerusalem. For prophetic calculations, a year has 360 days: 2300 days divided by 360 is 6 years, 4 months, and 20 days. Thus, the fulfillment of Daniel's 2300-day prophecy, aligns with Ezra's arrival in Jerusalem in the 7th year of Artaxerxes reign! A brief tarrying time then followed and the Sanctuary was cleansed on the 457 BC Day of Atonement according to the king's decree:

> I Artaxerxes the king, do make a decree... *whosoever will not do the law of thy God,* and the law of the king, *let judgment be executed speedily upon him* (Ezra 7:21, 26).

Ezra also wrote that the Temple had been *finished* "on the third day of the month Adar, which was in the sixth year of the reign of Darius" (Ezra 6:15). If the prophecy had been *completely* fulfilled during Darius's reign, when the *Temple was finished*, the decree from Artaxerxes would not have been needed. The prophecy was more completely fulfilled when, "The elders of the Jews builded... and finished it, according to the commandment of the God of Israel, and *according to the commandment of Cyrus, and Darius, and Artaxerxes* king of Persia" (Ezra 6:14).

After the 70 years were doubled (Jeremiah 29:10; 16:15-18), and after 2300 literal days (Daniel 8:14, with a brief tarrying time [Habakkuk 2:3] before and after the 140 years), Artaxerxes 457 BC decree fulfilled Bible prophecy. The Temple was *cleansed* on the 457 BC Day of Atonement.

Ezekiel also prophesied of the destruction of the Temple and Jerusalem – in *long-time*: A day for a year. "I have appointed thee each day for a year" (Ezekiel 4:6). A few years after Ezekiel's prediction, the Temple was destroyed when King Nebuchadnezzar "burnt the house of the LORD" (2 Kings 25:9). As it had been destroyed in fulfillment of a *long-time* prophecy, the prophecy of its restoration should be fulfilled in *long-time*. The 457 BC restoration and *cleansing of the Sanctuary* had not fulfilled Daniel 8:14 in *long-time*.

Cleanse is: *To be put or made right, i.e., to be justified.* The 457 BC *cleansed* Sanctuary *was not completely made right*, because it was cleansed yearly until it was destroyed again in 70 AD on the anniversary of its first destruction.

From the date of the decree of the king of Persia, found in Ezra 7...457 before Christ, the 2300 years of Daniel 8:14 must terminate with 1843 (LS80 185.2).

The decree of Artaxerxes for the restoration of Jerusalem, which formed the starting-point for the period of the 2300 days, went into effect in the autumn of the year B. C. 457... Reckoning from the autumn of 457, the 2300 years terminate in the autumn of 1844 (GC88 398.3).

Thus, in the early 1800's a Baptist preacher named William Miller understood that the 2300-years would end in 1843. Based on that understanding, he preached that Christ would come in 1843. Thousands of people called Millerites or Adventists believed his message and prepared for Christ's Advent. After Christ did not come, they reexamined the prophecies and found that the 2300 years ended in 1844.

Those faithful...ones, who could not understand why their Lord did not come, were not left in darkness. Again, they were led to their Bibles to search the prophetic periods... *They saw that the prophetic periods reached to 1844, and that the same evidence they had presented to show that the prophetic periods closed in 1843, proved that they would terminate in 1844.* Light from the word of God shone upon their position, and they discovered a tarrying time.--If the vision tarry, wait for it.--In their love for Jesus' immediate coming, they had overlooked the tarrying of the vision, which was calculated to manifest the true waiting ones (1SG 138.1).

How can the 2300 years end in 1843 and the *same evidence* prove that they end again in 1844? And if they really ended in 1844, why did Christ not Come in 1844?

For the *same evidence* to prove both dates: The 2300-years that began in 457 BC had to end twice: Once in 1843 and again in 1844. To end twice, the 2300 years had to have a *dual fulfillment*: Thus, the 2300 years that began on the same day (the Day of Atonement) in 457 BC had to run concurrently to end on two different dates. How can they end on two different dates?

When Christ did not come in 1843, after the 2300 years were fulfilled the first time, the Adventists assumed that the date was the error rather than the event, which was the real problem because of the traditional view that the earth was the sanctuary that was to be cleansed. The Adventists went back to the Bible to discover that when BC changed to AD, there was no year zero. Thus, when the missing year was added, it was clearly seen that the prophecy ended in 1844. Therefore, the 2300-year prophecy that had one start date, had two end dates. But Christ still did not come in 1844.

Further Bible study revealed that the sanctuary that was to be cleanse was not the earth but the Sanctuary in Heaven.

Our disappointment in 1844 was not because of failure in the reckoning of *prophetic periods*, but in the events to take place. The earth was believed to be the sanctuary. But the sanctuary which was to be cleansed at the end of the prophetic periods was the heavenly sanctuary and not the earth as we all supposed. The Saviour did enter the Most Holy Place in 1844 to cleanse the sanctuary and the investigative judgment had commenced for the dead (10MR 269.1).

It is while men are still dwelling upon the earth that the work of investigative judgment takes place in the courts of heaven. The lives of all His professed followers pass in review before God. All are examined according to the record of the books of heaven, and according to his deeds the destiny of each is forever fixed (COL 310.2).

When the 2300-year prophecy was fulfilled in 1843 and again in 1844, and it was understood that the Sanctuary to be cleansed was in heaven, a new problem arose. Since, Miller and the Adventists had misunderstood what was to be cleansed, when the Adventists got prophecy right, people did not believe it. Jesus had not come as they had predicted, so their corrected view was seen as back peddling. Folks said: "You got it wrong twice, now you are reinterpreting the prophecies. It is smoke and mirrors. You fooled me once and maybe twice, but you won't fool me again!"

After the Adventists organized the Seventh-day Adventist Church in 1863, to counteract the false narrative, the focus of the 2300-year prophecy became 1844. The memory of the 1843 date and "you were wrong twice" faded. Now many Seventh-day Adventists merely call themselves, Adventists. Even though, many of the founders, who waited for Christ to come in 1843 and 1844 are the very ones who founded the Seventh-day Adventist Church, some Adventists are now quick to say that the church has never set a date for the coming of Christ because it was not formed until almost 20 years after 1844. Today, the church stresses the 1844 date as if the 1843 date never happened. To forget 1843 as though it was not important, is to cast a shadow over the *tarrying time* that fulfilled Bible prophecy.

By God's clock, both dates are important to follow Bible prophecy. Some prophecies, before Christ, align with the 1843 date, while prophecies that are after Christ, align with the 1844 date. It is like friends in Nashville and Chattanooga (separated by a time zone) doing lunch at noon. The time zone must also be specified or one may be an hour early or an hour late because noon in Chattanooga, is not noon in Nashville. To arrive at the luncheon on time everyone needs to use the same clock.

> The 1843 chart was directed by the hand of the Lord, and that it should not be altered; that the figures were as He wanted them (ExV 61.1).

> They were correct in their reckoning of the prophetic periods; *prophetic time closed in 1844*, and Jesus entered the most holy place to cleanse the sanctuary at the ending of the days (EW 243.2).

Recapping, *three kings in Persia* (Daniel 11:2): Cyrus, Darius, and Artaxerxes (cf Ezra 6:14) issued decrees that began the 2300-years in 457 BC to cleanse the Temple. The appointed 2300 years ended in 1843 and again in 1844, which was the last end of the vision when the 2300-year prophecy was fulfilled. In the study of Daniel 11, the historical events that transpire during the 2300 years from 457 BC to 1844 AD are specified from the *three kings in Persia* to Michael standing for His people (12:1) to cleanse Heaven's Temple when the Investigative Judgment began in 1844: "He that overcometh ... I will not blot out his name out of the book of life, but I will confess his name before My Father, and before His angels" (Revelation 3:5).

Jesus rose up, and shut the door, and entered the Holy of Holies, at the 7th month 1844; but Michael's standing up (Daniel 12:1) *to deliver His people, is in the future* (WLF 12.4).

At the end of the 2300-years, Jesus stood for His people to confess their names before His Father and His angels. But Jesus will stand the final time (Daniel 12:1) at His Second Coming. "And behold, I come quickly; and My reward is with Me, to give every man according as his work shall be" (Revelation 22:12). Thus, history confirms that the 2300 days that were fulfilled in Ezra's Day foretold the 2300 years that were fulfilled from 457 to 1843; and they had a dual fulfillment when they ended in 1844. Thus, as Daniel 12:1 was fulfilled in 1844 when Christ stood for His people, Christ standing will have a dual fulfillment at His Second Advent. But all of this was not understood previously because the *book of Daniel* was expressly *sealed, closed-up,* and *shut-up* until the time of the end (cf Daniel 12:4, 9). "*Since 1798 the book of Daniel has been unsealed, knowledge of the prophecies has increased*" (GC88 356.2).

After the 2300-year prophecy was fulfilled in 1844, the meaning of Daniel 8 is to be understood. But there is a danger of misunderstanding the message and the time prophecies, and of not reading the prophecies aright. As knowledge has increased and is increasing, are we learning those things that God intends for us to understand as we approach the time of Christ's Coming? Or are the historical interpretations of Bible prophecies that have served past generations blocking us from increasing our knowledge of endtime prophecies that are being fulfilled around us?

I have been shown that just such phases of error as I was compelled to meet among Advent believers after the passing of the time in 1844, will be repeated in these last days. In our early experience, I had to go from place to place and bear message after message to disappointed companies of believers. The evidences accompanying my messages were so great that *the honest in heart received as truth the words that were spoken. The power of God was revealed in a marked manner, and men and women were freed from the baleful influence of fanaticism and disorder, and were brought into the unity of the faith* (3SM 376.4).

When the Thessalonian church received erroneous views concerning the coming of Christ, the apostle Paul counseled them to *carefully test their hopes and anticipations by the word of God. He cited them to prophecies revealing the events to take place before Christ should come,* and showed that they had no ground to expect Him in their day. "Let no man deceive you by any means," are his words of warning. *Should they indulge expectations that were not sanctioned by the Scriptures, they would be led to a mistaken course of action; disappointment would expose them to the derision of unbelievers, and they would be in danger of yielding to discouragement, and would be tempted to doubt the truths essential for their salvation.* The apostle's admonition to the Thessalonians contains an important lesson for those who live in the last days. *Many Adventists have felt that unless they could fix their faith upon a definite time for the Lord's coming, they could not be zealous and diligent in the work of preparation.* But as their hopes are again and again excited, only to be destroyed, their faith receives such a shock that it becomes well-nigh impossible for them to be impressed by the great truths of prophecy. The more frequently *a definite time is set for the Second Advent,* and the more widely it is taught, the better it suits the purposes of Satan. After the time has passed, he excites ridicule and contempt of its advocates, and thus casts reproach upon *the true time movement of 1843 and 1844.* Those who persist in this error will at last fix upon a date too far in the future for the coming of Christ. Thus, *they will be led to rest in a false security, and many will not be undeceived until it is too late* (4SP 290.2).

The history of ancient Israel is a striking illustration of the past experience of the Adventist body. God led His people in the Advent movement, even as he led the children of Israel from Egypt. *In the great disappointment their faith was tested as was that of the Hebrews at the Red Sea. Had they still trusted to the guiding hand that had been with them in their past experience, they would have seen of the salvation of God. If all who had labored unitedly in the work in 1844 had received the third angel's message, and proclaimed it in the power of the Holy Spirit, the Lord would have wrought mightily with their efforts. A flood of light would have been shed upon the world. Years ago, the inhabitants of the earth would have been warned, the closing work completed, and Christ would have come for the redemption of His people* (4SP 291.1).

It was not the will of God that Israel should wander forty years in the wilderness; He desired to lead them directly to the land of Canaan, and establish them there, a holy, happy people. But *"they could not enter in because of unbelief."* [Hebrews 3:19.] Because of their backsliding and apostasy, they perished in the desert, and others were raised up to enter the promised land. *In like manner, it was not the will of God that the coming of Christ should be so long delayed, and His people should remain so many years in this world of sin and sorrow. But unbelief separated them from God. As they refused to do the work which He had appointed them, others were raised up to proclaim the message. In mercy to the world, Jesus delays His Coming, that sinners may have an opportunity to hear the warning, and find in Him a shelter before the wrath of God shall be poured out* (4SP 292.1).

Now, as in former ages, the presentation of a truth that reproves the errors and sins of the times, will call forth a storm of opposition. "Every one that doeth evil hateth the light, neither cometh to the light, lest his deeds should be reproved." [John 3:20.] *Those who cannot sustain their position by the Scriptures are stubbornly determined that it shall be sustained at all hazards, and with a malicious spirit they attack the character and motives of those who stand in defense of unpopular truth.* Though very unbelieving in regard to the sure word of prophecy, they manifest the utmost credulity in accepting anything detrimental to the Christian integrity of those who dare to reprove fashionable sins. This spirit will increase more and more as we near the close of time (4SP 292.2).

The Endtime Meaning of Daniel 8

<u>*At the time appointed*</u>...*The ram having horns [are] the kings of Media and Persia (cf Daniel 8:19-20).* <u>*Are*</u> was supplied by the translators. In the vision, Daniel saw the ram *pushing* westward, northward, and southward, cf 8:4. *The ram was <u>pushing</u> toward the kings of Media and Persia.*

In Revelation 13, the endtime events depict the transition from the papal sea-beast to the American earth-beast with *lamblike horns.* That transition happened during the reign of Pope Benedict XVI and Presidents Bush II.

The ram in Daniel 8 is a *lamblike beast.* The ram's two endtime horns correlate with Bush II and Obama. Bush II *pushed* toward Medo-Persian provinces: Afghanistan and Iraq, which led to the death of Saddam Hussein. Obama, the other horn that came up last, continued *to push* toward Iraq and Afghanistan until Osama bin laden was killed.

As there are four primary horns in Daniel 8, the study of Daniel 7 and Revelation 13 showed that the *duo lamblike horns are four horns* or rulers. The "Four *living captains* came up *from out of the west*" (cf Daniel 7:2, from a Hebrew perspective). Historically, America, the *prophetic earth* from the *west,* correlates with that reading of Bible prophecy.

The rough goat [pushing toward] the king of Grecia: and the great horn that [is] between his eyes [is] the primary king (8:21, cf Strong's) relates to President Trump, who is pushing America from the west toward Iran, which was once conquered by the Greek, Alexander the Great. *Rough goat* is from *satyr,* a demon possessed goat, *devil goat.*

Now that being broken (8:22 part a): *President Trump will be broken*, i.e., maimed, crippled, wrecked; or crushed (fig, cf Strong). It has yet to happen. However, though President Trump's impeachment failed because Republicans controlled the Senate; at God's appointed time he will be broken. After Mr. Trump is broken, Daniel 11 predicts that the ships from Chittim will attack the king of the north's (America's) fleet. Then speaking of President Pence (Trump's successor from the executive branch) "He shall come up, and shall become strong with a small people" (11:22).

Whereas four stood up for it, four kingdoms shall stand up out of the nation, but not in his power (8:22 part b). After President Trump is broken, America's four *sovereign powers are*: The House of Representatives, the Senate, the Supreme Court, and the Executive branch without President Trump. From the Executive Branch, a little horn, President Michael Pence will arise. When ancient Babylon fell, there were two rulers with similar names: Belshazzar and Belteshazzar. Likewise, in the endtime, when Michael stands (12:1), Michael Pence stands first and then Michael (Christ) stands.

Revelation 13:11 describes the earth-beast as having *duo* horns. Presidents Bush II and Obama partially fulfilled that prophecy. After President Trump, who is about to be broken, came to office with Vice President *Michael* Pence on his team, it was discovered that *duo* is also *two and two* (cf Luke 10:1). As Isaiah named Cyrus before he was born, 500 years before Christ, Daniel wrote: *Michael will stand for his people! Michael Pence will also fulfill this prophecy to begin* Jacob's Time of Trouble. Then Christ will stand for His people!

> Satan...attempted what he has attempted... —to deceive and destroy the people by palming off upon them a counterfeit in place of the true... (GC88 186.1).

> Pence positioned himself as ... "a Christian, a conservative, and a Republican, in that order" (https://en.wikipedia.org/wiki/Mike_Pence).

Pence – a fervent Christian who urged the president to keep his pledge to his evangelical base and move the U.S. embassy to Jerusalem (http://www.philly.com/philly/columnists/trudy_rubin/trump-and-pence-unnerve-holy-land-christians-20171223.html).

On May 17, 2017, Pence filed FEC paperwork to form Great America Committee, a PAC... *This is the only time a vice president has started his own PAC while still in office.* Pence denied a New York Times article's allegations that *he will run for president in 2020*, calling them "laughable and absurd", and said the article was "disgraceful and offensive" (https://en.wikipedia.org/wiki/Mike_Pence).

As Governor of Indiana Michael Pence signed into law the *Religious Freedom Restoration Act (RFRA)*, "a law in the U.S. state of Indiana, which allows individuals and companies to assert that their exercise of religion has been, or is likely to be, substantially burdened as a defense in legal proceedings" (https://en.wikipedia.org/wiki/Religious_Freedom_Restoration_Act_(Indiana)

The *duo horned* earth-beast is in Bible prophecy! It speaks like a dragon, it calls fire down from heaven, and it exercised all the power of the first papal-beast.

I beheld another beast coming up *out of the earth*; and *he had <u>duo horns</u> like a lamb, and he <u>spoke as a dragon</u>. And he <u>exercised all the power of the first beast</u> before him, and <u>caused the earth and them which dwell therein to worship the first beast, whose deadly wound was healed</u>. And he doeth great wonders, so that <u>he maketh fire come down from heaven on the earth in the sight of men</u>* (Revelation 13:11-13).

He said, Behold, I will make thee know what shall be in the last end of the indignation: for *at the time appointed the end [shall be]* (Daniel 8:18-19).

All the virgins are watching for the bridegroom. Hour after hour passes, and they are still anxiously looking for His appearing. But at last the weary, watching ones fall asleep. And at midnight, the very darkest hour, when their lamps are most needed, the cry is heard, "Behold, the Bridegroom cometh; go ye out to meet Him" (RH, October 31, 1899 par. 4).

The bride constitutes the church that is waiting for the second appearing of our Lord and Saviour Jesus Christ. Some who have a nominal faith are not prepared for His coming. The oil of grace is not feeding their lamps, and they are not prepared to enter in to the marriage supper of the Lamb. The representation is such as to call forth our earnest study, that we may know what preparation we who are living in the last days are to make, that we may enter in and partake of the marriage supper of the Lamb. We are to accept the last message of mercy given to a fallen world: "Blessed are they that do His commandments, that they may have right to the tree of life, and may enter in through the gates into the city" (16MR 268.3).

Clearly, then, the bride represents the holy city, and the virgins that go out to meet the Bridegroom are a symbol of the church. In the Revelation the people of God are said to be the guests at the marriage supper. [Revelation 19:9.] If guests, they cannot be represented also as the bride. Christ, as stated by the prophet Daniel, will receive from the Ancient of days in Heaven, "dominion, and glory, and a kingdom," He will receive the New Jerusalem, the capital of His kingdom, "prepared as a bride adorned for her husband." [Daniel 7:14; Revelation 21:2.] Having received the kingdom, He will come in His glory, as King of kings, and Lord of lords, for the redemption of His people... (GC88 426.2).

And in the latter time of their kingdom, when the transgressors are come to the full, a king of fierce countenance, and understanding dark sentences, shall stand up. And his power shall be mighty, but not by his own power: and he shall destroy wonderfully, and shall prosper, and practice, and shall destroy the mighty and the holy people. And through his policy also he shall cause craft to prosper in his hand; and he shall magnify [himself] in his heart, *and by peace shall destroy many: he shall also stand up against the Prince of princes; but he shall be broken without hand.* And the vision of the evening and the morning which was told [is] true: wherefore shut thou up the vision; for it [shall be] for many days. (Daniel 8:23-27).

The mingling of churchcraft and statecraft is represented by the iron and the clay. This union is weakening all the power of the churches. This investing the church with the power of the state will bring evil results. Men have almost passed the point of God's forbearance. They have invested their strength in politics, and have united with the papacy. But the time will come when God will punish those who have made void His law, and their evil work will recoil upon themselves (4BC 1168.8).

Jesus stands before the ark, making His final intercession for all those for whom mercy still lingers and for those who have ignorantly broken the law of God. This atonement is made for the righteous dead as well as for the righteous living. It includes all who died trusting in Christ, but who, not having received the light upon God's commandments, had sinned ignorantly in transgressing its precepts (EW 254.1).

Daniel 9

¹In the first year of Darius the son of Ahasuerus, of the seed of the Medes, which was made king over the realm of the Chaldeans; ²In the first year of his reign I Daniel understood by books the number of the years, whereof the word of the LORD came to Jeremiah the prophet, that he would accomplish seventy years in the desolations of Jerusalem. ³And I set my face unto the Lord God, to seek by prayer and supplications, with fasting, and sackcloth, and ashes:

⁴And I prayed unto the LORD my God, and made my confession, and said, O Lord, the great and dreadful God, keeping the covenant and mercy to them that love Him, and to them that keep His commandments; ⁵We have sinned, and have committed iniquity, and have done wickedly, and have rebelled, even by departing from Thy precepts and from Thy judgments: ⁶Neither have we hearkened unto Thy servants the prophets, which spake in Thy name to our kings, our princes, and our fathers, and to all the people of the land.

⁷O Lord, righteousness [belongeth] unto Thee, but unto us confusion of faces, as at this day; to the men of Judah, and to the inhabitants of Jerusalem, and unto all Israel, [that are] near, and [that are] far off, through all the countries whither Thou hast driven them, because of their trespass that they have trespassed against Thee.

⁸O Lord, to us [belongeth] confusion of face, to our kings, to our princes, and to our fathers, because we have sinned against Thee. ⁹To the Lord our God [belong] mercies and forgivenesses, though we have rebelled against Him; ¹⁰Neither have we obeyed the voice of the LORD our God, to walk in His laws, which He set before us by His servants the prophets. ¹¹Yea, all Israel have transgressed Thy law, even by departing, that they might

not obey Thy voice; therefore, the curse is poured upon us, and the oath that [is] written in the law of Moses the servant of God, because we have sinned against Him. [12]And He hath confirmed his words, which He spake against us, and against our judges that judged us, by bringing upon us a great evil: for under the whole heaven hath not been done as hath been done upon Jerusalem.

[13]As [it is] written in the law of Moses, all this evil is come upon us: yet made we not our prayer before the LORD our God, that we might turn from our iniquities, and understand Thy truth. [14]Therefore hath the LORD watched upon the evil, and brought it upon us: for the LORD our God [is] righteous in all His works which He doeth: for we obeyed not His voice. [15]And now, O Lord our God, that hast brought Thy people forth out of the land of Egypt with a mighty hand, and hast gotten Thee renown, as at this day; we have sinned, we have done wickedly. [16]O Lord, according to all Thy righteousness, I beseech Thee, let Thine anger and thy fury be turned away from Thy city Jerusalem, Thy holy mountain: because for our sins, and for the iniquities of our fathers, Jerusalem and Thy people [are become] a reproach to all [that are] about us.

[17]Now therefore, O our God, hear the prayer of Thy servant, and his supplications, and cause Thy face to shine upon Thy sanctuary that is desolate, for the Lord's sake. [18]O my God, incline Thine ear, and hear; open Thine eyes, and behold our desolations, and the city which is called by Thy name: for we do not present our supplications before Thee for our righteousnesses, but for Thy great mercies. [19]O Lord, hear; O Lord, forgive; O Lord, hearken and do; defer not, for Thine own sake, O my God: for Thy city and Thy people are called by Thy name.

[20]And whiles I [was] speaking, and praying, and confessing my sin and the sin of my people Israel, and presenting my supplication before the LORD my God for

the holy mountain of my God; 21Yea, whiles I [was] speaking in prayer, even the man Gabriel, whom I had seen in the vision at the beginning, being caused to fly swiftly, touched me about the time of the evening oblation. 22And he informed [me], and talked with me, and said, O Daniel, I am now come forth to give thee skill and understanding. 23At the beginning of thy supplications the commandment came forth, and I am come to show [thee]; for thou [art] greatly beloved: therefore, understand the matter, and consider the vision [*mareh*].

24Seventy weeks are determined upon thy people and upon thy holy city, to finish the transgression, and to make an end of sins, and to make reconciliation for iniquity, and to bring in everlasting righteousness, and to seal up the vision and prophecy, and to anoint the most Holy. 25Know therefore and understand, [that] from the going forth of the commandment to restore and to build Jerusalem unto the Messiah the Prince [shall be] seven weeks, and threescore and two weeks: the street shall be built again, and the wall, even in troublous times. 26And after threescore and two weeks shall Messiah be cut off, but not for himself: and the people of the prince that shall come shall destroy the city and the sanctuary; and the end thereof [shall be] with a flood, and unto the end of the war desolations are determined. 27And he shall confirm the covenant with many for one week: and in the midst of the week he shall cause the sacrifice and the oblation to cease, and for the overspreading of abominations he shall make [it] desolate, even until the consummation, and that determined shall be poured upon the desolate.

Points to Ponder

1. Daniel's prayer
2. The interpretation of the time in Daniel 8 continues
3. The endtime meaning of the times
4. Taking away the Sacrifice and Oblation

Daniel's Prayer

After the fall of Babylon, Gabriel returned to Daniel to continue explaining the 2300 days. He arrived while Daniel was praying to confess his sins and those of his people. Daniel's prayer focused on God's grace because there is no merit in man that can earn God's forgiveness. It is granted only because of God's love, and His willingness to keep His covenant that He chose to extend to man, who willfully rebelled against Him and His will.

Daniel was concerned that Jerusalem's Sanctuary was no longer in existence because it had been indispensable to the Plan of Salvation. The Sanctuary Services included sinners offering sacrifices to atone for their sins, the priests offering morning and evening sacrifices daily, and the High Priest cleansing the Sanctuary yearly, which indicated that God had accepted their repentance and had forgiven their sins and removed the records of them from the Sanctuary. Its destruction was a big deal! King David expressed the importance of the Sanctuary in Psalms:

> The LORD hear thee in the day of trouble; the name of the God of Jacob defend thee; Send thee help from the Sanctuary (Psalms 20:1-2).

How would God's people be forgiven without a Temple and its Sanctuary Services? When Solomon dedicated the Temple, his prayer gave some insight into its importance:

> O LORD my God...That Thine eyes may be open toward this house night and day, [even] toward the place of which Thou hast said, My name shall be there: that Thou mayest hearken unto the prayer which Thy servant shall make toward this place. And hearken Thou to the supplication of Thy servant, and of Thy people Israel, when they shall pray toward this place: and hear Thou in heaven Thy dwelling place: and when Thou hearest, forgive...When Thy people Israel be smitten down before the enemy, because they have sinned against Thee, and

shall turn again to Thee, and confess Thy name, and pray, and make supplication unto Thee in this house: Then hear thou in heaven, and forgive the sin of Thy people Israel, and bring them again unto the land which Thou gavest unto their fathers (1 Kings 8:28-30, 33-34).

O Lord, according to all Thy righteousness...hear the prayer of Thy servant, and his supplications, and cause Thy face to shine upon Thy sanctuary that is desolate, for the Lord's sake (cf Daniel 9:16-17).

From Daniel to Jesus

The burden of Christ's preaching was, "The time is fulfilled, and the kingdom of God is at hand; repent ye, and believe the gospel." Thus, the gospel message, as given by the Saviour Himself, was based on the prophecies. The "time" which He declared to be fulfilled was the period made known by the angel Gabriel to Daniel. "Seventy weeks," said the angel, "are determined upon thy people and upon thy holy city, to finish the transgression, and to make an end of sins, and to make reconciliation for iniquity, and to bring in everlasting righteousness, and to seal up the vision and prophecy, and to anoint the most holy." Daniel 9:24. A day in prophecy stands for a year. See Numbers 14:34; Ezekiel 4:6. The seventy weeks, or four hundred and ninety days, represent four hundred and ninety years. A starting point for this period is given: "Know therefore and understand, that from the going forth of the commandment to restore and to build Jerusalem unto the Messiah the Prince shall be seven weeks, and threescore and two weeks," sixty-nine weeks, or four hundred and eighty-three years. Daniel 9:25. The commandment to restore and build Jerusalem, as completed by the decree of Artaxerxes Longimanus (see Ezra 6:14; 7:1, 9, margin), went into effect in the autumn of B. C. 457. From this time four hundred and eighty-three years extend to the autumn of A. D. 27. According to the prophecy, this period was to reach to the Messiah, the Anointed One. In A. D. 27, Jesus at His baptism received the anointing of the Holy Spirit, and soon afterward began His ministry. Then the message was proclaimed. "The time is fulfilled" (DA 233.1).

Then, said the angel, "He shall confirm the covenant with many for one week [seven years]." For seven years after the Saviour entered on His ministry, the gospel was to be preached especially to the Jews; for three and a half years by Christ Himself; and afterward by the apostles. "In the midst of the week He shall cause the sacrifice and the oblation to cease." Daniel 9:27. In the spring of A. D. 31, Christ the true sacrifice was offered on Calvary. Then the veil of the temple was rent in twain, showing that the sacredness and significance of the sacrificial service had departed. The time had come for the earthly sacrifice and oblation to cease (DA 233.2).

The one week--seven years--ended in A. D. 34. Then by the stoning of Stephen the Jews finally sealed their rejection of the gospel; the disciples who were scattered abroad by persecution "went everywhere preaching the word" (Acts 8:4); and shortly after, Saul the persecutor was converted, and became Paul, the apostle to the Gentiles (DA 233.3).

The time of Christ's coming, His anointing by the Holy Spirit, His death, and the giving of the gospel to the Gentiles, were definitely pointed out. It was the privilege of the Jewish people to understand these prophecies, and to recognize their fulfillment in the mission of Jesus. Christ urged upon His disciples *the importance of prophetic study*. Referring to the prophecy given to Daniel in regard to their time, He said, "Whoso readeth, *let him understand*." Matthew 24:15. After His resurrection He explained to the disciples in "all the prophets" "the things concerning Himself." Luke 24:27. The Saviour had spoken through all the prophets. "The Spirit of Christ which was in them" "testified beforehand the sufferings of Christ, and the glory that should follow." 1 Peter 1:11 (DA 234.1).

The Endtime Meaning

Not at first had God revealed the exact time of the first advent; and even when the prophecy of Daniel made this known, not all rightly interpreted the message (PK 700.1).

These prophecies had been literally fulfilled in Jesus of Nazareth...the sure word of prophecy (AA 124.3).

As the message of Christ's First Advent announced the kingdom of His grace, so the message of His Second Advent announces the kingdom of His glory. And the second message, like the first, is based on the prophecies. The words of the angel to Daniel relating to the last days were to be understood in the time of the end (DA 234.4).

The time has come for Daniel to stand in his lot. The time has come for the light given him to go to the world *as never before.* If those for whom the Lord has done so much will walk in the light, *their knowledge of Christ and the prophecies relating to Him will be greatly increased as they near the close of this earth's history* (21MR 407.3).

The message of Christ's First Advent was based on the prophecies in Daniel 9 and 11. The message of Christ's Second Advent is based on these same prophecies repeated.

The truth for this time, *the third angel's message, is to be proclaimed with a loud voice, meaning with increasing power, as we approach the great final test... The present truth for this time comprises the messages, the third angel's message succeeding the first and the second. The presentation of this message with all it embraces is our work. We stand as the remnant people in* <u>*these last days to promulgate the truth and swell the cry*</u>

of the third angel's wonderful distinct message, giving the trumpet a certain sound. Eternal truth, which we have adhered to from the beginning, is to be maintained in all its increasing importance to the close of probation. The trumpet is to give no uncertain sound (9MR 291.1).

Daniel shall stand in his lot at the end of the days. John sees the little book unsealed. Then *Daniel's prophecies have their proper place in the first, second, and third angels' messages* to be given to the world. *The unsealing of the little book was the message in relation to time* (1MR 99.2).

Based on the prophecies in Daniel 9, the "time" which is to be fulfilled in the endtime was the period made known by Gabriel to Daniel: "Seventy weeks are determined upon thy people and upon thy holy city, to finish the transgression, and to make an end of sins, and to make reconciliation for iniquity, and to bring in everlasting righteousness, and to seal up the vision and prophecy, and to anoint the most holy" (Daniel 9:24). In the endtime, the seventy weeks are four hundred and ninety literal days from this starting point: "Know therefore and understand, that from the going forth of the commandment to restore and to build Jerusalem unto the messiah the prince shall be seven weeks, and threescore and two weeks" (Daniel 9:25). Gabriel's words as recorded by Daniel have more than one meaning. When the alternate meanings of the words are studied, the endtime meaning is clearly explained after the book of Daniel is unsealed and opened. The alternate endtime meanings repeat and enlarge the prophecy to take it to the messiah, the anointed one.

Know therefore and understand that from the going forth of the command to apostatize by the mother to the children teaching peace unto the anointing of the ruler shall be seven weeks and threescore and two weeks. This is enlarged: from the mother's decree to the children, the time of anguish shall come again (Daniel 9:25, alternate wording cf Strong's).

Jerusalem means *Teaching of Peace.* The Roman mother church's endtime command to restore and build Jerusalem is her decree *teaching peace, Dies Domini* issued 31 (May 1998) that links Sunday to *peace.*

In the endtime, Daniel 9:25 is: From the going forth of the *command to apostatize* (31 May 1998), unto the anointing of the *ruler* shall be 69 weeks. *This time of anguish shall come again.* The 69 weeks double to 138. From the *command to apostatize* issued on Sunday, 31 May 1998, the 69 weeks doubled (138 weeks) ended on Saturday, 20 January 2001 when the Protestant counterfeit prince of America's covenant, George Walker Bush, was anointed as President of the USA! The endtime message of Daniel 9 began to proclaim "The time is fulfilled!" Prophecy has met endtime history.

And after threescore and two weeks shall messiah be cut off, but not for himself: and the people of the prince that shall come shall destroy the city and the sanctuary; and the end thereof [shall be] with a flood, and unto the end of the war desolations are determined (Daniel 9:26).

Threescore is translated originally as *six* multiplied by *ten. In certain* instances, the number can be added to *ten* rather than being multiplied by it (cf Strong's). The endtime fulfillment of Daniel 9:26 confirms that *sixteen* is the correct reading today. Following *sixteen,* the word is *two,* which is *twice* or *double* (cf Nehemiah 23:20 & 2 Kings 2:9; 6:10). Sixteen weeks doubled are 32 weeks. *Cut off* also means to *fail.* The endtime meaning of Daniel 9:26 is: *after 32 weeks, the anointed Protestant prince shall fail:* Bush II failed!

On 1 September 2001, President Bush II returned from vacation—exactly 32 weeks *after* being anointed the Prince of America's Constitution. Shortly after his vacation ended, he failed to keep America safe. On 11 September 2001, a surprise attack changed America and the world forever.

After thirty-two weeks, the anointed one [Bush II] shall fail. The prince's people shall attack and destroy the city's set apart places to cut them asunder. At the end of time, he will become incensed with anger even unto the end of the war that is appalling and decisive (Daniel 9:26, endtime alternate reading cf Strong's).

A *sanctuary* is a *set apart place, a treasure house.* One *Twin Tower* was set apart as a *treasure house* with a vault of gold. *Satan is the prince of this world. His men destroyed it.*

And *he shall confirm the constitution* [Strong's] *with many for one week: and in the midst of the week he shall cause the sacrifice and the oblation to cease,* and for the overspreading of abominations he shall make [it] desolate, even until the consummation, and that determined shall be poured upon the desolate (Daniel 9:27).

I, George W. Bush, President of the United States of America...do hereby proclaim...September 17 through September 23, 2001, as Constitution Week (www. presidency.ucsb.edu/ws/index.php?pid=61763).

In the midst of *Constitution Week* (September 17 thru 23, 2001) on Thursday (9/20/01), America's apostate Protestant prince of the covenant, Bush II, caused Christ's *Sacrifice* and *Oblation to cease.*

I also want to speak tonight directly to Muslims throughout the world. We respect your faith... *Its teachings are good* and peaceful, and those who commit evil in the name of Allah blaspheme the name of Allah (http://www.americanrhetoric.com/speeches/gwbush9 11jointsessionspeech.htm).

A popular view is that Jews, Muslims, and Christians worship the same God thru Abraham. The teachings of these religions are assumed to be all of equal value. But the Jews rejected their high calling when they rejected Jesus. "His blood [be] on us, and on our children" (cf Matthew 27:22-25). And like the Jews, though Muslims came from Abraham thru Ishmael, they departed from Abraham's God to become heathens. Salvation without Christ is a heathen idea that voids Christ's Sacrifice and Oblation.

> The idea that it is necessary only to develop the good that exists in man by nature, is a fatal deception. "The natural man receiveth not the things of the Spirit of God: for they are foolishness unto him: neither can he know them, because they are spiritually discerned." …1 Corinthians 2:14; 3:7. Of Christ it is written…the only "name under heaven given among men, whereby we must be saved." John 1:4; Acts 4:12 (SC 18.2).

Christ's *Sacrifice* on Calvary was to save us. The *Oblation* is the necessity for us to receive Jesus as our *personal Savior*. Christ's death is useless in our behalf unless we accept Him as the Atonement for our sins. Bush II's speech did away with Jesus as our personal Savior.

> The prosperity of the soul depends upon Christ's atoning sacrifice. He came to this world to obtain forgiveness in our behalf. Our first work is to strive most earnestly for spiritual blessings, in order that we may be kept loyal and true amidst the perils of these last days-- kept from yielding one inch to Satan's devices. It is the duty of every one to make straight paths for his feet, lest the lame be turned out of the way. We have no time to lose. The prosperity of the soul depends upon the oneness that Christ prayed might exist among those who believe in Him. They are to be one with Him as He is one with the Father. Drawing apart from one another is not God's plan, but the plan of the artful foe (TDG 74.3).

> We are to beware of those who…would if possible, deceive the very elect… Those who are departing from the faith are at work to undermine the confidence of others… Our warnings come from the One who…sees our dangers,

and is acquainted with the conniving of those who are opposed to His truth... He who is our Intercessor in the heavenly courts will purify His people (TDG 74.4 – 5).

The *Ten Days of Awe* precede Yom Kippur, the Day of Atonement. In ancient Israel, each day of awe was set aside to review one of the Ten Commandments to make sincere confession to God in preparation for Yom Kippur.

Yom Kippur came 27 September 2001. On the 3rd Day of Awe when God's ancient people would be confessing their sins regarding the 3rd commandment: "Thou shalt not take the name of the LORD thy God in vain (Ex 20:7), Bush II voided Christ's *Sacrifice* and *Oblation*. Christians, who are in name only, live a life that takes God's name in vain!

Today this sacrilegious work is being more than repeated. There will be messages borne; and those who have rejected the messages God has sent, will hear most startling declarations. The Holy Spirit will invest the announcement with a sanctity and solemnity which will appear terrible in the ears of those who have heard the pleadings of infinite love, and have not responded to the offers of pardon and forgiveness. Injured and insulted Deity will speak, proclaiming the sins that have been hidden. As the priests and rulers, full of indignation and terror, sought refuge in flight at the last scene of the cleansing of the temple, *so will it be in the work for these last days. The woes that will be pronounced upon those that have had light from heaven, and yet did not heed it, they will feel, but will have no power to act.* This is represented in the parable of the wise and foolish virgins. They cannot obtain a character from the wise virgins, and they have no oil of grace to discern the clear light or to accept it. They cannot light their lamps and join the procession that goes in to the marriage supper of the Lamb (SpTA07 54.2).

> Understand the words and the vision [*mareh*]:
> seventy weeks are determined 7 times
> upon thy people [Daniel 9:23-27]
>
> 1st 70...to awaken and prepare the people
> 31 May 1998 to 2 October 1999
>
> 2nd 70...to finish known rebellion
> 3 October 1999 to 3 February 2001
>
> 3rd 70...to seal the purification from sins
> 4 February 2001 to 8 June 2002
>
> 4th 70...to make atonement for iniquity
> 9 June 2002 – 11 October 2003
>
> 5th 70...to bring in everlasting righteousness
> 12 October 2003 to 12 February 2005
>
> 6th 70...to seal the vision and prophecy
> 13 February 2005 to 17 June 2006
>
> 7th 70...to anoint the Sanctuary
> 18 June 2006 to 20 October 2007

1.   70 weeks allotted "to awaken and prepare the people:" 31 May 1998 Pope John-Paul II issued *Dies Domini* to begin these 70 weeks. At their end, 2 October 1999 President Clinton "told hundreds of gay and lesbian supporters ...that it is time for the nation to rise up more vigorously against all forms of hate, which he called 'America's largest problem'" (http://www.remnantofgod. org/nl991017.htm).

Study the Revelation in connection with Daniel; for history will be repeated. We must be true and faithful amid the abounding iniquity that prevails. At no period of time are we in such danger as when prosperity seems to crown our efforts. Self must be hidden in God. We are living amid the perils of the last days, and many are insensible to the perils that threaten our world. *We, with all our religious advantages, ought to know far more today than we do know.* "Watch, and pray," said Jesus, "for ye know not when the time is." "Be ye therefore ready also: for the Son of Man cometh at an hour when ye think not." Repentance is not a desirable emotion. Christ said, "Except ye repent, ye shall all likewise perish." *...There is hidden depravity that needs to be carefully considered and uprooted. God help us individually to purify our souls by obeying the truth* (SpTA07 55.1).

The world is a second Sodom; the end is right upon us, and is it reasonable to think that there is no message to make ready a people to stand in the day of God's preparation? Why is there so little eyesight? So little deep, earnest, heartfelt labor? Why is there so much pulling back? Why is there such a continual cry of "peace and safety," and no going forward in obedience to the Lord's command? *Is the third angel's message to go out in darkness, or to lighten the whole earth with its glory?* Is the light of God's Spirit to be quenched and the church to be left as destitute of the grace of Christ...? All must admit that it is time that a vivifying, heavenly influence should be brought to bear upon our churches. It is time that unbelief, pride, love of supremacy, evil-surmising, depreciation of the work of others, licentiousness, and hypocrisy should go out of our ranks (1888 423.2).

On 2 October 1999, Johannes Hanselmann also died. "When the Lutheran-Roman Catholic project which led to the Joint Declaration on the Doctrine of Justification was in a decisive phase, with discussions going on whether the Declaration could be considered as having reached its goal and be officially confirmed, Hanselmann was...in the search for a positive and satisfactory outcome. This he did." (http://archive.wfn.org/1999/10/msg00063.html).

[The] Joint Declaration has this intention: namely, to show that on the basis of their dialogue the subscribing Lutheran churches and the Roman Catholic Church are now able to articulate a common understanding of our justification by God's grace through faith in Christ. ... basic truths of the doctrine of justification and shows that *the remaining differences... are no longer the occasion for doctrinal condemnations* (http://www.united inchrist.com/documents/JDDJ-Lutheran-Catholic-Joint-Accord-1999-United-In-Christ.pdf).

2.   70 weeks "to finish known rebellion:" 3 February 2001 Babylon's fornications that had been foretold in prophecy centuries earlier went public. "The church... denied any prior knowledge" [*even after the Roman Church had counseled him about this problem*] (http://www.thenorthernecho.co.uk/news/7118673.Paedophile_priest_s_victims_win_payout/).

3.   This endtime 70 weeks "to end sin and to seal up sinners" aligns with Daniel 9:26-27. President Bush II failed; he confirmed the Constitution with many for one week; in the midst of that week, he made the *sacrifice* and *oblation* to cease; and the belief in that lie that was established during these 70 weeks seals the fate of sinners.

4.   These 70 weeks "to make reconciliation for guilt or iniquity." The Greek equivalent for *iniquity* links to the *church* according to the *Theological Workbook of the Old Testament* (TWOT): At that time, *churches were reconciling.* "The pope expressed gratitude for the progress between Roman Catholics and Anglicans... The Archbishop expressed ... appreciation for the shared ecumenical journey between the two communions" (https://scholar.sun.ac.za/bitstream/handle/10019.1/1374/Lebruybib.pdf.txt?sequence=13). "A sign of the Anglican Communion's commitment to this dialogue and a means to our growth in deeper understanding and fellowship...until Our Lord's command is fulfilled that we may be one in him" (http://www.indcatholicnews.com/news.php?viewStory=8617).

5.   These 70 weeks were to "bring in everlasting righteousness." Jesus is the only One, who can bring in *everlasting righteousness!* But America's Protestant Prince of the Constitution did what some considered a righteous act. "President George W. Bush presents the Medal of Freedom to Pope John Paul II during a visit to the Vatican" (http://www. usa-patriotism.com/photos/special/pope-jp1.htm).

Protestantism shall stretch her hand across the gulf to grasp the hand of the Roman power (5T451.1).

Bush II also stood for biblical heterosexual marriage:

Because marriage is a sacred institution and the foundation of society, it should not be redefined by activist judges. For the good of families, children and society, *I support a constitutional amendment to protect the institution of marriage* (http://www.washingtonpost.com /wp-srv/politics/transcripts/bushtext 020205.html).

Unfortunately, many also died in their own *righteousness* (apart from Christ). A tsunami struck 26 December 2004. And most of the deaths resulting were in Sumatra (a Buddhist stronghold–now mostly Islamic); Sri Lanka (Buddhist with Hindu as its second most popular religion); India (birthplace of Buddhism and Hinduism); and Thailand (Theravada Buddhism is its national religion). These religions that deny salvation through Christ bore the brunt of that disaster with nearly 300,000 deaths that day.

Events cited during these 70-week periods aligning with Daniel's prophecy may appear subjective. There may be other events that also align. But the prophetic events in the next 70-weeks unquestionably fulfilled and sealed the prophecies.

6.   *In these 70 weeks from 13 February 2005 to 17 June 2006,* numerous prophecies were _sealed_. 1) The *season and time* (91 years, Daniel 7:12) that had ended on 9/11/01 had begun the 42 & 2-month countdown to the death of Pope John-Paul II (2 April 2005, Revelation 13:5). 2) After

President Bush II failed to keep America safe, he took away Christ's *Sacrifice* and *Oblation* 9/20/01, by setting up an abomination that destroys those who believe his lie. Exactly, 1290 days (Daniel 12:11) after Bush II set up this abomination of desolation; *the* daily (*the one who continues,* Revelation 13:5) *was taken away!* John-Paul II died (2 April 2005). 3) Pope Benedict XVI began his *short-space* reign (29 March 2006). 4) The promise, "Blessed is he that waiteth, and cometh to the thousand three hundred and five and thirty days" (Daniel 12:12) was fulfilled 17 May 2005. It was exactly 1335 days after Bush II set up his 9/20/01 abomination of desolation when it was confirmed that he was a liar in that he had lied about Iraq. 5) The same day it was confirmed that Pope Benedict XVI had also lied. 6) A Task Force on the Future of North America was set up to develop a North American Border Pass with biometric identifiers. [This will be understood more fully when the Mark of the Beast is implemented.] 7) Another 1335-day fulfillment of prophecy on 17 May 2005 included a prophetic warning from Ellen White: "There has been for years, in churches of the Protestant faith, a strong and growing sentiment in favor of a union based upon common points of doctrine. To secure such a union...a Bible standpoint—must necessarily be waived" (GC88 444.1). 8). Christ's words were partially fulfilled, "As it was in the days of Noe, so shall it be also in the days of the Son of man... As it was in the days of Lot..." (Luke 17:26, 28). 9) On the last day of these 70 weeks, 17 June 2006, the papal beast in Revelation 13 transitioned to President Bush II, who confirmed a prophecy in Daniel 11.

Each Gospel is a supplement to the others, every prophecy an explanation of another, every truth a development of some other truth (Ed 123.3).

In the prophecies, the future is opened before us as plainly as it was opened...by the words of Christ. *The events...are clearly presented. But multitudes have no more understanding of these important truths than if they had never been revealed* (GC88 594.1).

[The] Bush administration appeared intent on invading Iraq...it *"fixed" intelligence to fit its intention* (http://www.911insidejob.com/Iraqwar/Iraq-british memo.htm).

Bush II misstated "the information that might have stopped the invasion of Iraq" to justify it (http://www.salon.com/2007/09/06/bush_wmd/). "He wanted to remove Saddam, through military action...and facts were being fixed around the policy" (http://www.commondreams.org /views 05/0517-25.htm). Archbishop Desmond Tutu, a Nobel Peace Prize winner, lamented the deception: "The ex-leaders of Britain and the United States... *fabricated the grounds...* They have driven us to the edge of a precipice...with...Syria and Iran before us..." (http://www.nydailynews.com/news/world/desmond-tutu-george-bush-tony-blair-face-trial-hague-article-1. 1150170#ixzz2cqHUq1I4).

After Pope Benedict XVI had ignored the priests' fornications, he stated on 17 May 2005: *"The Church cannot cease to proclaim that in accordance with God's plans (cf. Mt 19:3-9), marriage and the family are irreplaceable and permit no other alternatives."*

When Pope Benedict XVI lied about the Roman Church *not allowing* homosexual alternatives, Massachusetts was 1) the most Catholic state in the USA, 2) the focal point of the Roman Catholic Church's priests' sex scandal; and 3) the first state in the USA to legalize homosexual marriage. This correlation of cause to effect is not a coincidence! The vision and prophecy were true, fulfilled and sealed!

On 17 May 2006, the 2nd anniversary of the legalization of homosexual *marriage* in Massachusetts there was a horrific flood that Governor Romney jokingly compared to Noah's Flood (http://en.wikipedia.org/wiki/New_England_Flood_of_May_2006#cite_ref-6). Christ said that at His Coming it would be: *As it was in Noah and Lot's Day!*

[17 May 2005] Anglican theologians accept Catholic devotion to Mary ... Anglican and Roman Catholic theologians... declared that one of the two faiths' most fundamental differences - the position of Mary, the mother of Christ - should no longer divide them. The move, aimed at reconciling Protestants to Catholicism's devotion to the Blessed Virgin (http://www. guardian.co.uk/uk/2005/may/17/religion.world).

[The] Task Force on the Future of North America... security and advance the well-being of citizens of all three countries [Canada, USA, and Mexico]... Develop a North American Border Pass with biometric identifiers (http://www.cfr.org/canada/task-force-urges-measures -strengthen-north-american-competitiveness-expand- trade-ensure-border-security/p8104).

17 June 2006, Bush II *sealed a vision and prophecy.* He restated that he had traveled to Baghdad on a personal visit, not with an invading army *as the former or as the latter.* [This prophecy will be studied more in Dan 11.]

I traveled to Baghdad to personally show our Nation's commitment to a free Iraq (https://2001- 2009.state.gov/p/nea/rls/rm/2006/67982.htm).

All heaven co-operates with Christ in His work of making plain the heavenward path... But this work is a solemn work, and unless we have the co-operation of heaven, we cannot do it effectually. *We may speak words of warning, but they will lack power. The words that are accompanied by the power of the Holy Spirit will find an assent in the judgment of candid, unprejudiced minds.* The consciences of those who hear these words will be awakened. *The soul hungering and thirsting after righteousness, admits the truth of the evidence presented by those who with power hold forth the words of life.* The truth is sought for as hidden treasure; the eye of faith, receiving the heavenly anointing, beholds the light of the knowledge of the glory of God in the face of Jesus Christ (ST, March 24, 1898 par. 11).

Has not the Lord Jesus opened to us the Scriptures, and presented to us things kept secret from the foundation of the world? Some have heard the reading of the evidence of the binding claims of the law of God, and the enjoined obedience to His commandments, and have felt their characters to be in such contrast to the requirements that had they been placed in circumstances similar to Jehoiakim, king of Judah, they would have done as he did. *A special message was sent to him to be read in his hearing, but after listening to three or four pages, he cut it out with a penknife, and cast in into the fire. But this could not destroy the message; for the word of God will never return unto Him void. The same Holy Spirit who had given the first testimony, which [was] refused and burned, came to the servant of God, who caused the first to be written in the roll, and repeated the very message that had been rejected, caused the latter to be written, and added a great deal more to* it (SpTB07 58.2).

It is now fully time that an advance move was made... We shall have to meet every form of opposition, and every manner of hindrance; *the history of the past will be repeated. It is not evidence of the truth of our cause that our enemies want;* for they are filled with fierce opposition to the truth itself, because they cannot controvert it. There are enemies without who are orga- nized to stop the work of God; but *let us move forward with well-concentrated effort, and overcome every difficulty. We must reach the people where they are...* (BEcho, Dec. 8, 1893 par. 9).

Many show plainly that it is not evidence they want, but an excuse for disregarding a plain "Thus saith the Lord." Instead of fearing and trembling before God, rejoicing that they have the privilege of listening to warnings and reproof, some inwardly wish that light had never come to them, to bring them to the test of decision (RH, November 13, 1900 par. 8).

7.   The final 70 weeks from18 June 2006 to 20 October 2007 were *to anoint the prepared or the most holy. Holy* is from a root that means to *consecrate*, to *sanctify* or to *prepare*. The *consecrated* will be *prepared* to be anointed.

As Bush II had clasped the hand of John-Paul II (June 2004), he grasped Dalai Lama's hand (17 October 2007) https://georgewbush-whitehouse.Archives.gov/news/releases/2007/10/20071017-3.html

> *Protestantism shall...grasp the hand of the Roman power...[and]...clasp hands with spiritualism* (5T 451).

During these 70 weeks to *anoint the prepared*, the Protestant counterfeit prince of America's Constitution in Revelation 13 prepared to yield his authority to Candidate Barack Obama, who was being set apart to be the next *prince of America's Constitution. "Arise, Barak, and lead thy captivity captive"* (Judges 5:11-12). As President Bush II's had mingled his religious views with politics, Mr. Obama proclaimed *America to be no longer a Christian nation!*

> We're no longer a Christian nation. At least not just. We are also a Jewish nation, a Muslim nation, and a Buddhist nation, and a Hindu nation, and a nation of nonbelievers (http://www.wnd.com/2008/06/67735/).

Remember *the "waymarks which show us our correct bearings, that we are near the close of this earth's history"* (3T 440.3). Prophetic history is about to be repeated! At the appointed time and in the correct way, historical prophetic events will have their final fulfillment: The first horn, Saddam Hussein, of the three in the remnants of the Eastern Roman Empire was killed 30 December 2006.

> Prophecies concerning the Savior's advent led the Hebrews to live in an attitude of constant expectancy. Many died in the faith, not having received the promises. But having seen them afar off, they believed and...kept alive the hope of His appearing (PK 699.3).

Study the great waymarks that point out the times in which we are living... Everything of a worldly nature should be secondary to the service of God. We should now pray most earnestly that we may be prepared for the struggles of the great day of God's preparation... The soul who accepts the truth will find... his grasp loosens from earthly things... He realizes that his trials are working out for him a far more exceeding and eternal weight of glory, and in comparison to the riches that are his to enjoy, he counts them light afflictions which are but for a moment (RH, June 23, 1896 par. 5).

Instead of living in expectation of some special season of excitement, we are wisely to improve present opportunities, doing that which must be done in order that souls may be saved... Yield ourselves to the control of the Holy Spirit, to do present duties, to *give the bread of life, unadulterated with human opinions, to souls who are perishing for the truth* (RH, March 22, 1892 par. 3).

All who love God may come to the Scriptures earnestly, prayerfully, with contrition of soul, searching for truth as for hidden treasures, fasting and praying for truth, and they will not be disappointed but be made wise unto salvation (1888 826.1).

A partial surrender to truth gives Satan free opportunity to work. Until the soul-temple is fully surrendered to God, it is the stronghold of the enemy. This influence is leading souls away from the grand old waymarks into false paths. *When the mind becomes confused, when right is considered unessential, and error is called truth, it is almost impossible to make these deceived souls see that it is the adversary who has confused their senses and polluted the soul-temple.* A tissue of lies is placed where truth, and truth alone, should be. The word of God is a dead letter to them, and the Savior's love is unknown (RH, November 28, 1899 par. 5).

The 490 weeks Repeat a Final Time

As the LORD had said of the 70 years, "first I will recompense their iniquity and their sin double" (Jeremiah 16:18), Gabriel's explanation of the 2300-day/year prophecy has essentials within it that have been doubled. The literal time (2300 days) that was fulfilled in Ezra's Day were doubled as 2300-years. The 2300 years were doubled again ending a second time in 1844. The 70 weeks of years were repeated seven times, as 490 years, and the initial 490 weeks of years were fulfilled as 70 weeks in the endtime that are doubled.

Understand the words and the vision:
seventy weeks are determined 7 times
upon thy people

1st 70...to awaken and prepare the people
21 October 2007 to 21 February 2009

2nd 70...to finish known rebellion
22 February 2009 to 26 June 2010

3rd 70...to seal the purification from sins
27 June 2010 to 29 October 2011

4th 70...to make atonement for guilt
30 October 2011 to 2 March 2013

5th 70...to bring in everlasting righteousness
3 March 2013 to 5 July 2014

6th 70...to seal the vision and prophecy
6 July 2014 to 7 November 2015

7th 70...to anoint the Sanctuary
8 November 2015 to 11 March 2017

Daniel 7 depicts Presidents Bush II and Obama as though they both are the *fourth earth-beast,* and when Revelation 6 *repeats,* in a sense, it treats them as joint *riders of the pale horse,* it would be odd if the 490-week prophecy focused so much on Bush II without giving equal time to Obama. The command in Revelation 10 to *prophesy again* also applies to this endtime prophecy in Daniel 9. *Prophecy explains itself when compared to the history that it foretells.*

1.   As President Bush II's term was ending and President Obama's term was beginning, the first 70 weeks *to awaken God's people* are from 10/21/2007 to 2/21/2009. To put it in prospective, some *coincidences* that are worthy of noting align history with prophecy. They are *significant because they grab our attention: To awaken God's people!* Though not necessarily evidence of prophecy fulfilled, *they are notable!*

As noted, during these 70 weeks, Bush II (the Protestant prince of America's Constitution reached his hand across the gulf to grasp the Roman Power again, after grasping the hand of the Roman Power and Spiritualism. He did this when Pope Benedict XVI visited the US on 15 April 2008 (https://www.youtube.com/watch?v=YVgrCm btrZk).

> When Protestantism shall stretch her hand across the gulf to grasp the hand of the Roman power, when she shall reach over the abyss to clasp hands with Spiritualism...*the end is near* (5T 451.1).

> The Protestants of the United States will be foremost in stretching their hands across the gulf to grasp the hand of Spiritualism; they will reach over the abyss to clasp hands with the Roman power...this country will follow in the steps of Rome in trampling on the rights of conscience (GC88 588.1).

As noted in White's earlier statement, President Bush II (America's Protestant prince of the covenant) clasped the hand of the Roman power, Pope John-Paul II, and then he clasped the hand of spiritualism, Dalai Lama. Then as White repeated herself and reversed the order of events, after Bush II clasped Dalai Lama's hand, he again took the hand of the Roman power, Pope Benedict XVI.

Then in 2008 Barack Obama became America's 44th President. In ancient Israel, the 44th ruler was the last. With the Russian meddling in America's election of President Trump, Mr. Obama was America's last President duly elected by the people. Fake news? A notable coincidence!

President Obama also aligns with the number 666 from Monroe to Obama. Coincidently, he was elected from Illinois. On the day that it was announced that he was President-elect, "The numbers 6-6-6 were the winning combination in an Illinois lottery" (https://www.snopes.com/fact-check/sorry-wrong-number-2/).

> The vision of the evening and the morning which was told [is] true: wherefore shut thou up the vision for it [shall be] for *many days* (Daniel 8:26).

Coincidently, *day[s]* in 8:26 is in the Bible 2008 times. Insert 2008 in the text: *The vision is true—shut up the vision; for it shall be for 2008*—[the year Obama was elected].

Another 2008 coincidence: Noah was a "preacher of righteousness" (2 Peter 2:5) for 120 years. The message about Righteousness by Faith was rejected by the Seventh-day Adventist Church in Minneapolis in 1888. Ellen White "SPOKE TWENTY TIMES IN MINNEAPOLIS...SHE PLEADED FOR OPEN-MINDED BIBLE STUDY. SHE HERSELF DID NOT SPEAK ON THE TOPIC OF RIGHTEOUSNESS BY FAITH." (3SM 158.3) "A. T. JONES, SPEAKING OF THE RECEPTION OF THE TRUTHS SET FORTH AT MINNEAPOLIS, REPORTED: 'I KNOW THAT SOME THERE ACCEPTED IT; OTHERS REJECTED IT ENTIRELY. YOU KNOW THE SAME THING. OTHERS TRIED TO STAND HALF WAY BETWEEN, AND GET IT THAT WAY'" (3SM 158.4). Thus, *The vision is true—shut up the vision; for it shall be for* 2008 is coincidentally the year that marks 120 years since Adventists shut out the message of Righteousness by Faith. As the Israelites rejected God's leading them into the promised land, and were made to wander in the wilderness for 40 years, the Seventh-day Adventist Church's rejection of Righteousness by Faith has delayed Christ's Advent for 120 years from 1888 to 2008, and this state of unbelief is not going to continue much longer. The final countdown in Bible prophecy has begun.

2.   The 2nd 70 weeks to *finish known rebellion* repeated from 2/22/2009 to 6/26/2010. God's faithful people were fleeing the priests' *known rebellion* in the Roman Church as God had commanded: "Come out of her, My people, that ye be not partakers of her sins" (Revelation 18:4). Benedict XVI tried to stop the exodus from the Roman Church by proclaiming the "Year for Priests" [June 2009-2010].

> This Year, meant to deepen the commitment of all priests to interior renewal for the sake of a stronger and more incisive witness to the Gospel in today's world (https://w2.vatican.va/content/benedict-xvi/en/letters/2009/documents/hf_ben-xvi_let_20090616_anno-sacerdotale.html).

During these 70 weeks, President Obama rebelled against his campaign promise to stop the war in Afghanistan. 13 December 2009, he defended his rebellion:

> I think it's the right thing to do... This is one of those situations where, having looked exhaustively at all the information available to me, after having consulted with military experts, the civilian experts, our allies, it was my strong conclusion [to fight on.] (http://www.cbsnews.com/news/transcript-president-barack-obama-part-1-13-12-2009/2/).

"There is a way that seemeth right unto a man, but the end thereof are the ways of death" (Proverbs 16:25). "LORD, who shall abide in Thy tabernacle? Who shall dwell in Thy holy hill? ...He that sweareth to his own hurt, and changeth not" (Psalms 15:1, 4).

3.   The 3rd 70 weeks *to purify sinners* repeated from 6/27/2010 to 10/29/2011. The war between Christ and

Satan raged on: Osama bin Laden was killed 2 May 2011. Pope Benedict XVI again tried to stop the RCC's exodus:

> Promoting New Evangelization, Benedict XVI announced...a forthcoming 'Year of Faith' (http://catholic exchange.com/pope-benedict-xvi-announces-the-year-of-faith).

Satan was fighting *to seal sinners in their sins... to keep sinners from being purified* through faith in Jesus. And the American state was involving itself in religion: Cf Executive Order 13498 that extended President Obama's Advisory Council on Faith-Based and Neighborhood Partnerships (http://www.presidency.ucsb.edu/ws/?pid=85734).

4.   The 4th 70 weeks *to make atonement for guilt* repeated 10/30/2011 to 3/2/2013. Heaven's Investigative Judgment Hour for the living ended!

The principle of *First Mention* studies a topic from where it is first in Scripture. To study creation and sin in relation to time, Genesis is where they are first mentioned. *Literal Time*: God created *The Day* that began in the evening.

> Evening and the morning...the first day (Gen 1:5)

After establishing Literal Time, Genesis refers to a DAY that is Not Literal Time that relates to Adam's Judgment: "In the *day* that thou eatest thereof thou shalt surely die" (Genesis 2:17). Adam did not die in Literal Time, i.e., the day that he sinned. Adam did not die in *long time, each day for a year* (Ezekiel 4:6), i.e., the year he sinned. He died in *Millennial Time*; in the day/1,000 years that he sinned.

> All the days that Adam lived were nine hundred and thirty years: *and he died* (Genesis 5:5).

First Mention links God's judgment of Adam to *Millennial Time,* therefore, a *Judgment Hour* links to *Millennial Time.* As Peter advised: Do not be ignorant of God's timing (a day with God is like 1,000 years or 1,000 years is like a day), God's judgment of Adam aligned with God's timing, i.e., *Millennial Time.* The same is true of God's Judgment of sin that is limited to 7,000 years: 6,000 years for Satan to tempt man, and 1,000 years for the earth to have its Sabbath rest.

The Judgment Hour of the dead began 22 October 1844. "Judgment must begin at the house of God" (1 Peter 4:17). It is written, "Of the church in Sardis...thou hast a name that thou livest, and art dead (Revelation 3:1). The Roman Catholic Church died in 1798: It was dead on 22 October 1844. "The Saviour did enter the Most Holy Place in 1844 to cleanse the sanctuary and the investigative judgment had commenced for the dead" (10MR 269.1).

Under the Mosaic system the cleansing of the sanctuary, or the great Day of Atonement, occurred on the tenth day of the seventh Jewish month (Leviticus 16:29-34) (GC 399.4).

That same Day: for it is a Day of Atonement (Leviticus 23:27).

In the day when God shall judge the secrets of men by Jesus Christ (Romans 2:16).

"Moses sat to judge the people...from the morning unto the evening" (Exodus 18:13).

On the Day of Atonement, the High Priest ministered in the Sanctuary during the daylight hours: From morning to evening. Jesus asked, "Are there not twelve hours in the day?" (John 11:9). *The length of an hour being determined by the length of the day is a Jewish principle called* <u>*Sha'ah Zemanit*</u>: "*Proportional hour... Total daylight hours divided by 12*" (http://www.chabad.org/library/article_cdo/aid/134527/jewish/About-Zmanim.htm).

Fear God, and give glory to Him; for *the hour of His Judgment is Come*: And worship Him that made heaven, and earth, and the sea, and the fountains of waters (Revelation 14:7).

How long is a Judgment HOUR? A literal hour is 60-minutes. In prophecies that use a day for a year, an hour can be a month (1/12th of a 360 day/prophetic year = 30 days). An hour is 15 days based on a 24-hour day in a 360-day/prophetic year. Josiah Litch used 1/24th of a day to precisely calculate the fall of the Ottoman Empire foretold in Rev 9. Based on Adam's *Millennial Judgment* and the fact that the Temple's Day of Atonement services took place during the daylight hours: The length of a *Judgment Hour* is *1/12th of a 1000-year day: 83 years and 4 months.*

An HOUR (cf Strong):

1) **A certain definite time**
2) **The daytime**
3) **A twelfth part of the day-time, an hour**
4) **Any definite time, point of time, moment**

Was the Roman Catholic Church dead for the Judgment HOUR of the dead, the 83 years 4 months from 22 October 1844 until 22 February 1928? Yes, the dead Roman Church confirms the length of that judgment Hour!

When the time allotted for the Judgment Hour of the dead ended, there was a brief tarrying time in which the papacy's deadly wound was healed by Mussolini, who restored a secular kingdom to Pope Pius XI via the Lateran Treaty. The healing process began in February 1929 and was completed by June. After the deadly wound was healed, the Day of Atonement in 1929 was on 14 October. The Roman Church was alive for the 83 years 4 months from 14 October 1929 until 14 February 2013.

When the Day of Atonement arrived 14 October 1929, Pope Pius XI had had his kingdom, Vatican City, restored. Exactly seven popes: Pius XI & XII, John XXIII, Paul VI,

John-Paul I & II, and Benedict XVI; reigned as solo kings for the 83-year 4-month Judgment Hour of the living papacy from 14 October 1929 thru 14 February 2013.

When Pope Benedict resigned, the papacy became a dual monarchy with two living popes as ancient Babylon had been a dual monarchy prior to its fall. When the Judgment Hour allotted for the living papacy ended, the history of the post-1929 papacy confirms the duration of the Judgment Hour of the living in Bible prophecy! The times allotted for the Judgment Hours of the dead and living have ended!

During the 70 weeks allotted *to anoint the Sanctuary* from 10/30/2011 to 3/2/2013, the *Hour allotted to Judge the Living ended on 14 February 2013. Christ's saints, who have been judged faithful during the Investigative Judgment of the Living are being sealed while the Third Angel's message sounds*: Do not take the *Mark of the Beast*!

Satan is now using every device in this sealing time to keep the minds of God's people from the present truth and to cause them to waver. I saw a covering that God was drawing over His people to protect them in the time of trouble; and every soul that was decided on the truth and was pure in heart was to be covered with the covering of the Almighty (EW 43.2).

"And he causeth all, both small and great, rich and poor, free and bond, to receive a mark in their right hand, or in their foreheads and that no man might buy or sell, save he that had the mark, or the name of the beast, or the number of his name" (1888 700.2).

This is the test that the people of God must have before they are sealed. All who prove their loyalty to God by observing His law, and refusing to accept a spurious Sabbath, will rank under the banner of the Lord God Jehovah, and will receive the seal of the living God. Those who yield the truth of heavenly origin, and accept the Sunday Sabbath, will receive the Mark of the Beast. What need will there be of the solemn warning not to receive the Mark of the Beast, when all the saints of God are sealed and ticketed for the New Jerusalem? "O consistency, thou art a jewel!" (1888 701.1).

5.   The 70 weeks *to bring in everlasting righteousness* repeated from 3/3/2013 to 7/5/2014. President Obama said, "It's a reminder, as Scripture often is, that God has a plan, and it's important, though, that we also recognize that we're an instrument of His will" (https://historymusings. wordpress.com/2013/05/26/full-text-obama-presidency-may-26-2013-president-barack-obamas-speech-after-touring-the-tornado-damage-in-moore-oklahoma/).

Everlasting righteousness (right doing) includes obeying God's Commandments; the Sabbath Commandment as well as the other nine...not the whims of tradition or the commands of presidents or popes. On 5 July 2014, *Pope Francis I rejected everlasting righteousness for a papal tradition having its foundation in pagan sun worship.*

Abandoning of the traditionally Christian practice of not working on Sundays...has a negative impact on families and friendships (http://www.nydailynews.com /news/world/pope-francis-sundays-article-1.1856433).

The day of the sun, Sunday, was a day devoted to the most vile of the heathen worship, for it was celebrated in connection with sun-worship (ST, Nov. 19, 1894 par. 5).

"It was an essential principle of the Babylonian system, that the Sun or Baal was the one only God." "As the sun in the heavens was the great object of worship, so fire was worshipped as its earthly representative." "According to the fundamental doctrine of the Mysteries, as brought from Pergamos to Rome, the sun was the one only god" (http://ldolphin.org/PDFs/The_Two_Babylons-Alexander_Hislop.pdf).

"Baal worship was accompanied with sinful sexual acts; behavior expressly forbidden in Jehovah's law." "Baal worship is giving free-reign to the carnal nature. It expresses itself in gluttony, drunkenness and sinful sexual acts"

(http://www.avoiceinthewilderness.org/snotes/pdf/
sermon197.pdf).

The pope's lamenting that Sunday-working is harmful to relationships between family and friends because it forsakes *a traditional Christian practice* is a perverted recognition of the harm that has come to the world because it abandoned God's holy Seventh-day Sabbath. Christ rested in His tomb on Sabbath. To sanctify Christ's Resurrection Day (the day that Jesus ended His rest and began to work again), as THE DAY of rest and worship in place of the day that God sanctified and blessed is turning God's word on its head!

> And God blessed the seventh day, and sanctified it: because that in it He had rested from all His work which God created and made (Genesis 2:3).

"The importance of the Sabbath as the memorial of creation is that it keeps ever present the true reason why worship is due to God," because He is the Creator, and we His creatures. "The Sabbath therefore lies at the very foundation of divine worship; for it teaches this great truth in the most impressive manner, and no other institution does this. The true ground of divine worship, not of that on the seventh day merely, but of all worship, is found in the distinction between the Creator and His creatures. This great fact can never become obsolete, and must never be forgotten." It was to keep this truth ever before the minds of men, that God instituted the Sabbath in Eden; and so long as the fact that He is our Creator continues to be a reason why we should worship Him, so long the Sabbath will continue as its sign and memorial. *Had the Sabbath been universally kept, man's thoughts and affections would have been led to the Creator as the object of reverence and worship, and there would never have been an idolater, an atheist, or an infidel. The keeping of the Sabbath is a sign of loyalty to the true God, "Him that made heaven and earth, and the sea, and the fountains of waters." It follows that the message which commands men to worship God and keep His commandments, will especially call upon them to keep the fourth commandment* (GC88 437.2).

Righteousness is right doing. Keeping the Sabbath that is now being kept in Heaven, the Sabbath that will be kept on the New Earth for eternity, is Everlasting Righteousness.

6.   These 70 weeks *to seal the vision and prophecy* were repeated from 7/6/2014 to 11/7/2015. The vision of the other angel (Revelation 18:1) was sealed, he is sounding: *Babylon is fallen! Babylon is the cage of unclean spirits*!

On 9 December 2015: Pope Francis I had a light show that projected unclean birds onto the façade of St Peter's Basilica that displayed them as being caged by its columns. [https://www.youtube.com/watch?v=WtI6P9R3x4E]

President Obama fulfilled Revelation 18:9! As the prophetic earth's king, he embraced Babylon's lust. "The kings of the earth, *who have committed fornication* and lived deliciously with her" (papal Babylon).

June 27, 2015 WASHINGTON — In a long-sought victory for the gay rights movement, the Supreme Court ruled by a 5-to-4 vote on Friday that the Constitution guarantees a right to same-sex marriage. "No longer may this liberty be denied," Justice Anthony M. Kennedy wrote   (https://www.nytimes.com/2015/06/27/us/supreme-court-same-sex-marriage.html).

The successor to the Protestant prince of the covenant, President Obama, "welcomed the decision!" (http://www.nytimes.com/2015/06/27/us/supreme-court-same-sex-marriage.html?_r=0). It happened at the time prophesied!

As prophesied, President, Obama tried to stop Iran's nuclear aspirations. The prophecy: "And both these kings' hearts shall be to do mischief, and they shall speak lies at one table; but it shall not prosper: for yet the end shall be at the time appointed" (Dan 11:27) was also sealed.

Their agreement was a lie. Iran wanted sanctions lifted. President Obama wanted a non-nuclear Iran. When the talking points were presented to the people of these two nations, the deal sounded totally different respectively, but a deal was forged within these 70 weeks: They were far apart on July 2014; but April 2015, a framework was announced. And "July 14, 2015 - World powers and Iran announce long-term, comprehensive nuclear agreement" (https://www.cbsnews.com/media/iran-nuclear-agreement-timeline/4/).

This agreement that *sealed the vision and prophecy* in these 70 weeks: *shall not prosper*. President Obama did not negotiate a treaty that required Congressional approval, because they would not approve it. In fact, Congress enacted H.R.1191 - Iran Nuclear Agreement Review Act of 2015 that required the President to certify every 180 days that Iran is complying. 13 October 2017 President Trump declined to certify their compliance: The deal collapsed.

The other angel is sounding His message in fulfillment of prophecy! Consider the parable of the ten virgins:

> Five were wise and five were foolish. The truth should have been proclaimed by the ten virgins, but only five had made the provision essential to join that company who walked in the light that had come to them. *The third angel's message was needed. This proclamation was to be made. Many who went forth to meet the Bridegroom under the messages of the first and second angels, refused the third angel's message, the last testing message to be given to the world* (16MR 269.3).

The identity of the one, who will form the image beast is known. Will you refuse to declare the third angel's message? Will you wait in doubt and unbelief until all doubt is removed when it is too late to receive and to give the warning?

> And *the third angel followed them, saying with a loud voice, If any man worship the beast and his image, and receive [his] mark in his forehead, or in his hand, The same shall drink of the wine of the wrath of God* (Revelation 14:9-10).

Are we to wait until the fulfillment of the prophecies of the end before we say anything concerning them? Of what value will our words be then? Shall we wait until God's judgments fall upon the transgressor before we tell him how to avoid them? Where is our faith in the word of God? Must we see things foretold come to pass before we will believe what He has said? In clear, distinct rays light has come to us, showing us that the great day of the Lord is near at hand, "even at the doors." Let us read and understand before it is too late (9T 20.1).

A similar work will be accomplished when that other angel, represented in Revelation 18, gives his message. The first, second, and third angels' messages will need to be repeated. The call will be given to the church, "Come out of her, My people, that ye be not partakers of her sins." "Babylon, the great, is fallen, is fallen, and is become the habitation of devils, and the hold of every foul spirit, and a cage of every unclean and hateful bird. For all nations have drunk of the wine of the wrath of her fornication, and the kings of the earth have committed fornication with her, and the merchants of the earth are waxed rich through the abundance of her delicacies... Come out of her, My people, that ye be not partakers of her sins, and that ye receive not of her plagues: for her sins have reached unto heaven, and God hath remembered her iniquities" [Revelation 18:2-5] (16MR 270.1).

7.   The final, 7th 70 weeks *to anoint the Sanctuary* or *to anoint the prepared* repeated from 11/8/2015 to 3/11/2017. President Trump was prepared and inaugurated 20 January 2017. He became the anointed Protestant counterfeit prince of America's Constitution identified from the prophecies of Daniel and Revelation.

It is not a coincidence that Republicans dominate all three branches of the US government: The Congress (makes the law), the majority Catholic Supreme Court (Republican appointees...interprets it), and the Whitehouse (Republican ...enforces it). Republicans have had a heritage that upheld traditional Protestant values like honesty, truthfulness, caring for the poor and needy, etc.

> *Our country shall repudiate every principle of its Constitution as a Protestant and republican government, and shall make provision for the propagation of papal falsehoods and delusions...* (5T 451.1).

The rulers of the land will take their position above the great Creator of the world. The claims of a false sabbath will be brought to the front, and the rulers and the people will act upon the principle of a short-sighted policy. The false sabbath, the first day of the week, will be accepted, and the rulers will unite with the man of sin to restore his lost ascendancy. Laws enforcing the observance of Sunday as the Sabbath, will bring about *a national apostasy from the principles of republicanism upon which the government has been founded.* The religion of the Papacy will be accepted by the rulers, and the law of God will be made void (7MR 192.1).

Our land is in jeopardy. The time is drawing on when its legislators shall so abjure the principles of Protestantism as to give countenance to Romish apostasy. The people for whom God has so marvelously wrought, strengthening them to throw off the galling yoke of popery, will by a national act give vigor to the corrupt faith of Rome, and thus arouse the tyranny which only waits for a touch to start again into cruelty and despotism. *With rapid steps are we already approaching this period.* When Protestant churches shall seek the support of the secular power, thus following the example of that apostate church, for opposing which their ancestors endured the fiercest persecution, then will there be a national apostasy which will end only in national ruin (4SP 410.2).

> *Romanism in the Old World, and apostate Protestantism in the New, will pursue a similar course toward those*

who honor all the divine precepts. This is the mystery of iniquity, the devising of satanic agencies, carried into effect by the man of sin (ST, February 22, 1910 par. 6).

President Trump is steering America toward the final conflict with Iran that Obama avoided. Is his destabilization of the world economy a harbinger for the Time of Trouble?

"If we don't win in 2020, everything that we have done – seriously, though — everything that we have done, your 401(k)s, they are going to crash. The whole thing, it's going to come down like a stack of cards," Trump told a North Carolina rally (http://access pressmag.com/ trumps-new-economic-message-reelect-him-or-it-all-goes-down-the-tubes/).

The prophecies identify our place in this world's history. Have some events been left sealed to test our faith in God's word? Daniel wrote, "I heard, but I understood not: then said I, O my Lord, what shall be the end of these things? And he said, Go thy way, Daniel: for the words are closed up and sealed till the time of the end" (Dan 12:7-8).

God's word warns: "Lying lips are abomination to the LORD: but they that deal truly are His delight" (Proverbs 12:22). Are President Trump's lips an abomination to God? Does President Trump speak the truth and deal truly? Should this cause us concern? "We speak of what we know, and we testify to what we have seen" (John 3:11, NIV).

The 70 weeks (11/8/2015 to 3/11/2017) allotted *to seal the prepared* or *to seal the Sanctuary*: Have been fulfilled. The 3rd Angel's Message is being proclaimed to prepare God's people for the anointing of the Holy Spirit, the *latter rain*, and to prepare them to resist the pending Mark of the Beast.

The last day of these 490 weeks was Sabbath, 11 March 2017, the day before Purim. "A Jewish Holiday which commemorates Jewish people being saved from extermination in Persia" (http://www.wincalendar.com/Purim).

As President Bush II had done at the beginning of his 490 weeks, at the end of the final 490 weeks, President Obama also confirmed the covenant with many for a week.

> I, BARACK OBAMA... do hereby proclaim... September 17 through September 23, 2016, as Constitution Week (https://www.whitehouse. gov/the-press-office/2016/09/16/presidential-proclamation-constitution-day-and-citizenship-day).

When President Bush II spoke (20 September 2001), he took away Christ's *Sacrifice* and *Oblation* in the midst of the week. 20 September 2016, in a speech to the United Nations, President Obama condemned fundamentalism that included Christians, who believe in salvation thru Christ, accept Him as their personal Savior, and honor His Sabbath. They will not worship the beast or take the Image of the Beast because of their belief in the sure word of God, the Bible!

> Religious fundamentalism...more often from the far right -- which seeks to restore what they believe was a better, simpler age free of outside contamination... *We must reject any forms of fundamentalism....that makes our traditional identities irreconcilable with modernity.* Instead we need to embrace the tolerance that results from respect of all human beings (https://www.White house.gov/the-press-office/2016/09/20/address-president-obama-71st-session-united-nations-general-assembly).

Without distinguishing between religions, his view: *We must reject any forms of fundamentalism...as intolerant, irreconcilable with modernity*, supposes that modernity is *tolerant and respects all human beings*. That proved to be untrue after President Trump occupied the Oval Office. Thus, *to reject Christian fundamentalists whose goal in life is to serve Christ is an abomination that will lead to the destruction of those who reject the truths that Christian fundamentalists bring from God's word!*

> The LORD hath sent unto you all His servants the prophets, rising early and sending [them]; but ye have not hearkened, nor inclined your ear to hear... I will persecute them with the sword, with the famine, and with the pestilence, and will deliver them to be removed to all the kingdoms of the earth, to be a curse, and an astonishment, and an hissing, and a reproach, among all the nations whither I have driven them: Because they have not hearkened to My words, saith the LORD, which I sent unto them by My servants the prophets, rising up early and sending [them]; but ye would not hear, saith the LORD (Jeremiah 25:4; 29:18,19).

20 September 2016 President Obama set up an abomination that will desolate those, who will not hear of Christ's *Sacrifice,* and who will not accept Christ as their personal Savior. In the midst of this Constitution week, President Obama established a rationale for taking away *Fundamentalist Christians,* whose belief in God's sure word is *irreconcilable with modernity.* Their belief established at creation that will endure thru eternity are that the Seventh-day is the Sabbath and Jesus is our only Savior.

After this speech, did President Obama fail? He failed to get Hillary elected. His executive acts (apart from Congress) are failing because President Trump is annulling them.

By their fulfillment in these last days, the prophecies in Daniel and Revelation are explaining themselves. Christian fundamentalism that is derived from sound Bible study is soon to be in mortal conflict with religious modernity.

Will the USA persecute Christians? Many Americans now adamantly believe that separating immigrant children from their parents, who enter America illegally, is the consequence for breaking the law. If these people will treat desperate children this way, what will they do to Christians who refuse to yield their God given right to worship as their conscience directs when it is against the dictates of America?

Too many professed Christians regard one whom they deem in error with an unfeeling, relentless spirit, which is the fruit of pride, self-sufficiency, and hardness of heart; thus, they show that God's great love for them is not appreciated; for it has not softened their hearts (HM, January 1, 1892 par. 16).

The majority of professed Christians are serving other gods besides the Lord (4SP 237.3).

The unprepared inhabitants of earth know what to expect. Satan cannot pay a ransom for their souls; and poor, deluded, professed Christians, who have been content to let the ministers search the Scriptures for them, see that they will receive as their works have been. Those, too, who have wrested the Scriptures, and taught for doctrines the commandments of men, see that they must answer for the souls of those who have been led into error and apostasy. A wail of agony and despair reaches heavenward, but it echoes back to earth. Louder, far louder, than any human cry, is the last trumpet's sound; and far above all is heard the voice of Omnipotence: "Depart from Me, ye that work iniquity" (RH, November 22, 1898 par. 15).

Are all religions of equal value? Do all religions lead to God? "Enter ye in at the strait gate: for wide [is] the gate, and broad [is] the way, that leadeth to destruction, and many there be which go in there at: Because strait [is] the gate, and narrow [is] the way, which leadeth unto life, and few there be that find it (Matthew 7:13, 14). Thus, the view that all religions are as good as the next—though popular is not biblical. True fundamental biblical beliefs are *irreconcilable with modernity*! Should you be concerned if President Trump is removed or leaves office prematurely and Mr. Michael Pence becomes President of the United States of America?

Daniel 9 foretold that Christ would be anointed the Prince of the Covenant in 27 AD, and the prophecy repeated in the endtime on 20 January 2001, when Bush II was anointed the counterfeit *Prince of America's Covenant*. Later, he set up his abomination that desolates on 20 September 2001 that counted down to the death of the one who was to *continue*, Pope John-Paul II on 2 April 2005.

When President Obama repeated history 20 September 2016, he set up his abomination of desolation that rejected ALL fundamentalism that refuses to yield the consciences to modernity. It will not go well for Christians, who cling to a belief in salvation doctrines like God's Seventh-day Sabbath and Christ's *sacrifice* and *oblation*. From Obama's setting up of his abomination that desolates, the 1290 days in Daniel 12:11 count down to 2 April 2020.

The continual Sabbath from eternity past to eternity future was the reason that the shew bread was said to be set in order *continually* (cf Lev 24:8). Since Daniel is prophesying about the continual Sabbath, on 2 April 2020, the day that President Trump announced that America would give free money to people to keep America afloat during the pandemic, is a harbinger of the Mark of the Beast and a National Sunday Law that will take away the Sabbath. Daniel warns that preparations for the Sabbath *to be taken away, and the abomination that maketh desolate to be set up, in a thousand two hundred and ninety days* (12:11) are in progress!

The things in Daniel's prophecies that are yet to happen will be better understood after the prophecies are fulfilled. But there is ample prophetic evidence to know that the time has arrived for the endtime prophecies to be fulfilled. As it was in the days of Noah: He knew when to go into the ark. Then he waited for seven days for the rain to come.

Pope Benedict resigned on 14 February 2013 when the Judgment Hour of the living ended. A day is a year in some Bible prophecy. As Noah waited 7 days in the ark, on 14 February 2020 (7years later), the rains came: Two hurricanes merged in the Atlantic to create a bomb cyclone that struck Iceland, and moved on to England and Europe. The World Health Organization declared COVID-19 a global pandemic on that very day. COVID-19 is a judgment from God just as sure as the flood in Noah's Day!

14 February 2020 was about 47 days before 2 April 2020. There is the promised blessing to those who wait for the 45 days that end on 17 May 2020. The global meeting that Pope Francis I intended to convene in Rome to exalt Sunday sacredness, was cancelled. This blessing was a direct result of the COVID-19 pandemic.

The title *Prince of the Covenant* passed successively from Bush II, to Obama, and Trump; and when he is broken, Michael Pence will be the *Prince of the Covenant*. When President Michael Pence becomes America's Prince of the Constitution, he will set up the National Sunday Law abomination of desolation!

And at that time shall Michael stand up, the great prince which standeth for the children of thy people: and there shall be a time of trouble, such as never was since there was a nation even to that same time: and at that time thy people shall be delivered, every one that shall be found written in the book (Daniel 12:1).

[Someone once urged] that nothing should be taught in the college contrary to that which has been taught, I felt deeply, for I knew whoever framed that resolution was not aware of what he was doing (1888 258.4).

A time is coming when the law of God is, in a special sense, to be made void in our land. The rulers of our nation will, by legislative enactments, enforce the Sunday law, and thus, God's people be brought into great peril. When our nation, in its legislative councils, shall enact laws to bind the consciences of men in regard to their religious privileges, enforcing Sunday observance, and bringing oppressive power to bear against those who keep the seventh-day Sabbath, the law of God will, to all intents and purposes, be made void in our land; and national apostasy will be followed by national ruin (RH December 18, 1888).

When the law of God is being made void, when His name is dishonored, when it is considered disloyal to the laws of the land to keep the seventh day as the Sabbath, when wolves in sheep's clothing, through blindness of mind and hardness of heart, are seeking to compel the conscience, shall we give up our loyalty to God? No, no. The wrongdoer is filled with a Satanic hatred against those who are loyal to the commandments of God, but the value of God's law as a rule of conduct must be made manifest. The zeal of those who obey the Lord will be increased as the world and the church unite in making void the law. They will say with the Psalmist, "I love Thy commandments above gold; yea above fine gold" [Psalms 119:127]. This is what will be sure to occur when the law of God is made void by a national act. When Sunday is exalted and sustained by law, then the principle that actuates the people of God will be made manifest, as the principle of the three Hebrews was made manifest when Nebuchadnezzar commanded them to worship the golden image in the plain of Dura. We can see what our duty is when the truth is overborne by falsehood (13MR 71.1).

Are we by repentance and confession sending our sins beforehand to Judgment, that they may be blotted out...? This is an individual work,--a work which we cannot safely delay. We should take hold of it earnestly; our salvation depends upon our sincerity and zeal. Let the cry be awakened in every heart, "What must I do to be saved?" (RH, August 28, 1883 par. 20)

Daniel 10

¹In the third year of Cyrus king of Persia a thing was revealed unto Daniel, whose name was called Belteshazzar; and the thing [was] true, but the time appointed [was] long: and he understood the thing, and had understanding of the vision [*mareh*].

²In those days I Daniel was mourning three full weeks. ³I ate no pleasant bread, neither came flesh nor wine in my mouth, neither did I anoint myself at all, till three whole weeks were fulfilled. ⁴And in the four and twentieth day of the first month, as I was by the side of the great river, which [is] Hiddekel; ⁵Then I lifted up mine eyes, and looked, and behold a certain man clothed in linen, whose loins [were] girded with fine gold of Uphaz: ⁶His body also [was] like the beryl, and his face as the appearance of lightning, and his eyes as lamps of fire, and his arms and his feet like in color to polished brass, and the voice of his words like the voice of a multitude.

⁷And I Daniel alone saw the vision [form of *mareh*]: for the men that were with me saw not the vision [form of *mareh*]; but a great quaking fell upon them, so that they fled to hide themselves. ⁸Therefore, I was left alone, and saw this great vision [form of *mareh*], and there remained no strength in me: for my comeliness was turned in me into corruption, and I retained no strength.

⁹Yet heard I the voice of his words: and when I heard the voice of his words, then was I in a deep sleep on my face, and my face toward the ground. ¹⁰And, behold, an hand touched me, which set me upon my knees and [upon] the palms of my hands. ¹¹And he said unto me, O Daniel, a man greatly beloved, understand the words that I speak unto thee, and stand upright: for unto thee am I now sent. And when he had spoken this word unto me, I stood trembling.

¹²Then said he unto me, Fear not, Daniel: for from the first day that thou didst set thine heart to understand, and to chasten thyself before thy God, thy words were heard, and I am come for thy words. ¹³But the prince of the kingdom of Persia withstood me one and twenty days: but, lo, Michael, one of the chief princes, came to help me; and I remained there with the kings of Persia. ¹⁴Now I am come to make thee understand what shall befall thy people in the latter days: for yet the vision [*chazon* is] for [many] days.

¹⁵And when he had spoken such words unto me, I set my face toward the ground, and I became dumb. ¹⁶And, behold, [one] like the similitude of the sons of men touched my lips: then I opened my mouth, and spake, and said unto him that stood before me, O my lord, by the vision [form of *mareh*] my sorrows are turned upon me, and I have retained no strength. ¹⁷For how can the servant of this my lord talk with this my lord? for as for me, straightway there remained no strength in me, neither is there breath left in me.

¹⁸Then there came again and touched me [one] like the appearance of a man, and he strengthened me, ¹⁹And said, O man greatly beloved, fear not: peace [be] unto thee, be strong, yea, be strong. And when he had spoken unto me, I was strengthened, and said, Let my lord speak; for thou hast strengthened me.

²⁰Then said he, Knowest thou wherefore I come unto thee? and now will I return to fight with the prince of Persia: and when I am gone forth, lo, the prince of Grecia shall come. ²¹But I will show thee that which is noted in the scripture of truth: and [there is] none that holdeth with me in these things, but Michael your prince.

Points to Ponder

1. During Cyrus' rule Daniel received this *long-time* vision
2. Daniel was mourning and fasting for 3 weeks
3. Gabriel returned to explain the time in the earlier vision
4. Daniel received this vision by the Hiddekel River
5. It is endtime specific and chapter 11 fills in the details

Commentary

Daniel understood from Jeremiah's "Scripture of truth" that the 70 years of Jerusalem's desolation had ended when Cyrus began to reign. He is the Prince of Persia. Daniel fasted and prayed "three full weeks" that God would fulfill His word and restore the Temple (cf Daniel 9).

The Hebrew Calendar is arranged differently than the Gregorian Calendar. Firstly, it is a lunar calendar. The year starts in the month of Nissan. But the first day of the seventh month (Tishrei) is New Year's Day. This is because Nissan counts time from the Exodus from Egypt and Tishrei marks time from creation (earth's beginning).

The *First Month* is cited as such 29 times in Scripture. The first month is "the month Nisan" (Esther 3:7). Daniel fasted until the 24th of the *First Month,* but Daniel did not fast until Nissan 24. For Daniel to have completed three full weeks of fasting immediately prior to Nissan 24, his fast would have had to have been during Passover, Nissan 14. Daniel would not fast when God commanded him to eat the Passover lamb:

> This month shall be unto you the beginning of months: it shall be *the first month of the year...* Your lamb shall be without blemish...the *fourteenth day of the same month*: and the whole assembly of the congregation of Israel shall *kill it in the evening...*And *they shall eat the flesh...* (cf Exodus 12:1-11).

> But the man that...forbeareth to keep the Passover ...shall bear his sin (cf Numbers 9:13).

Daniel's three-week fast was in Tishrei. The first two days of Tishrei are Rosh Hashanah (Jewish New Year). They are not fast days, but feast days. Together these two days are as one long day and they are linked with the eating of certain foods like apples and honey to signify that the New Year will be a sweet one. They also begin the ten Days of Awe when God's faithful people search their souls in regards to the Ten Commandments in preparation for Yom Kippur, the Day of Atonement. It aligns with September-October on the Gregorian Calendar. Daniel fasted from Tishrei 3 thru Tishrei 23, which are exactly *three full weeks*. Immediately after Daniel fasted for 21-days, Gabriel's coming to him on Tishrei 24 fits the context that aligns with his concern about the desolation of the Sanctuary and its suspended Services to make atonement for sins.

While Daniel fasted, Gabriel was working with Cyrus. "From the first day that thou didst set thine heart to understand, and to chasten thyself before thy God, thy words were heard... But the prince of the kingdom of Persia withstood me *one and twenty days*" (Daniel 10:12-13). Gabriel left Cyrus to go to Daniel at the end of the three weeks, after Jesus interceded with Cyrus. The elderly Daniel, who was also weakened by fasting, collapsed at the glorified appearance of Gabriel (and Jesus).

> So great was the divine glory revealed to Daniel that he could not endure the sight. Then the messenger of Heaven veiled the brightness of his presence and appeared to the prophet as "one like the similitude of the sons of men." By his divine power he strengthened this man of integrity and of faith, to hear the message sent to him from God (RH, February 8, 1881 par. 32).

> The prophet Daniel was an example of true sanctification. His long life was filled up with noble service for his Master. He was a man "greatly beloved" [Daniel 10:11.] of Heaven. Yet instead of claiming to be pure and holy, this honored prophet identified himself with the really sinful of Israel, as he pleaded before God in behalf

of his people: "We do not present our supplications before Thee for our righteousnesses, but for Thy great mercies." "We have sinned, we have done wickedly." He declares, "I was speaking, and praying, and confessing my sin and the sin of my people." And when at a later time the Son of God appeared, to give him instruction, he declares, "My comeliness was turned in me into corruption, and I retained no strength." [Daniel 9:18, 15, 20; 10:8.] (GC88 470.3).

We do not understand as we should the great conflict going on between invisible agencies, the controversy between loyal and disloyal angels. Evil angels are constantly at work, planning their line of attack, controlling as commanders, kings, and rulers, the disloyal human forces... Do not indulge in fanciful speculations. The written Word is our only safety. We must pray as did Daniel, that we may be guarded by heavenly intelligences. As ministering spirits angels are sent forth to minister to those who shall be heirs of salvation. *Pray, my brethren, pray as you have never prayed before. We are not prepared for the Lord's coming. We need to make thorough work for eternity* (4BC 1173.7).

When our brethren and ministers shall feel the burden that should rest upon them, they will not be content with a few surface truths. They will sink the shaft deep, and will have the spirit that Daniel possessed. There will be no frivolous spirit: no cheap, superficial sanctification, prated from unsanctified lips, and coming from hearts that are destitute of purity, of consecration and wholehearted surrender to God. There will be earnest prayer that the truth may be so indelibly stamped upon the heart that the entire man may be brought, with all his ways, into conformity to the truth. "With the heart man believeth unto righteousness; and with the mouth confession is made unto salvation" (Romans 10:10) (9MR 365.2).

Daniel 11

¹Also I in the first year of Darius the Mede, [even] I, stood to confirm and to strengthen him. ²And now will I show thee the truth.

Behold, there shall stand up yet three kings in Persia; and the fourth shall be far richer than [they] all: and by his strength through his riches he shall stir up all against the realm of Grecia.

³And a mighty king shall stand up, that shall rule with great dominion, and do according to his will. ⁴And when he shall stand up, his kingdom shall be broken, and shall be divided toward the four winds of heaven; and not to his posterity, nor according to his dominion which he ruled: for his kingdom shall be plucked up, even for others beside those. ⁵And the king of the south shall be strong, and [one] of his princes; and he shall be strong above him, and have dominion; his dominion [shall be] a great dominion.

⁶And in the end of years they shall join themselves together; for the king's daughter of the south shall come to the king of the north to make an agreement: but she shall not retain the power of the arm; neither shall he stand, nor his arm: but she shall be given up, and they that brought her, and he that begat her, and he that strengthened her in [these] times.

⁷But out of a branch of her roots shall [one] stand up in his estate, which shall come with an army, and shall enter into the fortress of the king of the north, and shall deal against them, and shall prevail: ⁸And shall also carry captives into Egypt their gods, with their princes, [and] with their precious vessels of silver and of gold; and he shall continue [more] years than the king of the north.

⁹So the king of the south shall come into [his] kingdom, and shall return into his own land. ¹⁰But his sons shall be stirred up, and shall assemble a multitude of great forces: and [one] shall certainly come, and overflow, and pass through: then shall he return, and be stirred up, [even] to his fortress. ¹¹And the king of the south shall be moved with choler, and shall come forth and fight with him, [even] with the king of the north: and he shall set forth a great multitude; but the multitude shall be given into his hand. ¹²[And] when he hath taken away the multitude, his heart shall be lifted up; and he shall cast down [many] ten thousands: but he shall not be strengthened [by it].

¹³For the king of the north shall return, and shall set forth a multitude greater than the former, and shall certainly come after certain years with a great army and with much riches. ¹⁴And in those times there shall many stand up against the king of the south: also, the robbers of thy people shall exalt themselves to establish the vision [*chazon*]; but they shall fall.

¹⁵So the king of the north shall come, and cast up a mount, and take the most fenced cities: and the arms of the south shall not withstand, neither his chosen people, neither [shall there be any] strength to withstand. ¹⁶But he that cometh against him shall do according to his own will, and none shall stand before him: and he shall stand in the glorious land, which by his hand shall be consumed. ¹⁷He shall also set his face to enter with the strength of his whole kingdom, and upright ones with him; thus, shall he do: and he shall give him the daughter of women, corrupting her: but she shall not stand [on his side], neither be for him. ¹⁸After this shall he turn his face unto the isles, and shall take many: but a prince for his own behalf shall cause the reproach offered by him to cease; without his own reproach he shall cause [it] to turn upon him. ¹⁹Then he shall turn

his face toward the fort of his own land: but he shall stumble and fall, and not be found.

20Then shall stand up in his estate a raiser of taxes [in] the glory of the kingdom: but within few days he shall be destroyed, neither in anger, nor in battle. 21And in his estate shall stand up a vile person, to whom they shall not give the honor of the kingdom: but he shall come in peaceably, and obtain the kingdom by flatteries. 22And with the arms of a flood shall they be overflown from before him, and shall be broken; yea, also the prince of the covenant. 23And after the league [made] with him he shall work deceitfully: for he shall come up, and shall become strong with a small people.

24He shall enter peaceably even upon the fattest places of the province; and he shall do [that] which his fathers have not done, nor his fathers' fathers; he shall scatter among them the prey, and spoil, and riches: [yea], and he shall forecast his devices against the strong holds, even for a time. 25And he shall stir up his power and his courage against the king of the south with a great army; and the king of the south shall be stirred up to battle with a very great and mighty army; but he shall not stand: for they shall forecast devices against him. 26Yea, they that feed of the portion of his meat shall destroy him, and his army shall overflow: and many shall fall down slain. 27And both these kings' hearts [shall be] to do mischief, and they shall speak lies at one table; but it shall not prosper: for yet the end [shall be] at the time appointed. 28Then shall he return into his land with great riches; and his heart [shall be] against the holy covenant; and he shall do [exploits], and return to his own land.

29At the time appointed he shall return, and come toward the south; but it shall not be as the former, or as the latter. 30For the ships of Chittim shall come against him: therefore, he shall be grieved, and return, and have indignation against the holy covenant: so, shall he do; he shall even return, and have intelligence with them that forsake the holy covenant. ³¹And arms shall stand on his part, and they shall pollute the sanctuary of strength, and shall take away the daily [continual, margin], and they shall place the abomination that maketh desolate.

³²And such as do wickedly against the covenant shall he corrupt by flatteries: but the people that do know their God shall be strong, and do [exploits]. ³³And they that understand among the people shall instruct many: yet they shall fall by the sword, and by flame, by captivity, and by spoil, [many] days. ³⁴Now when they shall fall, they shall be holpen with a little help: but many shall cleave to them with flatteries. ³⁵And [some] of them of understanding shall fall, to try them, and to purge, and to make [them] white, [even] to the time of the end: because [it is] yet for a time appointed.

³⁶And the king shall do according to his will; and he shall exalt himself, and magnify himself above every god, and shall speak marvellous things against the God of gods, and shall prosper till the indignation be accomplished: for that that is determined shall be done. ³⁷Neither shall he regard the God of his fathers, nor the desire of women, nor regard any god: for he shall magnify himself above all.

³⁸But in his estate shall he honor the God of forces: and a god whom his fathers knew not shall he honor with gold, and silver, and with precious stones, and pleasant things. ³⁹Thus shall he do in the most strong holds with a strange god, whom he shall acknowledge [and] increase with glory: and he shall cause them to rule over many, and shall divide the land for gain.

⁴⁰And at the time of the end shall the king of the south push at him: and the king of the north shall come against him like a whirlwind, with chariots, and with horsemen, and with many ships; and he shall enter into

the countries, and shall overflow and pass over. ⁴¹He shall enter also into the glorious land, and many [countries] shall be overthrown: but these shall escape out of his hand, [even] Edom, and Moab, and the chief of the children of Ammon. ⁴²He shall stretch forth his hand also upon the countries: and the land of Egypt shall not escape. ⁴³But he shall have power over the treasures of gold and of silver, and over all the precious things of Egypt: and the Libyans and the Ethiopians [shall be] at his steps. ⁴⁴But tidings out of the east and out of the north shall trouble him: therefore, he shall go forth with great fury to destroy, and utterly to make away many. ⁴⁵And he shall plant the tabernacles of his palace between the seas in the glorious holy mountain; yet he shall come to his end, and none shall help him.

Points to Ponder

1. Chapter 11 is in Cyrus' reign; it begins with a caveat
2. Gabriel had been working during the reign of Darius
3. Kings (3 including Cyrus) stood to restore the Temple
4. Daniel 11 begins the 2300 years at 457 BC
5. The 2300 years ended in 1844 AD when Jesus stood
6. Dan 11:2 to 12:1 foretells events from 457BC–1844AD
7. After 1844, Dan 11 repeats as directed in Rev 10
8. The repetition of Dan 11 is not linked to *long-time*
9. Dan 11 repeats at the end of years, after 1844
10. The prophecy begins repeating at Daniel 11:6
11. Repeated history depicts events thru Christ's Advent
12. Daniel 11 repeated does not link to time
13. Daniel 11 does not reveal the time of Christ's Advent
14. Chapter 11 shows that Christ's Advent is imminent
15. Understanding Daniel 11 is vitally important today
16. Aligning prophetic history requires much prayer
17. Daniel was opened after 1844: God knows the meaning

Daniel 11 is to Prophesy Again

Daniel stood in his lot to bear his testimony which was sealed until the time of the end (TM 115.3).

It [Daniel] carries us forward to the last scenes of this earth's history (CTr 334.5).

These matters are of infinite importance in these last days (TM 115.3).

Christ urged upon His disciples the importance of prophetic study. Referring to the prophecy given to Daniel in regard to their time, He said, "Whoso readeth, let him understand." Matthew 24:15. (DA 234.1).

This prophecy (Daniel 11:1-12:1) began with the *three kings in Persia* (11:2), Cyrus, Darius, and Artaxerxes, who issued decrees to rebuild Jerusalem and the Temple. Thus, the 2300-years began in 457 BC that ended in 1844 when Michael stood for His people (12:1) to cleanse Heaven's Sanctuary at the beginning of the Investigative Judgment.

The coming of Christ here described is not His Second Coming to the earth. He comes to the Ancient of days in Heaven to receive dominion, and glory, and a kingdom, which will be given Him at the close of His work as a mediator. It is this coming, and not His Second Advent to the earth, that was foretold in prophecy to take place at the termination of the 2300 days, in 1844 (GC88 479.3; cf RH, May 9, 1893 par. 8).

When that time comes, Mikha'el, the great prince who champions your people, will stand up (Daniel 12:1, CJB).

The prophetic periods ended in 1844... The ministration of Jesus in the Holy place ended...He stood by the ark (1SG 158.1).

Jesus rose up, and shut the door, and entered the Holy of Holies, at the 7th month 1844; but Michael's standing up (Daniel 12:1) *to deliver His people, is in the future* (WLF 12.4).

The prophecies of the eleventh of Daniel <u>have</u> almost reached <u>their final fulfillment</u> (RH, Nov. 24, 1904 par. 8).

The prophecy in the eleventh of Daniel has nearly reached its complete fulfillment. *Much of the history that has taken place in fulfillment of this prophecy will be repeated* (13MR 394.1).

The time has come for the light given him [Daniel] to go to the world *as never before*. If those for whom the Lord has done so much will walk in the light, *their knowledge of Christ and the prophecies relating to Him will be greatly increased as they near the close of this earth's history* (21MR 407.3).

There are those now living who in studying the prophecies of Daniel and John, received great light from God as they passed over the ground where special prophecies were in process of fulfillment in their order. <u>*They bore the message of time to the people*</u>. The truth shone out clearly as the sun at noonday. *Historical events, showing the direct fulfillment of prophecy, were set before the people, and the prophecy was seen to be a figurative delineation of events leading down to the close of this earth's history... The people now have a special message to give to the world* (17MR 1.3).

Jesus Stands

Daniel 11:40-45 explains what took place immediately before Christ stood in 1844 (Dan 12:1). The King of the South title went from Egypt to France and the King of the North title went from the Ottoman Empire to England. While France was conquering Europe, it claimed to be a friend of the Ottoman Empire. It had an ambassador at Istanbul when Napoleon suddenly invaded Egypt, a province of the King of the South. Napoleon claimed to *liberate* the Egyptians from Ottoman *oppression,* but his Egyptian invasion endangered the British trade routes to India.

Simultaneously, General Berthier invaded Rome. "Pius VI...is the pope specified in prophecy, which received the deadly wound" (5MR 318.1). "In 1798...a French army entered Rome, and made the pope a prisoner" (GC88 266.2). As prophesied of the papacy, "One of his heads as it were wounded to death" (Revelation 13:3). Prophetically, the subjected Roman Church became the daughter of the King of the South, France.

France ruled the Mediterranean and its European ports. For safety sake, Admiral Nelson kept the British fleet harbored near the fortress at Gibraltar. When the French fleet was located, Nelson crossed the Mediterranean in 30 days (whirlwind speed for sailing ships of that era). "And at the time of the end shall the king of the south push at him: and the king of the north shall come against him like a whirlwind, with chariots, and with horsemen, and with many ships" (Daniel 11:40). Nelson sank the French fleet off the coast of Egypt in the battle at Abuqir 1 August 1798.

Without his fleet, Napoleon attempted to go back to Europe over land. On the way, he besieged Acre (Akka), a strategic Ottoman fortress between Egypt and Syria. The British flotilla joined forces with the Ottoman forces. From off shore, the British fleet shelled the French position. Because the Ottomans depended on England's naval might to fight Napoleon, England prophetically became the King of the North. And when Napoleon retreated to Egypt, the British fleet pursued him as Daniel's prophecy had foretold:

> He shall enter also into the glorious land, and many countries shall be overthrown: but these shall escape out of his hand, even Edom, and Moab, and the chief of the children of Ammon. He shall stretch forth his hand also upon the countries: and the land of Egypt shall not escape (Daniel 11:41-42).

Napoleon returned to Egypt (without fighting in Jordan, Moab, or Edom), and then he escaped with his army. The British then dominated the Mideast to secure its routes to India. "He shall have power over the treasures of gold and of silver, and over all the precious things of Egypt: and the Libyans and the Ethiopians shall be at his steps" (11:43).

"Tidings out of the east and out of the north shall trouble him: therefore, he shall go forth with great fury to destroy, and utterly to make away many" (11:44). Britain was fighting in the *east* and the *north*: 1803-India, 1812-USA, and 1815-France. Henry John Temple, 3rd Viscount Palmerston, Britain's Foreign Secretary, feared a Russian-French alliance would shift the European balance of power and he feared a Russian expansion in the *north* through Afghanistan into India. He used the Ottoman Empire to keep Russia from accessing the Mediterranean Sea.

Without consulting France, Palmerston convinced Russia, Prussia, and Austria 15 July 1840 that Egypt was about to topple the Ottoman Empire. In his view, this would upset the balance of power; he preferred a weak sultan rather than a strong military leader that would strengthen and enlarge the Ottoman Empire. On 11 August 1840, they gave Egypt an ultimatum to stand down or face their allied forces. Muhammad Ali of Egypt refused, and war followed.

"Josiah Litch in 1838, two years before the expected event was to occur. In that year he predicted that the Turkish power would be overthrown "in A.D. 1840, sometime in the month of August;"[Josiah Litch, The Probability of the Second Coming of Christ About A.D. 1843, p. 157] "but a few days before the fulfillment of the prophecy he concluded more definitely from his study that the period allotted to the Turks would come to an end on August 11, 1840" (Daniel and the Revelation, Uriah Smith, p. 513). It happened when the allies helped the Ottomans in their war with Egypt.

Daniel 11:45 is highly supplemented by the translators. Daniel literally wrote: *To plant dwelling palace sea glorious holy mountain to come end of time to help.*

The British fleet partially fulfilled this prophecy when it positioned itself on the sea between Mount Carmel and Acre to plan their assault of Acre. They then occupied Acre in November 1840. "In the face of European military might, Muhammad Ali acquiesced" (https://en.wikipedia.org/wiki

/Muhammad_Ali_of_Egypt). Soon thereafter, Palmerston's government *came to its end* in 1841: It was voted out of office.

William Miller recognized that Daniel 11 was to end at Christ's Advent, which he initially dated in 1843. He also understood that the *Kings of the North and South* had become European powers. He linked them to "*Spain, in the south, and Great Britain, in the north...*" Then "Spain...joined the *French*" (Evidence From Scripture and History of the Second Coming of Christ About the year 1843, William Miller (1841) p. 105). Miller was correct, the *Kings of the North and South* had transitioned from the Ottoman Empire and Egypt to Great Britain and France.

Repeating the Prophetic history in Daniel 11

I pray earnestly that the work we do at this time shall impress itself deeply on heart and mind and soul. Perplexities will increase; but let us, as believers in God, encourage one another. Let us not lower the standard, but keep it lifted high, looking to Him who is the Author and Finisher of our faith... I am encouraged and blessed as I realize that the God of Israel is still guiding His people, and that He will continue to be with them, even to the end (LS 437.3).

Thou must prophesy again before many peoples, and nations, and tongues, and kings (Revelation 10:11).

In the end of years (Daniel 11:6), after 1844.

And in the end of years they shall join themselves together; for the king's daughter of the south shall come to the king of the north to make an agreement: but she shall not retain the power of the arm; neither shall he stand, nor his arm: but she shall be given up, and they that brought her, and he that begat her, and he that strengthened her in [these] times (Daniel 11:6).

After France (King of the South) had taken Pope Pius VI captive in 1798, prophetically speaking, the Roman Church became the daughter of the *King of the South*. "A woman, representing the Lord's chosen church on the earth" (RH, February 26, 1914 par. 7). France assumed the role as the *Protector of the Catholics*, who once were Christ's Church.

In Britain (King of the North), Palmerston came back into office (1846). The Tsar wrote him of the Ottoman Empire: "We have on our hands a very sick man, perhaps it would be as well to arrange for his funeral" (Caesar to Churchill p. 42). Palmerston refused to remove the Ottoman Empire from buffering Russia from the Mediterranean. The Tsar protested that Orthodox Christians in Palestine were being endangered by the Catholics, and the Crimean War (1854-1856) followed. As prophesied, *in the end of years* (after 1844)*, the Kings of the North (Britain) and South (France), *shall join themselves* together: They united to oppose Russia in the Crimean War.

Count Cavour was on a mission to unify Italy under King Victor Emanuel II. He had joined the allies in the Crimean War just in time to sit at the peace table. He settled a border dispute between France and Italy that put Italian unification in motion. The pope opposed it because he would lose secular rule over the *Papal States*.

After 1844, as prophesied, "the king's daughter of the south shall come to the king of the north to make an agreement: but she shall not retain the power of the arm; neither shall he stand, nor his arm: but she shall be given up" (Daniel 11:6). Though British warships were off Italy's coast during the struggle for unification (in case British nationals had to be evacuated), England refused to help the papacy keep the Papal States. And France also refused.

By 1870, "France was stripped of its Italian territories... Meanwhile, the Italian king had driven the pope into the Vatican City and was thereafter excommunicated from the Catholic Church" (http://www.heritage-history.com/?c=academy&s=char-dir&f=emmanuel1i). When France lost its Italian territories, Italy became the King of the South.

But out of a branch of her roots shall [one] stand up in his estate, which shall come with an army, and shall enter into the fortress of the king of the north, and shall deal against them, and shall prevail. And shall also carry captives into Egypt their gods, with their princes, [and] with their precious vessels of silver and of gold; and he shall continue [more] years than the king of the north. (Daniel 11:7-8).

The Roman Church had had two roots or branches: the religious (church) and secular (state). Mussolini (*a branch of the state/political roots*) seized Italy's government in 1922. Prior to this (1885-1889), Italy had entered into alliances with the African kingdoms: Zanzibar, Obbia, and Caluula, and its influence extended to Ethiopia. In 1908, official borders existed between Italian Somaliland and Kenya.

But out of a branch of her roots shall [one] stand up in his estate, which shall come with an army, and shall enter into the fortress of the king of the north, and shall deal against them, and shall prevail (Daniel 11:7).

As the King of the South, Mussolini unilaterally seized the Jubaland Province of Kenya and the town and port of Kismayo from Britain. England did not respond to his attack with a war, but it relinquished the territory to Italy (cf http:// bearcatspage.50megs.com/custom3.html). After World War I, expansion of the colonial Italian Empire was directed toward Egypt by Benito Mussolini (http://en.wikipedia. org/wiki/Italian_Egyptians#cite_note-9).

Though Muslims saw belief in God and Jesus as many gods, the Italian-Catholics got along with the Egyptians; too well from the British perspective. In WWII, Britain alleged that Egypt's Prime Minister favored the Axis powers. King Farouk I was given the ultimatum to replace him or be replaced. The king told Britain's Ambassador that he would get rid of his *Italian advisors* when the ambassador got rid of his *Italian advisor* (his wife).

After World War II, Egypt's British trained generals ousted Farouk. He was granted asylum in Italy. But during the war, when Britain had been about to fall to the Axis powers, President Roosevelt (FDR) had rescued Britain from certain destruction and became the King of the North.

He shall continue [more] years than the king of the north (Daniel 11:8).

Mussolini became King of the South in 1922, when he seized Italy's government, and he died 28 April 1945. FDR had become President in 1933, and he died 12 April 1945.

King of South Outlives King of North			
Mussolini Seized Power	FDR President	FDR Died	Mussolini Died
▼	▽	▽	▼
1922	1933	4/12/45	4/28/45

"So, the king of the south shall come into [his] kingdom, and shall return into his own land" (11:9). After Mussolini died, King Farouk was banished to Italy. And the King of the South title *returned* to *his own land,* Egypt.

But his sons shall be stirred up, and shall assemble a multitude of great forces: and [one] shall certainly come, and overflow, and pass through: then shall he return, and be stirred up, [even] to his fortress (11:10).

Jews Return to Israel in 1948

In the Bible, sons can be literal or members of a class (cf Strong). King Farouk's son, Ahmed Fuad was made king of Egypt, but within a year he was replaced by the *sons*, who held the real power in Egypt: Generals Nasser and Sadat. Israel was America's fortress in the region.

In 1945, at British prompting, Egypt, Iraq, Lebanon, Saudi Arabia, Syria, Transjordan, and Yemen formed the Arab League to coordinate policy between the Arab states (http://en.wikipedia.org/wiki/1948_Arab-Israeli_War).

Prior to WW II, the British had confiscated weapons from both Jews and Palestinians. During WW II, they armed both groups to fight the Axis powers. After the war, Great Britain resumed seizing arms and meddling in Mideast politics. Then 29 November 1947, the United Nations (UN) and USA decided to partition Palestine into a Jewish and Palestinian state. Egypt and the Palestinians opposed it. Then, hours before the British mandate over Palestine expired 15 May 1948, Israel declared itself a state. Truman, the King of the North, abruptly recognized Israel (America's fortress). And Egypt *assembled a multitude of great forces* against Israel.

"The Arab Legion joined the war in May 1948. It fought only in the areas that king Abdullah wanted to secure for Transjordan: The West Bank and East Jerusalem." "On 8 July, before the expiration of the truce, Egyptian General Naguib renewed the war." "In 1949, Israel signed separate armistices with Egypt on 24 February" (https://en.wikipedia.org/wiki/1948_Arab%E2%80%93Israeli_War).

And the king of the south shall be moved with choler, and shall come forth and fight with him, [even] with the king of the north: and he shall set forth a great multitude; but the multitude shall be given into his hand (Daniel 11:11).

The King of the South (Egypt with the Arab League) *assembled a multitude of forces*, which can be read, *made multiple attempts* to move against America's fortress, Israel. But the UN kept the peace on the Egyptian Sinai until the funding ceased in 1967. Egypt prepared to invade Israel as prophesied: The 1967 six-day war fulfilled this prophecy.

Then shall he return, and be stirred up, [even] to his fortress. And the king of the south shall be moved with choler, and shall come forth and fight with him, [even] with the king of the north: and he shall set forth a great multitude; but the multitude shall be given into his hand (Daniel 11:10-11).

Egypt amassed 1000 tanks and 100,000 soldiers on the border, closed the Straits of Tiran to all ships flying Israeli flags or carrying strategic materials, and called for unified Arab action against Israel. In response, on June 5, 1967, Israel launched a pre-emptive attack against Egypt's air force. Jordan...attacked... U. S. Secretary of Defense [under President Johnson] Robert McNamara revealed that a carrier battle group, the U. S. 6th Fleet... was re-positioned towards the eastern Mediterranean to defend Israel (https://en.wikipedia.org/wiki/Controversies_relating_to_the_Six-Day_War).

[And] when he hath taken away the multitude, his heart shall be lifted up; and he shall cast down [many] ten thousands: but he shall not be strengthened [by it] (Daniel 11:12).

[In 1973] Golda Meir, Moshe Dayan, and Israeli general David Elazar met...6 hours before the war was to begin... There would be no preemptive strike. Israel might be needing American assistance soon and it was imperative that it not be blamed for starting the war (http://en.wikipedia.org/wiki/Yom_Kippur_War).

On October 6, 1973, Yom Kippur, the holiest day in the Jewish calendar, the Egyptian and Syrian armies launched a surprise attack against Israel. The war ended on October 26 with Israel successfully repelling Egyptian

and Syrian forces but suffering great losses (http://en.
wikipedia.org/wiki/Israel).

Israel pushed toward Damascus. *Jordan and Iraq joined
with Syria to drive them back.* After the war ended, Sadat
became the first Arab head of state to make peace with Israel,
and the King of the South moved to Saddam Hussein.

King of the South, Saddam Hussein

> For the king of the north shall return, and shall set
> forth a multitude greater than the former, and shall
> certainly come after certain years with a great army and
> with much riches. And in those times, there shall many
> stand up against the king of the south: also, the robbers
> of thy people shall exalt themselves to establish the
> vision [*chazon*]; but they shall fall (Daniel 11:13-14).

America stayed out of the 1973 war. Saddam Hussein,
as the King of the South, eventually invaded Kuwait. Bush I,
King of the North, rallied the world against the Iraqis
(http://www.pbs.org/wgbh/americanexperience/features/g
eneral-article/bush-gulf-war/). And when Iraq's army was
pushed from Kuwait, it set the oil fields ablaze. Bush I got
the UN to sanction Iraq to make reparations and to punish
their global environmental vandalism. President Bush I had
envisioned the New World Order of "peace and security,
freedom, and the rule of law" (http://www.infoplease.com/
ipa/A0900156.html). On 6 March 1991, Bush I announced
his vision that eventually failed as prophesied.

> What is at stake is more than one small country, it
> is a big idea—a new world order, where diverse nations
> are drawn together in common cause to achieve the
> universal aspirations of mankind: peace and security,
> freedom, and the rule of law (http://en.wikipedia.org/
> wiki/Saddam_Hussein).

King of the South, Osama bin Laden

After Bush I and the world defeated Saddam Hussein, the King of the South moved to Osama (Usama) bin Laden, a wealthy Saudi Arabian. He declared war on America from Afghanistan. In 1979, he had "joined mujahideen forces in Pakistan fighting against the Soviet Union in Afghanistan" (http://en.wikipedia.org/wiki/Osama_bin_Laden).

Two upheavals in the Middle East would determine the future course of bin Laden's life. The first was the October War. On Oct. 6, 1973, Egyptian and Syrian forces—supported by Jordan and Iraq and *funded by Saudi Arabia*—launched an attack on Israeli forces (http://www.scribd.com/doc/83008925/Enemies-by-Design).

In 1993, the first World Trade Center bombing killed six people. In 1998, the bombing of two U. S. embassies in Africa killed 224. Both were the work of al-Qaida and bin Laden, who in 1998 declared holy war on America (http://www.msnbc.msn.com/id/4540958/ns/nbcnightlynews/t/osama-bin-laden-missed-opportunities/#.UGwxyOFfF_Y).

In response to bin Laden's attacks 21 August 1998: "U. S. cruise missiles struck targets in Afghanistan… Thursday in what President Clinton described as an act of self-defense against imminent terrorist plots and of retribution for the bombings of U. S. embassies" (http://partners.nytimes.com/library/world/africa/082198attack-us.html).

President Clinton and Monica

The King of the North had become President Clinton. He attacked bin Laden (Daniel 11:15) in 1998. After his missile attack on bin Laden's citadel, the King of the South reverted to Iraq, who Clinton also attacked in 1998. After Daniel's narration arrives at 1998, the prophetic explanation (11:16-19) is given to tell what led up to that conflict.

So, the king of the north shall come, and cast up a mount, and take the most fenced cities: and the arms of the south shall not withstand, neither his chosen people, neither [shall there be any] strength to withstand.

But he that cometh against him shall do according to his own will, and none shall stand before him: and he shall stand in the glorious land, which by his hand shall be consumed. He shall also set his face to enter with the strength of his whole kingdom, and upright ones with him; thus, shall he do: and he shall give him the daughter of women, corrupting her: but she shall not stand [on his side], neither be for him. After this shall he turn his face unto the isles, and shall take many: but a prince for his own behalf shall cause the reproach offered by him to cease; without his own reproach he shall cause [it] to turn upon him. Then he shall turn his face toward the fort of his own land: but he shall stumble and fall, and not be found (Daniel 11:15-19).

October 26-29, 1994: President Clinton attended the signing of the Israel-Jordan peace agreement... And spoke to the Knesset in Jerusalem (http://www.state. gov/r/pa/ho/trvl/pres/5188.htm).

Then President Clinton became embroiled in a scandal as Daniel had foretold: *He shall give him the daughter of women* (Daniel 11:17). Unlike the symbolic daughter of the King of the south (the 1798 papacy that had fulfilled 11:6 when it repeated in the endtime), this is a literal woman.

Did someone *give* or introduce Monica to Bill Clinton? She has not said. If so, who? Is there an Israeli connection? "May 5-8, 1995 Prime Minister Yitzhak Rabin Israel Met with President Clinton during a private visit" (http:// www.state.gov/r/pa/ho/15735.htm). "Monica will go down in history as the woman who had sex with an American president and saved an Israeli prime minister" (http://www.meforum.org 471/monica-lewinsky-in-middle-eastern-eyes). Mr. Clinton admitted to having had an "inappropriate relationship" while Lewinsky worked at the White House in 1995. She is of Russian Jewish descent (http://en.wikipedia.org/wiki/Monica_Lewinsky). She did *not stand on his side.* She produced that infamous dress that caught him in a lie. *The glorious land was consumed. Land*: its root links to *a moral sense: the impurity of lustful...profligate living* (cf Strong). While the USA was *consumed* with Clinton's Lewinsky scandal: "On November 4, 1995, Rabin was assassinated... leaving a mass rally in Tel Aviv in support of the Oslo process" (http://en.wiki pedia.org/wiki/Yitzhak_Rabin).

President Clinton stood in the *glorious land* pushing the peace process that led to Rabin's death! Clinton returned to Israel for Rabin's funeral with *upright ones with him* (11:17).

In... *Living History* Hillary Rodham Clinton shows a picture of Bill Clinton, Dole, and Gingrich...on the plane going to Yitzhak Rabin's funeral in Israel (http://en.wiki pedia.org/wiki/Newt_Gingrich).

While the scandal was infatuating America, Clinton went to the British Isles as prophesied (Daniel 11:18; http://www. state.gov/r/pa/ho/trvl/pres/5188.htmUK,Sept.3-5,1998). Public focus was redirected to Iraq (http://en.wikipedia. org/wiki/Bill_Clinton#cite_note-46Dec.1998).

The December 1998 bombing of Iraq (code-named Operation Desert Fox) was a major four-day bombing campaign on Iraqi targets from 16 December 1998, to 19 December 1998, by the United States and United Kingdom https://en.wikipedia.org/wiki/Bombing_of_Iraq_(1998)

As prophesied (11:18), Gingrich, Speaker of the House of Representatives (a prince in America's line of succession) caused Clinton's reproach to cease when the House im-peached him for the Monica affair (http://en.wikipedia .org/wiki/Newt_Gingrich). "A year before Gingrich became House speaker" he began an affair (http://articles.chicago

tribune.com/1999-11-11/news/9911110139_1_callista-bis
ek-georgia-republican-house-speaker-newt-gingrich).

The Republican Senate acquitted President Clinton
(http://edition.cnn.com/ALLPOLITICS/stories/1999/02/1
2/impeachment/). Was it political suicide to impeach a
popular president? Or that "Incumbents tend to win
elections" (http://www.npr.org/templates/story/story.php?
storyId=204745388).

If Vice President Gore would have become President, with
the incumbent advantage, he would have run for president
shortly thereafter. To avoid that scenario, the Senate let
Clinton finish his term. After Clinton lied to America (and
apologized), public opinion turned against Gingrich: *he
caused it to turn upon him* (Da 11:18). Though *fallen*, Clinton
remained in office. Gingrich resigned (http://www.nytimes.
com/1998/11/07/us/speaker-steps-down-overview-facing-
revolt-gingrich-won-t-run-for-speaker -will.html).

The statement: *Then he shall turn his face toward the fort
of his own land: but he shall stumble and fall, and not be
found* (11:18-19) was fulfilled. It could have more than one
meaning aligning with the prophecy: 1) Rabin went back to
Israel and was killed. 2) After returning to America from
Israel, Gingrich was ousted from his Speaker role. 3) After
Clinton finished his term, he left the political scene. Some
secondary fulfillments relate to Rabin and Clinton.

The Raiser of Taxes

Then shall stand up in his estate a raiser of taxes [in]
the glory of the kingdom: but within few days he shall be
destroyed, neither in anger, nor in battle (Daniel 11:20).

Prime Minister Benjamin Netanyahu followed Rabin.
Netanyahu caused 22-40 million tax dollars to be *taken
away* from the Palestinian Authority in 1998 (http://
community.seattletimes.nwsource.com/archive/?date=199
70812&slug=2554373). He had been installed in 1996, and
destroyed, broken, maimed, crippled, or wrecked (cf Strong)
when he was ousted a few days later (prophetic years) in July

1999 because of corruption allegations. Prophecy fulfilled! Then, he returned. Will he again be *broken within a few* years by Christ's glory? Or more political corruption? In 2019, in spite of two elections back to back, neither he nor his rival, Benny Gantz, could form a government. On 21 November 2019, Netanyahu was indicted for bribery and fraud while anticipating an unprecedented third election.

America is, in a sense, political Babylon. As the head of gold on the idol in Daniel 2 symbolized Nebuchadnezzar, President Reagan (the creator of Reaganomics) was also the endtime head of gold. Thus, as prophecy was fulfilled about ancient Babylon, it will be repeated concerning America:

> "And now have I given all these lands into the hand of...the king of Babylon, My servant; and the beasts of the field have I given him also to serve him. And all nations shall serve him, and his son, and his son's son, until the very time of his land come: and then many nations and great kings shall serve themselves of him...And it shall come to pass, when seventy years are accomplished, [that] I will punish the king of Babylon, and that nation, saith the LORD, for their iniquity, and the land of the Chaldeans, and will make it perpetual desolations" (Jeremiah 27:6-7, 25).

In 1950, Israel was an established nation. The Knesset established Jerusalem as Israel's capital and moved from Tel Aviv to the King George Hotel in Jerusalem. "The Law of Return, granting every Jew in the world the right to settle in Israel, was passed by the Knesset..." And Israel had its "first nationwide municipal elections after independence" (https://www.jewishvirtuallibrary.org/ timeline-of-modern-israel-1950-1959-2). Seventy years later, in 2020, America recognized Jerusalem as Israel's capital.

Israel's 70-years of servitude to the United States of America extend from 1950 to 2020. Thus, the failure of Israel's politicians to form a government aligns with the end of the prophetic period. As does increased military activity in the area: "Israel strikes Iran-backed fighters in Syria, killing more than 20" ([https://www.foxnews.com/world/ israel-strikes-iran-backed-fighters-in-syria-killing-more-than-20-monitor-says](https://www.foxnews.com/world/israel-strikes-iran-backed-fighters-in-syria-killing-more-than-20-monitor-says)). Fox News 6 Feb 2020.

Daniel's statement *then he shall turn his face toward the fort of his own land: but he shall stumble and fall, and not be found* (11:18-19) also aligns with President Clinton, he was crippled politically when he left office. All of his past popularity was forgotten when his wife ran for President.

Then shall stand up in his estate a raiser of taxes would be about President George Bush II, who turned the Clinton tax surplus into a massive deficit. *But within few days he shall be destroyed, neither in anger, nor in battle* (11:20).

A few days can be a few years in Bible prophecy. It has been almost 12 years since Bush II was President: He is still alive. Even though Daniel 7:11 states of him (the fourth earth king) that he is to be "destroyed, and given to the burning flame" that accompany Christ's Advent: It is very close.

Standing in His Estate

And in his estate shall stand up a vile person, to whom they shall not give the honour of the kingdom: but he shall come in peaceably, and obtain the kingdom by flatteries (Daniel 11:21).

In Daniel 9, Bush II, who was the Protestant prince of America's Constitution, became the King of the North. Then prophecy moved to President Obama. Daniel 11 expands and explains earlier visions, like chapter 2 where the brass midsection aligns with President Clinton; Bush II and Obama correspond to the iron legs. But the order in Daniel 11 is not chronological; *estate* means *foot* 8 of the times that it is in the Bible. Presidents Trump and Pence correspond with the feet in Daniel 2. Daniel's narration has moved directly from Clinton to the two feet in Daniel 11:20-21.

The first foot is President Trump: "In his estate a raiser of taxes [in] the glory of the kingdom: but within a few days he shall be destroyed, neither in anger, nor in battle." He has been in office almost 4 years. He has been impeached, which correlates with the context: a *few days* (prophetic years), being *destroyed* or *broken*, but he has not yet been removed from office. And the second foot corresponds to President Michael Pence, who is yet to be America's President:

> And in his estate shall stand up a vile person, to whom they shall not give the honor of the kingdom: but he shall come in peaceably, and obtain the kingdom by flatteries. And with the arms of a flood shall they be overflown from before him, and shall be broken; yea, also the prince of the covenant. And after the league [made] with him he shall work deceitfully: for he shall come up, and shall become strong with a small people (11:21-23).

Thus, after President Trump is broken, President Michael Pence is described as *vile*, which is *despised* or *despicable*. He does not have the honor of the kingdom: He was not elected, but put in office after President Trump is *broken*. President Michael Pence is to come into power peaceably while making fine promises. *Then with the force of a flood, the* Fundamentalist Christians *shall be swept away before him, and he shall be broken by the Prince of the Covenant*; Jesus comes to rescue His saints!

Presidents Bush II and Obama'

Daniel 11:24-28 can be seen both as sequential (as it pertains to President Pence), and as a caveat as it relates to Presidents Bush II and Obama. Bush II's peaceful entry into Iraq was fulfilled on Thanksgiving Day 2003. Then 17 June 2006 (the day identified in Daniel 9:25, when the 70 weeks *determined to seal up the vision and prophecy* were fulfilled), he stated that his Thanksgiving Day visit to a free Iraq was one of his accomplishments in his effort to bring peace. Then Daniel recaps the events that led up to that trip.

Father. Head or founder of a household, group, family, or clan as well as a male parent (cf Strong). Bush II had done something that (fathers) Bush I and Reagan have not done. *Province* is from a root linking to Lord of the whole earth. A time is generally a year of 360 days for prophetic calculation, but a year can be 12 months on the Hebrew calendar unless it is a leap year: It is a lunar calendar and Adar I has to be added periodically to keep it aligned with the earth's orbit around the sun. *Even for a time* is like saying, *next year*. Thus, President Bush II *forecast his devices against the strong holds, even for a time/year*. The year after America passed the law in October, Saddam Hussein was captured in December 2003 (http://en. wikipedia.org/wiki/Iraq_War).

The authorization was sought by President George W. Bush. Introduced as H. J. Res. 114 ... It was signed into law by President Bush on October 16, 2002 (http://en.wikipedia.org/wiki/Iraq_Resolution).

Saddam Hussein, Iraq's fleeing *strongman*, was captured hiding in a *stronghold*, a hole in the ground. Then Daniel pauses to tell what led up to it.

And he shall stir up his power and his courage against the king of the south with a great army; and the king of the south shall be stirred up to battle with a very great and mighty army; but he shall not stand: for they shall forecast devices against him. Yea, they that feed of the portion of his meat shall destroy him, and his army shall overflow: and many shall fall down slain (Daniel 11:25-26).

President Bush II stirred up a great army against Iraq. Then "Interrogating Saddam Hussein's former bodyguards and relatives of people close to Saddam provided most of the information that led U.S. forces to Saddam" (http://www. cnn.com/2003/WORD/meast/12/14/sprj.irq.main/index. html).

And both these kings' hearts [shall be] to do mischief, and they shall speak lies at one table; but it shall not prosper: for yet the end [shall be] at the time appointed (Daniel 11:27).

Speaking lies at one table is about negotiations between the US and Iraq. Bush II invented reasons to invade Iraq, and Hussein fabricated reports of weapons of mass destruction.

> Then shall he return into his land with great riches; and his heart [shall be] against the holy covenant; and he shall do [exploits], and return to his own land (11:28).

President Bush II's heart was against the covenant (America's Constitution) when he signed the Patriot Act on 26 October 2001. It severely limits Constitutional freedoms.

> No person shall be held...nor shall be compelled in any criminal case to be a witness against himself, nor be deprived of life, [or] liberty...without due process of law (US Constitution, Bill of Rights, Article V).

No person being deprived of liberty has not included the foreign nationals that Bush II imprisoned in Guantanamo Cuba for eons without trials or legal recourse. What is happening to America's Constitution in plain sight?

"Why did George Bush invade Iraq? ...Was he evil, looking out only for business interests and intent on making money for himself and his friends off the disaster that is Iraq - military contractors, security industries, corrupt rebuilding ...? (http://www.theseminal.com/2008 /05/26/afternoon-open-thread-george-bush-stupid-or-evil/). The War was profitable to Halliburton, the firm that Mr. Chaney ran before becoming Vice President.

Then came President Obama. "This is an odd turn of events, says Bill Galston of the Brookings Institution. Suddenly, Obama and Bush are seeing things eye to eye" (http://www.npr.org/blogs/itsallpolitics/2013/07/15/201571729/in-second-term-obama-takes-softer-tone-toward-bushes). The prophecy about Bush II repeats about Obama.

> He shall enter peaceably even upon the fattest places of the province; and he shall do [that] which his fathers have not done, nor his fathers' fathers; he shall scatter

among them the prey, and spoil, and riches: [yea], and he shall forecast his devices against the strong holds, even for a time (Daniel 11:24).

President Obama peacefully entered the ancient Persian province of Iraq 7 April 2009, a year after being inaugurated. He *forecast his devices* [plans] *even for a time*; he told the Iraqis that he was going to withdraw American forces. A year later, August 2010, he confirmed that America's troops have been mostly withdrawn from Iraq.

He shall stir up his power and his courage against the king of the south with a great army; and the king of the south shall be stirred up to battle with a very great and mighty army; but he shall not stand: for they shall forecast devices against him (Daniel 11:25).

After Saddam Hussein was killed, the king of the South became Osama bin Laden (leader of Al Qaeda), who was killed by US forces in 2011. Then Iran and Abū Bakr al-Baghdadi, the leader of ISIS, shared the King of the South title alternately. *President Obama stirred up his power and his courage with a great army to fight against Abū Bakr al-Baghdadi. With a great army of political allies, President Obama had Europe, China, and Russia join him to pressure Iran to make a nuclear agreement. Iran was stirred up to battle for the best deal; but the king of the south shall not stand: for they shall forecast devices against him.*

And both these kings' hearts [shall be] to do mischief, and they shall speak lies at one table; but it shall not prosper: for yet the end [shall be] at the time appointed (Daniel 11:27).

During the negotiations to limit Iran's nuclear program, a deal was struck. But the hyperbole to America and Iran sounded as if they were pitching different deals.

Iran's past President [ruler/king], Akbar Hashemi Rafsanjani, who was an influential moderate that kept the hard-liners from taking Iran to extremes died suddenly 8 January 2017. The next day a US warship fired warning shots at Iranian speedboats (http://www.cnn.com/2017/01/09/politics/us-iran-warning-shots/). In time, this conflict will go ballistic.

> Then shall he return into his land with great riches; and his heart [shall be] against the holy covenant; and he shall do [exploits], and return to his own land (Daniel 11:28).

When President Obama returned to Washington from Laos in September 2016, he turned against God's Covenant in his UN speech 20 September. He said that the beliefs of fundamentalists were *irreconcilable with modernity*. Thus, he established a rational to take away fundamentalist Christians, who believe in the *Sacrifice* and *Oblation* of Christ: They refuse to yield to the dictates of the state.

Chronology from President Trump to Pence

As Daniel 11:24-28 was a caveat about Presidents Bush II and Obama. It then flows to President Pence. But it is also a caveat about President Trump.

> And he shall stir up his power and his courage against the king of the south with a great army; and the king of the south shall be stirred up to battle with a very great and mighty army; but he shall not stand: for they shall forecast devices against him. Yea, they that feed of the portion of his meat shall destroy him, and his army shall overflow: and many shall fall down slain (11:25-26).

The King of the South had become Abū Bakr al-Baghdadi the leader of ISIS along with Iran. American troops focused on ISIS as America's primary enemy. Then Abū Bakr al-Baghdadi was killed. "They that feed of the portion of his meat shall destroy him." "The surprising information about Islamic State leader Abu Bakr al-Baghdadi's general location

...came following the arrest and interrogation of one of Baghdadi's wives and a courier" (https://www.msn.com/en-us/news/world/cia-got-tip-on-al-baghdadi-e2-80-99s-location-from-arrest-of-a-wife-and-a-courier/ar-AAJrI7a).

> And both these kings' hearts [shall be] to do mischief, and they shall speak lies at one table; but it shall not prosper: for yet the end [shall be] at the time appointed (Daniel 11:27).

The pro-ISIS Taliban in Afghanistan was negotiating with America. When they were supposed to come to Camp David to finalize the deal, President Trump abruptly called off the talks because the Taliban had killed a US worker.

The King of the South has become Iran. France has tried to get the Trump Administration and Iran to negotiate an end to their escalating hostilities. They refuse, but "The intermediaries... secretly have been relaying messages between Washington and Tehran for months in hopes of getting the sides talking at a time of heightened hostility on a range of issues" (https://www.reuters.com/article/us-usa-iran-afghanistan-exclusive-idUSKCN1V60B2).

> Then shall he return into his land with great riches; and his heart [shall be] against the holy covenant; and he shall do [exploits], and return to his own land (11:28).

After killing al-Baghdadi, President Trump kept Syria's oil to support the Kurdish fighters that he had abandoned and to pay for the internment of the ISIS fighters in Syria. "We want to keep the oil, $45 million a month, keep the oil. We've secured the oil" (https://www.rawstory.com/2019/10/trump-attacks-obama-and-gloats-about-keeping-the-oil-in-rambling-speech-to-chicago-cops/).

President Trump was then impeached for abusing his constitutional authority. His defense reinterpreted the Constitution to prevent his removal from office.

President Michael Pence

Thus, Daniel 11:21 explains the second foot, President Pence. Verses 22-28 are specifically about him. Daniel's prophecy is explaining the past, present, and future.

Power will transfer peacefully from President Trump to Pence. Then "with the arms of a flood shall they be overflown from before him, and shall be broken; yea, also the prince of the covenant" (11:22). President Pence as America's Protestant Prince of the Covenant, wages war on God's Church. He encounters Jesus and is broken at Christ's Advent.

"After the league [made] with him [President Pence] he shall work deceitfully: for he shall come up, and shall become strong with a small people" (Daniel 11:23, enhanced). His political allies? Or is it the Space Force that he organized?

> He shall enter peaceably even upon the fattest places of the province; and he shall do [that] which his fathers have not done, nor his fathers' fathers; he shall scatter among them the prey, and spoil, and riches: [yea], and he shall forecast his devices against the strong holds, even for a time. And he shall stir up his power and his courage against the king of the south with a great army; and the king of the south shall be stirred up to battle with a very great and mighty army; but he shall not stand: for they shall forecast devices against him (Daniel 11:24, 25).

This is the war with Iran. Remember when President Trump threatened North Korea with *Fire and Fury* like the world has never seen. Vice President Pence was instrumental in setting up the US Space Force in 2019. Its weapons are unlike anything that the world has ever seen. Without going into specific details about the weapons from my years of tracking the Ballistic Missile Defense program: America has spent $10 billion a year on SDI since the 1980's (that evolved into BMD). While publicly saying, "It does not work," the US has hidden the expenses in plain sight as frivolous $10,000 toilet seats for jets and $750 claw hammers. Then Bush II withdrew America from the ABM Treaty to deploy BMD.

Ballistic missile defense has been revived by the George W. Bush administration as the National Missile Defense and Ground-based Midcourse Defense (http:// en.wikipedia.org/wiki/Strategic_Defense_Initiative#X-ray_laser).

The Anti-Ballistic Missile Treaty (ABM Treaty or ABMT) was a treaty between the United States of America and the Soviet Union on the limitation of the anti-ballistic missile (ABM) systems used in defending areas against missile-delivered nuclear weapons....[The treaty was in force for thirty years: May 26, 1972 until June 13, 2002, six months after giving the required notice of intent, the US withdrew from the treaty] (http://en.wikipedia .org/wiki/Anti-Ballistic_Missile_Treaty).

[George Bush II] Today, I have given formal notice to Russia, in accordance with the treaty, that the United States of America is withdrawing from this almost 30 year old treaty (http://www.whitehouse.gov/news/ releases/2001/12/20011213-4.html).

The treaty was undisturbed until Ronald Reagan announced his Strategic Defense Initiative (SDI) on March 23, 1983 (http://en.wikipedia.org/wiki/Anti-Ballistic_Missile_Treaty).

We have no time to lose. Troublous times are before us. The world is stirred with the spirit of war. Soon the scenes of trouble spoken of in the prophecies will take place. The prophecy in the eleventh of Daniel has nearly reached its complete fulfillment. Much of the history that has taken place in fulfillment of this prophecy will be repeated. In the thirtieth verse a power is spoken of that "shall be grieved, and return, and have indignation against the holy covenant: so, shall he do; he shall even return, and have intelligence with them that forsake the holy covenant" [Verses 31-36, quoted] (13MR 394.1).

At the time appointed he shall return, and come toward the south; but it shall not be as the former, or as the latter. For the ships of Chittim shall come against him: therefore, he shall be grieved, and return, and have indignation against the holy covenant: so, shall he do; he shall even return, and have intelligence with them that forsake the holy covenant. And arms shall stand on his part, and they shall pollute the sanctuary of strength, and shall take away the daily [continual, margin], and they shall place the abomination that maketh desolate. And such as do wickedly against the covenant shall he corrupt by flatteries: but the people that do know their God shall be strong, and do [exploits]. And they that understand among the people shall instruct many: yet they shall fall by the sword, and by flame, by captivity, and by spoil, [many] days. Now when they shall fall, they shall be holpen with a little help: but many shall cleave to them with flatteries. And [some] of them of understanding shall fall, to try them, and to purge, and to make [them] white, [even] to the time of the end: because [it is] yet for a time appointed. And the king shall do according to his will; and he shall exalt himself, and magnify himself above every god, and shall speak marvellous things against the God of gods, and shall prosper till the indignation be accomplished: for that that is determined shall be done (Daniel 11:29-36).

Chittim is "from an unused name denoting Cyprus: a general term for all islanders of the Mediterranean Sea; the descendants of Javan" (cf Strong). Javan "is universally used by the nations of the East as the generic name of the Greek race" (cf Easton's Bible Dictionary). Chittim may once have denoted the island of Cyprus, which is now divided between Greece and turkey. The Greek empire which included Cyprus extended to Iran. The endtime Chittim is most likely an island near Iran. The Iranians are protective of their islands.

What is happening in the region?

Persian Gulf is home to many islands...and some utilized for communication, military, or as ship docks... Recent wars and political unrest has also made these islands strategic military locations (http://en.wikipedia.org/wiki/List_of_islands_in_the_Persian_Gulf).

"Iran is building a replica of a Nimitz-class aircraft carrier at a shipyard on the Persian Gulf near the Strait of Hormuz (http://www.stripes.com/news/iran-s-replica-of-a-us-air craft-carrier-puzzles-navy-officials-1.273877). It is being constructed at Bandar Abbas—not far from Iran's Qeshm Island: "an underground military facility... [that may] house Iran's Ghadir-Nahang class submarines" (http://en.wikipedia.org/wiki/Qeshm).

A US fleet is stationed in the Gulf (http://usnews.nbcnews.com/news/2012/07/16/12769568-aircraft-carrier-uss-stennis-going-to-persian-gulf-early-staying-longer?lite) Iranian ships are blocked from docking at a Yemen seaport. America's navy intercepts and boards boats in the Persian Gulf (http://www.history.navy.mil/wars/dstorm/sword-shield.htm). Iran claims to be ready to engage America.

Iran will target American aircraft carriers in the Persian Gulf should a war between the two countries ever break out, the naval chief of Iran's powerful Revolutionary Guard warned today as the country completes work on a large-scale mock-up of a U. S. carrier... "Aircraft carriers are the symbol of America's military might" ... "The carriers are responsible for supplying America's air power. So, it's natural that we want to sink the carriers." ..."the Nimitz-class carriers used by the United States could be seriously damaged or destroyed if 24 missiles were fired simultaneously (http://www.columbiatribune.com/news/u-s-carriers-will-be-target-iranian-warns/article_62424e62-d54a-11e3-bbad-10604b9ffe60.html).

President Obama's advisors shrugged off Iran's ability to sink America's aircraft carriers. January 2016, Iran demonstrated that it has a strategy to sink America's aircraft carriers when the likelihood of a conflict arises.

The Iranian Navy locked its missiles on an American aircraft carrier deployed in the region... Iran seized and detained two US Navy boats on Farsi Island in the Persian Gulf. Tehran claims the personnel were in Iranian territorial waters illegally when they were captured. The Americans have since been released (http://www.liveleak.com/view?i=fe0_1452751875) (http://sputniknews.com/middleeast/20160114/1033094565/iran-navy-missiles-us-carrier.html).

Suicide bombers invented by Iran against America are widely used. Iran allegedly supplies remote road-side bombs for use against US troops (http://www.cnn.com/2007/WORLD/meast/02/15/iran.iraq/). And Iran claims to have reverse engineered a US drone (http://www.theguardian.com/world/2012/apr/22/iran-reverse-engineer-spy-drone). Pirates have used speed boats to hijack tankers near Somalia (https://en.wikipedia.org/wiki/Piracy_off_the_coast_of_Somalia) The USS Cole was almost sunk by a floating bomb (http://www.al-bab.com/yemen/cole1.htm). "Iranian drone buzzes U. S. aircraft carrier in Persian Gulf" (http://dailycaller.com/2014/03/03/video-iranian-drone-buzzes-u-s-aircraft-carrier-in-persian-gulf/).

Daniel is clear: the ships from Chittim will attack the US ships, America's President will return, *have indignation against the holy covenant* (America's Constitution), and he will go *beyond his* Constitutional restraints. But exactly what that means is yet to be seen.

President Trump is escalating the tensions with Iran to the point that Iran allegedly has begun attacking oil tankers in the Persian Gulf and oil facilities in Saudi Arabia. As if to say, "If we cannot sell our oil you cannot sell yours."

Now, just now, it is time for us to be watching, working, and waiting. *The word of the Lord reveals the fact that the end of all things is at hand, and its testimony is most decided that it is necessary for every soul to have the truth planted in the heart so that it will control the life and sanctify the character.* The Spirit of the Lord is working to take the truth of the inspired word and stamp it upon the soul so that the professed followers of Christ will have a holy, sacred joy that they will be able to impart to others. The opportune time for us to work is now, just now, while the day lasts. But there is no command for anyone to search the Scripture in order to ascertain, if possible, when probation will close. God has no such message for any mortal lips. He would have no mortal tongue declare that which He has hidden in His secret councils (RH, Oct 9, 1894 par. 11).

Transgression has almost reached its limit. Confusion fills the world, and a great terror is soon to come upon human beings. The end is very near. We who know the truth should be preparing for what is soon to break upon the world as an overwhelming surprise (8T 28.1).

When the judgment shall sit and the books be opened, there will be many astonishing disclosures. Men will not then appear as they now appear to human eyes and finite judgments. Secret sins will then be laid bare to the view of all. Motives which have been hidden in the dark chambers of the heart will then be revealed. Designing ambitions, selfish purposes, will be seen where outward appearances told only of a desire to honor God and to do good to all men. What revelations will then be made! Men of pure motives and true and noble purposes may now be neglected, slandered, and despised; but they will then appear in their true character, and will be honored with the commendation of God (Ms14-1889).

Daniel 12

¹And at that time shall Michael stand up, the great prince which standeth for the children of thy people: and there shall be a time of trouble, such as never was since there was a nation [even] to that same time: and at that time thy people shall be delivered, every one that shall be found written in the book. ²And many of them that sleep in the dust of the earth shall awake, some to everlasting life, and some to shame [and] everlasting contempt. ³And they that be wise shall shine as the brightness of the firmament; and they that turn many to righteousness as the stars for ever and ever.

⁴But thou, O Daniel, shut up the words, and seal the book, [even] to the time of the end: many shall run to and fro, and knowledge shall be increased.

⁵Then I Daniel looked, and, behold, there stood other two, the one on this side of the bank of the river, and the other on that side of the bank of the river. ⁶And [one] said to the man clothed in linen, which [was] upon the waters of the river, How long [shall it be to] the end of these wonders? ⁷And I heard the man clothed in linen, which [was] upon the waters of the river, when he held up his right hand and his left hand unto heaven, and sware by him that liveth for ever that [it shall be] for a time, times, and an half; and when he shall have accomplished to scatter the power of the holy people, all these [things] shall be finished.

⁸And I heard, but I understood not: then said I, O my Lord, what [shall be] the end of these [things]? ⁹And he said, Go thy way, Daniel: for the words [are] closed up and sealed till the time of the end.

¹⁰Many shall be purified, and made white, and tried; but the wicked shall do wickedly: and none of the wicked

shall understand; but the wise shall understand. ¹¹And
from the time [that] the daily [sacrifice] shall be taken
away, and the abomination that maketh desolate set up,
[there shall be] a thousand two hundred and ninety days.
¹²Blessed [is] he that waiteth, and cometh to the
thousand three hundred and five and thirty days. ¹³But
go thou thy way till the end [be]: for thou shalt rest, and
stand in thy lot at the end of the days.

Points to Ponder

1. The sealed book of Daniel is opened
2. Michael stands
3. The partial understanding is removed
4. Knowledge increases
5. Daniel's last time prophecy
6. Only the wise will understand
7. The wicked will do wickedly

Michael Shall Stand

Immediately before Michael stands: 1) The *duo* horns on
the earth-beast in Revelation 13 are Presidents Bush II,
Obama, and Trump; with Michael Pence to follow from the
executive branch of government when the Trump lamblike
horn is broken; 2) After the Trump horn, President Pence
becomes America's Prince of the Constitution, the ships from
Iran attack America's fleet. 3) This war morphs into
Armageddon. 4) President Michael Pence will void America's
Constitution as well as God's Covenant, the Ten
Commandments and implements the 666 Mark of the Beast.

Michael standing for His people in Daniel 12:1 is Christ
standing for His saints. Matthew Henry taught it: "Michael is
simply another of the many names for Jesus Himself"
(https://www.amazingfacts.org/media-library/book
/e/85/t/who-is-michael-the-archangel-#AN-AMAZING-
FACT). That is true, but it is not the whole truth. Why did
Ellen White teach it if it is not the whole truth?

Yet while it was not given to the prophets to understand fully the things revealed to them, they **earnestly sought to obtain all the light which God had been pleased to make manifest** (GC 344.3).

Jesus rose up, and shut the door, and entered the Holy of Holies, at the 7th month 1844; but Michael's standing up (Daniel 12:1) to deliver his people, is in the future (WLF 12.4).

Michael had not stood up, and that the time of trouble, such as never was, had not yet commenced. The nations are now getting angry, but when our High Priest has finished His work in the sanctuary, He will stand up, put on the garments of vengeance, and then the seven last plagues will be poured out (EW 36.1).

"The commencement of that time of trouble," here mentioned does not refer to the time when the plagues shall begin to be poured out, but to a short period just before they are poured out, while Christ is in the sanctuary. At that time, while the work of salvation is closing, trouble will be coming on the earth, and the nations will be angry, yet held in check so as not to prevent the work of the third angel. At that time the "latter rain," or refreshing from the presence of the Lord, will come, to give power to the loud voice of the third angel, and prepare the saints to stand in the period when the seven last plagues shall be poured out (EW 85.3).

These statements explain the sequence of endtime events in conjunction with Daniel 12:1. "At that time shall Michael stand up, the great prince which standeth for the children of thy people: and there shall be a time of trouble, such as never was since there was a nation..." "The commencement of that time of trouble," here mentioned does not refer to the time when the plagues shall begin to be poured out, but to a short period just before they are poured out..." Notice that Michael stands and the Time of Trouble begins before "our High Priest has finished His work in the sanctuary," and a short time later "He will stand up, put on the garments of vengeance, and then the seven last plagues will be poured out." Thus, Michael stands the first time after 1844 to begin the Time of Trouble, and a second time when Christ declares "It is finished." He then puts "on the garments of vengeance" and the seven last plagues begin. Then He Comes to the earth for His saints!

A careful study of endtime events in the Bible clearly indicates that Jesus does not stand twice after 1844. But the writings of Ellen White indicate that when Michael stands the Time of Trouble begins and when Michael stands the seven last plagues begin. White definitely states that Michael standing brings each of these events. And in Early Writings p. 85.3, White clearly stated that after the Time of Trouble begins the Holy Spirit will be poured out on God's people before Christ stands to begin the Seven Last Plagues.

Daniel 12:1 says Michael is "THE GREAT PRINCE." In Daniel, Prince Michael is the name of two people. The Prince of America's Constitution: A title passed from President Bush II to Presidents Obama and Trump; and that will apply to Michael Pence after President Trump is broken. And Michael, Heaven's Prince of the Covenant is Jesus Christ.

> *The light that Daniel received direct from God was given especially for these last days. The visions he saw by the banks of the Ulai and the Hiddekel...are now in process of fulfillment, and all the events foretold will soon have come to pass* (4BC 1166.5).

> *I was by the side of the great river, which [is] Hiddekel...*Michael, <u>one of the chief princes</u>, came to help me (Daniel 10:4, 13).

Daniel's endtime specific vision by the Hiddekel River reveals that Michael is one of the chief princes in the endtime. Christ lived in Daniel's Day and He helped Gabriel deal with the Persian prince. He is alive in the endtime as well. President Michael Pence, the Protestant Prince of America's Constitution, is also an endtime Prince Michael that will stand to begin the Time of Trouble. Then Michael, Christ will stand to begin the Seven Last Plagues.

Michael: "Who is like God." Lucifer wanted to be "like the Most High" (Isaiah 14:14). The war in Heaven (cf Rev 12:7) was between *Michael and the dragon* (Lucifer). Satan thru his agent will stand for his people to bring on the Time of Trouble, prior to Michael standing in Heaven.

> Satan...attempted what he has attempted... —to deceive and destroy the people by palming off upon them a counterfeit in place of the true (GC88 186.1).

> Satan is fast obtaining the control of human minds who have not the fear of God before them. Let all read and understand the prophecies of this book, for we are now entering upon the time of trouble spoken of: *"And at that time shall Michael stand up, the great prince which standeth for the children of thy people: and there shall be a time of trouble, such as never was since there was a nation [even] to that same time*: and at that time thy people shall be delivered, every one that shall be found written in the book. And many of them that sleep in the dust of the earth shall awake, some to everlasting life, and some to shame [and] everlasting contempt. And they that be wise shall shine as the brightness of the firmament; and they that turn many to righteousness as the stars forever and ever. But thou, O Daniel, shut up the words, and seal the book, [even] to the time of the end: many shall run to and fro, and knowledge shall be increased" [Daniel 12:1-4] (13MR 394.2).

> Precious, vital truths, are bound up with man's eternal well-being both in this life and in the eternity that is opening before us. "Sanctify them through Thy truth: Thy word is truth." John 17:17. The word of God is to be practiced. It will live and endure forever. While worldly ambitions, worldly projects, and the greatest plans and purposes of men will perish... (7T 249.1).

From the condition of things in our world, we can see that we are indeed living in the last days (https://egw writings.org/, Lt70-1906.3).

We are close to the time spoken of by Daniel the prophet (14MR 136.4).

The last times in Daniel 12:11 are the 1290 days from 20 September 2016 when President Obama denounced all forms of fundamentalism, which includes pure Christianity. And *as it was in the days of Noah, it will be in the endtimes*. When God's judgment was about to fall on the world, Noah knew when to go into the ark and he waited for 7 days. Since the Judgment Hour of the living ended on 14 February 2013, 14 February 2020 is the end of our seven year wait. What then? And when the 1290 days end on 2 April 2020, there is a promised blessing to those who endure for 1335 days, until 17 May 2020. What blessing?

The Vatican had planned an event 14 May 2020. Cardinal Burke links it to *a single global government*:

"...There are those who propose and work for a single global government, that is, for the elimination of individual national governments, so that all of humanity would be under the control of a single political authority," said Burke. "For those who are convinced that the only way to achieve the common good is the concentration of all government in a single authority, loyalty to one's homeland or patriotism has become an evil" (www.dailywire.com/news/ pope-francis-invites-political-leaders-sign-global-paul-bois).

We have only a little while to urge the warfare; then Christ will come, and this scene of rebellion will close. Then our last efforts will have been made to work with Christ and advance His kingdom. Some who have stood in the forefront of the battle, zealously resisting incoming evil, fall at the post of duty; others gaze sorrowfully at the fallen heroes, but have no time to cease work. They must close up the ranks, seize the banner from the hand palsied by death, and with renewed energy vindicate the truth and the honor of Christ. As never before, resistance must be made against sin,--against the powers of darkness. The time demands energetic and determined activity on the part of those who believe present truth. They should teach the truth by both precept and example. If the time seems long to wait for our Deliverer to come, if, bowed by affliction and worn with toil, we feel impatient for our commission to close, and to receive an honorable release from the warfare, let us remember-- and let the remembrance check every murmur--that God leaves us on earth to encounter storms and conflicts, to perfect Christian character, to become better acquainted with God our Father and Christ our elder Brother, and to do work for the Master in winning many souls to Christ, that with glad heart we may hear the words: "Well done, good and faithful servant; enter thou into the joy of thy Lord" (RH, October 25, 1881 par. 10).

Study Daniel 12

[Re: Bible prophecy] *The meaning was to be unfolded, from age to age, as the people of God should need the instruction therein contained* (GC88 344.1).

Daniel 12. Read attentively this chapter. *"Hear the word of the LORD, ye children of Israel: for the LORD hath a controversy with the inhabitants of the land, because [there is] no truth, nor mercy, nor knowledge of God in the land.* By swearing, and lying, and killing, and stealing, and committing adultery, they break out, and blood toucheth blood. Therefore, shall the land mourn, and every one that dwelleth therein shall languish, with the beasts of the field, and with the fowls of heaven; yea, the fishes of the sea also shall be taken away. Yet let no man strive, nor reprove another: for thy people [are] as they that strive with the priest. *Therefore, shalt thou fall in the day, and the prophet also shall fall with thee in the night, and I will destroy thy mother. My people are destroyed for lack of knowledge: because thou hast rejected knowledge, I will also reject thee, that thou shalt be no priest to me: seeing thou hast forgotten the law of thy God, I will also forget thy children"* Hosea 4:1-6 (18MR 220.4).

The great burden of every soul should be, Is my heart renewed? Is my soul transformed? Are my sins pardoned through faith in Christ? Have I been born again? Am I complying with the invitation, "Come unto me, all ye that labor and are heavy laden, and I will give you rest. Take My yoke upon you, and learn of Me; for I am meek and lowly in heart: and ye shall find rest unto your souls. For My yoke is easy, and My burden is light" [Matthew 11:28]. Do you count all things but loss for the excellency of the knowledge of Christ Jesus? And do you feel it your duty to believe every word that proceeds out of the mouth of God? (17MR 23.3).

The unprepared condition of our churches...The Lord showed...many things that it is not lawful for a man to utter. Why could he not tell the believers what he had seen? Because they would have made a misapplication of the great truths presented. They would not have been able to comprehend these truths...God gave him to bear to the churches (15MR 228.1).

The people of God need to study what characters they must form in order to pass through the test and proving of the last days. Many are living in spiritual weakness and backsliding. They know not what they believe. Let us read and study the twelfth chapter of Daniel. It is a warning that we shall all need to understand before the time of the end. There are ministers claiming to believe the truth who are not sanctified through the truth (15MR 228.2).

We must know for ourselves that the Spirit of God is abiding in our hearts, and that we can hold communion with God. Then if He should come to us quickly, if by any chance our life should suddenly be ended, we should be ready to meet our God. Now, while it is called today, let us set our house in order. "Today if ye will hear His voice, harden not your hearts as in the provocation." Because of their unbelief of God's Word, the children of Israel who left Egypt perished in the wilderness. God grant that we may not through unbelief fail of entering into the Promised Land. Let us keep step with Jesus Christ (GCB, April 6, 1903 par. 2).

The signs of the times are fulfilling in our world, yet the churches generally are represented as slumbering. Shall we not take warning from the experience of the foolish virgins, who when the call came, "Behold the bridegroom cometh; go ye out to meet him," found that they had no oil in their lamps? And while they went to buy oil, the bridegroom went in to the marriage supper with the wise virgins, and the door was shut. When the foolish virgins reached the banqueting hall, they received an unexpected denial. The master of the feast declared, "I know you not." They were left standing without in the empty street, in the blackness of the night (15MR 229.1).

Now, while our great High Priest is making the atonement for us, we should seek to become perfect in Christ. Not even by a thought could our Saviour be brought to yield to the power of temptation. Satan finds in human hearts some point where he can gain a foothold; some sinful desire is cherished, by means of which his temptations assert their power. But Christ declared of Himself, "The prince of this world cometh, and hath nothing in Me." Satan could find nothing in the Son of God that would enable him to gain the victory. He had kept His Father's commandments, and there was no sin in Him that Satan could use to his advantage. This is the condition in which those must be found who shall stand in the time of trouble (RH, March 14, 1912 par. 8).

When the third angel's message closes, mercy no longer pleads for the guilty inhabitants of the earth. The people of God have accomplished their work. They have received "the latter rain," "the refreshing from the presence of the Lord," and they are prepared for the trying hour before them. Angels are hastening to and fro in heaven. An angel returning from the earth announces that his work is done; the final test has been brought upon the world, and all who have proved themselves loyal to the divine precepts have received "the seal of the living God." Then Jesus ceases His intercession in the sanctuary above. He lifts His hands and with a loud voice says, "It is done;" and all the angelic host lay off their crowns as He makes the solemn announcement: "He that is unjust, let him be unjust still: and he which is filthy, let him be filthy still: and he that is righteous, let him be righteous still: and he that is holy, let him be holy still." Revelation 22:11. Every case has been decided for life or death. Christ has made the atonement for His people and blotted out their sins. The number of His subjects is made up; "the kingdom and dominion, and the greatness of the kingdom under the whole heaven," is about to be given to the heirs of salvation, and Jesus is to reign as King of kings and Lord of lords (GC 613.2).

When He leaves the sanctuary, darkness covers the inhabitants of the earth. In that fearful time the righteous must live in the sight of a holy God without an intercessor. The restraint which has been upon the wicked is removed, and Satan has entire control of the finally impenitent. God's long-suffering has ended. The world has rejected His mercy, despised His love, and trampled upon His law. The wicked have passed the boundary of their probation; the Spirit of God, persistently resisted, has been at last withdrawn. Unsheltered by divine grace, they have no protection from the wicked one. Satan will then plunge the inhabitants of the earth into one great, final trouble. As the angels of God cease to hold in check the fierce winds of human passion, all the elements of strife will be let loose. The whole world will be involved in ruin more terrible than that which came upon Jerusalem of old (GC 614.1).

Will you receive the gift of God brought by Jesus Christ of everlasting life and hear from the lips of Him who died for you, "Well done, good and faithful servant; ... enter into the joy of thy Lord?" Matthew 25:23. What joy is here spoken of? That joy of seeing souls redeemed in the kingdom of glory. That joy being yours of seeing souls saved through your instrumentality. Will this joy be yours? Will you live an aimless life of self-gratification longer, and in the end reap death and see souls lost through your example and influence who might have been saved? (https://egwwritings.org/, Lt6-1869.14)

Whenever the will of God is violated by nations or by individuals, a day of retribution comes, as surely as rivers that burst their banks carry devastation before them (19MR 391.2).

Remember that you will never reach a higher standard than you yourselves set. Set your mark high, and then step by step, even though it be by painful effort, by self-denial and self-sacrifice, ascend the whole length of the ladder of progress. Let nothing hinder you. Christ will be to you a present help in every time of trouble. Stand like Daniel, the faithful statesman, a man whom no temptation could corrupt... Do not disappoint Him who so loved you that He gave His own life to cancel your sins. He says: "Without Me ye can do nothing." *Remember this, If you have made mistakes, you certainly gain a victory if you see these mistakes, and regard them as beacons of warning.* I need not tell you that thus you turn defeat into victory, disappointing the enemy and honoring your Redeemer (1NL 81.5).

Have faith in God. We dishonor Him by our unbelief. Pray, and watch unto prayer. He is touched with the feelings of our infirmities. He is merciful, one who can have compassion on the ignorant, and on them that are out of the way (https://egwwritings.org/, Lt72-1897.16).

We are not to be dependent on the world in a manner to compromise the truth; we are not to be bribed or to attain the world's favor by bowing to the laws of men and setting aside the law of God; we are not to be brought in bondage to the world; and yet we are in the world to live as long as God shall permit, and the Lord has given us a special work to do to save the world (19MR 101.1).

There have been presented before me the very many precious opportunities to save souls, which have been unheeded and lost. Let us now see how many souls we can save for our Saviour (19MR 4.3).

What is done through the co-operation of men with God is a work that shall never perish, but endure through the eternal ages. He that makes God his wisdom, that grows up into the full stature of a man in Christ Jesus, will stand before kings, before the so-called great men of the world, and show forth the praises of Him who hath called him out of darkness into His marvelous light. Science and literature cannot bring into the darkened mind of men the light which the glorious gospel of the Son of God can bring. The Son of God alone can do the great work of illuminating the soul. No wonder Paul exclaims, "For I am not ashamed of the gospel of Christ; for it is the power of God unto salvation to everyone that believeth." [Romans 1:16.] The gospel of Christ becomes personality in those who believe, and makes them living epistles, known and read of all men. In this way the leaven of godliness passes into the multitude. The heavenly intelligences are able to discern the true elements of greatness in character; for only goodness is esteemed as efficiency with God (CE 97.1).

We are not one-half awake. We have not the power that is essential to the doing of the work that must be done. We must come into life, come into union. Now, just now, we must stand in that position where repentance and pardon shall be the striking features of our work. There must be no quarrelling. It is too late to engage with Satan in his work of blinding eyes. It is too late to give heed to seducing spirits and doctrines of devils (AUCR, March 11, 1907 par. 11).

I am instructed to say that when the Holy Spirit gives tongue and utterance, we shall see a work done similar to that done on the day of Pentecost. The representatives of Christ will work intelligently. There will not be found one man here and another there seeking to tear down and destroy (AUCR, March 11, 1907 par. 12).

The Lord is about to do a short and effectual work in the earth. Oh, that our leading workers would realize this, and shun their work of criticizing and forbidding. When the Judge of all the earth shall come to render to every man his reward, those who have laid plans that have hindered the cause of truth will be held responsible for their actions, with all the evil that has resulted therefrom (14MR 137.1).

Before the decree bring forth, before the day pass as the chaff, before the fierce anger of the Lord come upon you, before the day of the Lord's anger come upon you, seek ye the Lord, all ye meek of the earth, which have wrought His judgment; seek righteousness, seek meekness: it may be ye shall be hid in the day of the Lord's anger (AUCR, March 11, 1907 par. 13).

Unless our people arouse to their duties for missions at home, they will be found wanting in the day of God (14MR 137.2).

The cross stands where two roads diverge. One is the path of obedience leading to heaven. The other leads into the broad road, where man can easily go with his burden of sin and corruption, but it leads to perdition. In His sermon on the mount, Christ exhorts His hearers, "Therefore whatsoever ye would that men should do to you, do ye even so to them: for this is the law and the prophets. Enter ye in at the strait gate: for wide is the gate, and broad is the way that leadeth to destruction: and many there be that go in thereat: because strait is the gate, and narrow is the way that leadeth unto life, and few there be that find it." And another time one came to Christ and said, "Lord, are there few that be saved? And He said unto them, Strive to enter in at the strait gate: for many I say unto you shall seek to enter in, and shall not be able" (https://egwwritings.org/, Ms50-1898.12).

Take heed to yourselves, lest at any time your hearts be overcharged with surfeiting, and drunkenness, and cares of this life, and so that day come upon you unawares. For as a snare shall it come on all them that dwell on the face of the whole earth. Watch ye therefore, and pray always, that ye may be accounted worthy to escape all these things, and to stand before the Son of man (Luke 21:34-36).

Do not Take the Mark of the Beast!

In addition to the Ten Commandments, God has given other commands in the Bible. "Command thou the people, saying...Ye shall buy" (Deut. 2:4, 6). "The command must be obeyed, 'Sell that ye have...' (Luke 12:33) {8MR 206.2}.

And the third angel followed them, _saying with a loud voice, If any man worship the beast and his image, and receive his mark in his forehead, or in his hand,_ The same shall drink of the wine of the wrath of God, which is poured out without mixture into the cup of His indignation; and he shall be tormented with fire and brimstone in the presence of the holy angels, and in the presence of the Lamb: And the smoke of their torment ascendeth up for ever and ever: and they have no rest day nor night, who worship the beast and his image, and whosoever receiveth the mark of his name. *Here is the patience of the saints: here are they that keep the commandments of God, and the faith of Jesus* (Revelation 14:9-12).

The decree is to go forth that *all who will not receive the mark of the beast shall neither buy nor sell* and finally that they shall be put to death (ST, Nov. 8, 1899 par. 11).

Those who, after the light regarding God's law comes to them, continue to disobey, and exalt human laws above the law of God in the great crisis before us, will receive the mark of the beast (KC 148.4).

If we receive this mark *in our foreheads or in our hands*, the judgments pronounced against the disobedient must fall upon us (RH, April 27, 1911 par. 26).

An apostate church will unite with the powers of earth and hell to place upon the forehead or in the hand, the mark of the beast, and prevail upon the children of God to worship the beast and his image. They will seek to compel them to renounce their allegiance to God's law, and yield homage to the papacy (RH, Nov. 8, 1892 par. 7).

By this first beast is represented the Roman Church ...The image to the beast represents another religious body...the United States. Here is to be found an image of the Papacy. When the churches of our land, uniting upon such points of faith as are held by them in common, shall influence the State to enforce their decrees and sustain their institutions, then will Protestant America have formed an image of the Roman hierarchy. Then the true church will be assailed by persecution, as were God's ancient people (SR 381.2).

The beast with lamblike horns commands "all, both small and great, rich and poor, free and bond, to receive a mark in their right hand, or in their foreheads: and that no man might buy or sell, save he that had the mark, or the name of the beast, or the number of his name." Revelation 13:16, 17. This is the mark concerning which the third angel utters his warning. It is the mark of the first beast, or the Papacy, and is therefore to be sought among the distinguishing characteristics of that power (SR 382.1).

The light that we have upon the third angel's message is the true light. The mark of the beast is exactly what it has been proclaimed to be. Not all in regard to this matter is yet understood, and will not be understood until the unrolling of the scroll; but a most solemn work is to be accomplished in our world. The Lord's command to His servants is: 'Cry aloud, spare not, lift up thy voice like a trumpet, and show My people their transgression, and the house of Jacob their sins.' [Isaiah 58:1] A message that will arouse the churches is to be proclaimed. Every effort is to be made to give the light, not only to our people, but to the world... *The prophecies of Daniel and the Revelation...with the necessary explanations...should be sent all over the world. Our own people need to have the light placed before them in clearer lines* (8T 159.3).

In the issue of the contest, all <u>Christendom will be divided into two great classes</u>,—those who keep the commandments of God and the faith of Jesus, and those who worship the beast and his image and receive his mark. Although church and State will unite their power to compel 'all, both small and great, rich and poor, free and bond,' to receive 'the mark of the beast,' [Revelation 13:16.] yet the people of God will not receive it (GC88 450.1).

Not all who profess to keep the Sabbath will be sealed. There are many even among those who teach the truth to others who will not receive the seal of God in their foreheads. They had the light of truth, they knew their Master's will, they understood every point of our faith, but they had not corresponding works. These who were so familiar with prophecy and the treasures of divine wisdom, should have acted their faith. They should have commanded their households after them, that by a well-ordered family they might present to the world the influence of the truth upon the human heart (CET 189.1).

Ponder well the paths your feet are treading. Search your Bibles carefully and prayerfully. Study the waymarks, and inquire diligently whether your feet are in the path leading heavenward, or in the path leading to perdition (1MR 318.1).

The Closing Work

By Mrs. E. G. White (RH, October 13, 1904)

We see before us a special work to be done. We are now to pray as never before for the Holy Spirit's guidance. Let us seek the Lord with the whole heart that we may find Him. We have received the light of the three angels' messages; and we need now to come decidedly to the front, and take our position on the side of truth.

The fourteenth chapter of Revelation is a chapter of the deepest interest. This scripture will soon be understood in all its bearings, and the messages given to John the revelator will be repeated with distinct utterance.

The prophecies in the eighteenth of Revelation will soon be fulfilled. During the proclamation of the third angel's message, "another angel" is to "come down from heaven, having great power," and the earth is to be "lighted with his glory." The Spirit of the Lord will so graciously bless consecrated human instrumentalities that men, women, and children will open their lips in praise and thanksgiving, filling the earth with the knowledge of God, and with His unsurpassed glory, as the waters cover the sea.

Those who have held the beginning of their confidence firm unto the end will be wide-awake during the time that the third angel's message is proclaimed with great power. During the loud cry, the church, aided by the providential interpositions of her exalted Lord, will diffuse the knowledge of salvation so abundantly that light will be communicated to every city and town. The earth will be filled with the knowledge of salvation. So abundantly will the renewing Spirit of God have crowned with success the intensely active agencies, that the light of present truth will be seen flashing everywhere.

The saving knowledge of God will accomplish its purifying work on the mind and heart of every believer. The Word declares: "Then will I sprinkle clean water upon you, and ye shall be clean: from all your filthiness, and from all your idols, will I cleanse you. A new heart also will I give you, and a new spirit will I put within you: and I will take away the stony heart out of your flesh, and I will give you an heart of flesh. And I will put my Spirit within you, and cause you to walk in my statutes." This is the descent of the Holy Spirit, sent from God to do its office work. The house of Israel is to be imbued with the Holy Spirit, and baptized with the grace of salvation.

Amid the confusing cries, "Lo, here is Christ! Lo, there is Christ!" will be borne a special testimony, a special message of truth appropriate for this time, which message is to be received, believed, and acted upon. It is the truth, not fanciful ideas, that is efficacious. The eternal truth of the Word will stand forth free from all seductive errors and spiritualistic interpretations, free from all fancifully drawn, alluring pictures. Falsehoods will be urged upon the attention of God's people, but the truth is to stand clothed in its beautiful, pure garments. The Word, precious in its holy uplifting influence, is not to be degraded to a level with common, ordinary matters. It is always to remain uncontaminated by the fallacies by which Satan seeks to deceive, if possible, the very elect.

The proclamation of the gospel is the only means in which God can employ human beings as His instrumentalities for the salvation of souls. As men, women, and children proclaim the gospel, the Lord will open the eyes of the blind to see His statutes, and will write upon the hearts of the truly penitent His law. The animating Spirit of God, working through human agencies, leads the believers to be of one mind, one soul, unitedly loving God and keeping His commandments,-- preparing here below for translation.

There have been conflicts, and there will be until in heaven the voice of the Lord is heard, saying, "It is done." And after the redeemed are taken to heaven, God the Father will be glorified in crowning the Lord Jesus, who gave His life a ransom for the world.

Let the work of proclaiming the gospel of Christ be made efficient by the agency of the Holy Spirit. Let not one believer, in the day of trial and proving that has already begun, listen to the devising of the enemy. The living Word is the sword of the Spirit. Mercies and judgments will be sent from heaven. The working of providence will be revealed both in mercies and in judgments.

If we watch and pray and trust God's living Word, we shall gain victories "Watch and pray," Christ said, "that ye enter not into temptation." The day dawns. We must enter each battle with full faith that through Christ we shall be more than conquerors. As faithful watchmen we must diligently guard against the dangers threatening God's people. Other chapters will open before us, and in order to discern their meaning, we shall need keen perception. We are not to be depressed or discouraged, but filled with holy boldness. We are not to be disheartened by the prevalence of sin, or by the difficulties that arise on the right hand and on the left. We must put on the whole armor of God, and stand firm for the right. In the future, Satan's deceptions will assume new forms. False theories, clothed with garments of light, will be presented to God's people. Thus, Satan will try to deceive, if possible, the very elect. Our watchword is to be, "To the law and to the testimony: if they speak not according to this word, it is because there is no light in them." [Isaiah 8:20]

Appendix:

Elihu on the Sabbath

http://en.wikisource.org/wiki/Elihu_on_the_Sabbath,
By Benjamin Clark about 1862

This is the love of God, that we keep His commandments (1 John 5:8).

In reviewing the subject of the Sabbath, I design not to follow any previous writer, but simply, plainly, and briefly, to convince sinners of sin, let their profession be what it may. And this I hope and pray may be done without giving offense to those who love the truth more than error; for God has many servants on earth who would gladly exchange error for truth, and many who do exchange their former traditions for the precious and everlasting truths of God as contained in His Word.

Now, the New Testament witnesses to the law and to the prophets; and that book is said to have been written thus: Matthew's Gospel, six years after the resurrection of Christ; Mark's Gospel, ten years after the church commenced; Luke's Gospel, twenty-eight years after; John's Gospel, sixty-three years after; the Acts of the Apostles, thirty years after; Romans, First and Second Corinthians, and Galatians, twenty-four years after; Ephesians, Colossians, and Hebrews, twenty-nine years after; to Timothy, Titus, and the second epistle of Peter, thirty years after; the Revelation of John, sixty-one years after; his three epistles, about sixty-five years after the resurrection; and the church had properly commenced. And it is easy for us to understand how these apostles understood and practiced with regard to the Sabbath, and they are the "foundation" next after Christ Himself. Therefore, if there was any such institution known and frequently spoken of in the church as "Sabbath," in those different ages of the church, we can easily know what was then meant by it. Some say, if we keep the seventh day of the week, we shall keep a "Jewish Sabbath." Well, we have no Savior to trust in but Jesus Christ, who was, according to the flesh, a Jew; no other apostles and prophets but Jewish; no other than Jewish Scriptures; and, indeed, Jesus said Himself that "salvation is of the Jews." John 4:22. And what did the writers of the New Testament mean by the words "Sabbath" and "Sabbath day"?

What did Matthew mean in the sixth year of the Christian church? He certainly did not mean the first day of the week, but he meant the day before the first day of the week. See Matthew 28:1. He meant what all other Jewish writers ever meant; viz., "the seventh day is the Sabbath of the Lord thy God." But neither Matthew nor any of the apostles ever told us a word about the Sabbath's being changed from the seventh to the first day of the week. Now, if the Scriptures cannot be broken, but everywhere mean one and the same thing; viz. , "the seventh day is the Sabbath of the Lord," then, if ministers contradict this, and say the seventh day is not the Sabbath of the Lord, but the first day of the week is the Sabbath, will they not in this bear witness clearly and positively against themselves, unless they bring forward the chapter and verse where God commanded the Sabbath to be changed?

What did Mark mean by the word "Sabbath"? He meant, also, that the Sabbath was the day before the first day of the week. See Mark 16:1, 2. Surely, if the Sabbath had been changed at the resurrection of Christ, Mark would have known it within ten years afterwards.

What did Luke mean, who wrote twenty-eight years after the resurrection of Christ? He also meant that the Sabbath was the day before the first day of the week; for he says that the women who prepared the ointment rested the Sabbath day, according to the command merit. See Luke 23:56. Thus Luke understood the words "Sabbath day," in the fifty-eighth year of the Christian era, to mean the day immediately preceding the first day of the week.

How did John understand this subject in the sixty-third year of the Christian church? He not only speaks of the Sabbath day as the others did, but he shows plainly that the first day of the week was considered a business day by the disciples after the resurrection. See John 20:1; also Luke 24:13.

But what did the writer of the Acts of the Apostles mean by the words "Sabbath" and "Sabbath day," thirty years after the Christian church was fully commenced? In writing, he often mentions the Sabbath, and once mentions the first day of the week as meaning quite another thing in plain distinction from the Sabbath. See Acts 13:14, 42, 44; 20:7. The practice of the Jews was then, as it is now, to meet in the synagogue on the seventh day. And again: "The next Sabbath day came almost the whole city together to hear the word of God." He does not say this was the Jewish Sabbath, but the Sabbath day; this was the seventh day; and the first day of the week was not then known as a Sabbath by this writer, because he says the next Sabbath day most all of the Jews and Gentiles came together again. I say there would not have been any "next Sabbath" in the week till the next seventh day. Again, see Acts 16:13. "And on the Sabbath we went out of the city by a riverside, where prayer was wont to be made." He does not say on the Jewish Sabbath, nor on one of the Sabbaths, as though there were two Sabbaths then, but on the Sabbath, i.e., the seventh day, as understood by all Jewish writers of this day. Again, see Acts 17:2, where Paul, as his manner was, went in among the Jews, and three Sabbath days reasoned with them out of the Scriptures.

Thus have I proved that the apostles of Christ understood that one day in the week should be called the Sabbath day; and, further, I have proved that this day was the day before the first day of the week, which is the seventh day; and you cannot deny it, nor by the Scriptures disprove it; consequently, if the apostles of our Lord always called the Seventh day the Sabbath day, six, ten, twenty-eight, thirty, and sixty-three years after the church was fully commenced, then it must be the Sabbath day now. And every one of the Lord's ministers who calls any other day the Sabbath besides the one so called by the writers of the New Testament, gives it a title which is nowhere found in the Scriptures; for when they say the Sabbath day, they mean something very different from what the New Testament means. It is already proved that the apostles called the seventh day of the week the Sabbath, and the Sabbath day, for many years after the church was fully commenced.

Now we are to show what sin is; and we are not left to guess at it or to suppose it; but we have a given rule to know with certainty what constitutes sin. "By the law," then, "is the knowledge of sin." By what law was the knowledge of sin twenty-four years after the resurrection of Christ? Answer. — The very same law that was given when it was said, "Thou shalt not covet." The law, then, by which sin is known, is the Ten Commandments; and you cannot deny it! This law says, "The seventh day is the Sabbath of the Lord thy God: in it thou shalt not do any work, thou, nor thy son, nor thy daughter, thy manservant, nor thy maidservant, nor thy cattle, nor thy stranger that is within thy gates: for in six days the Lord made heaven and earth, the sea, and all that in them is, and rested the seventh day: wherefore the Lord blessed the Sabbath day, and hallowed it." See Exodus 20:10, 11. Now, until this law is altered or abrogated (and Christ says He came not "to destroy the law") by the same power that enacted it, a willful transgression of it is a willful sin, let your profession be what it may; for "sin is the transgression of the law." He that offends in one point, or in one of these commandments, is guilty of all, i.e., he is a transgressor of the law, a sinner in the sight of God. But a regenerated soul, a true-hearted Christian, says with Paul: "I delight in the law of God after the inward man." See Romans 7:22. "The law is holy, and the commandment holy, and just, and good." See Romans 7:12. And any person, who is not willing to keep the commandments of God, when plainly understood, has still a carnal mind, which "is not subject to the law of God, neither indeed can be." See Romans 8:7.

Will you say this is judging too hard? Or, "This is an hard saying; who can hear it?" I wish to judge no man; but the word that the Lord has spoken, the same shall judge you in the last day. See John 12:48. "As many as have sinned in the law shall be judged by the law; ...in the day when God shall judge the secrets of men by Jesus Christ according to my gospel." See Romans 2:12-16. Then those who shall hold the truth in unrighteousness, those who pretend to keep the law differently from what God appointed it, those who, in fact, lay aside the commandments of God (the fourth or any other command) and teach for doctrine the commandments of men (the observance of the first day instead of the seventh), such, the Word says, are vain worshipers. See Mark 7:7.

But you say, it makes no difference which day is kept or called the Sabbath day, provided we keep one seventh part of the time! This is not correct, because God never said so. God is not to be mocked in this way. He has been very good and kind to make the Sabbath for man, to appoint the day, and the particular time of the day when the Sabbath is to commence and when it is to end; it is the seventh day in order from the creation — the seventh day in the creation; and He said, "From even unto even, shall ye celebrate your Sabbath" (see Leviticus 23:32); as the evening and the morning were reckoned for the day. God did not leave this subject undecided, so that His people would appoint different days, and then everyone call his own the Sabbath day. But God blessed and sanctified the seventh day, and proved that particular day to be designated by Him, in the face and eyes of about six hundred thousand witnesses, by a miracle directly from heaven, in withholding the manna on that day, and in giving the food for that day on the day before; and it cannot be denied or disproved.

Again, you ask, How shall we know which is the seventh day? I answer, Do you wish to know? Then ask the Jews; for God has committed the lively oracles to them, and then scattered them among the nations. Do you know when the first day of the week comes? Well, the Sabbath is always the day before the first day of the week. See Matthew 28:1. But you may say, Do not the majority of honest-hearted Christians keep the first day of the week? And have they not for centuries done common labor on the seventh day, and observed the first in obedience to the fourth command, and still been honest in their motives, and living Christians? I answer, "What is that to us, so long as the true light of the Sabbath did not come to their minds?"

Now, we certainly know what sin is, not by what popular writers say — not by the popular traditions of our fathers — not altogether by our feelings — but by the law of God is this knowledge; for sin is the transgression of the law; and all who have the law of God have an infallible and everlasting rule to know what sin is. Art thou a willful transgressor of the law of God? Then by the law is the knowledge that thou art a willful sinner before God. But if thou art an ignorant transgressor of the law of God, then by the law is the knowledge that thou art an ignorant sinner before God. To say nothing of presumptuous sin, I say, If thou hast ignorantly sinned, then repent and reform, and God will heal you. See Lev. 4:2, 13.

By the law of God, then, is the clear knowledge of sin. I speak to you, Protestants, who keep the Sunday, a day formerly dedicated to the worship of the sun by the pagans, and afterwards brought into the Church by Constantine and Roman Catholics, and called the Christian Sabbath, a name never known for the first day of the week by any of the writers of the New Testament. I speak to you, Protestants, and ask you if you have any given rule to know what sin is. Have you any certain rule to know whether Roman Catholics sin or not, in bowing down to images? They say they do not sin! You say you know they do sin. But how do you know it is sin to bow down to images, when they say it is not sin? Answer— By the law, you say, you know this is sin, and you know it by no other rule; for you "had not known sin, but by the law." Well, by the same rule, I know what sin is. You say it is not sin to work and do common labor on the seventh day. But we know, not by your assertion, but by the law, whether you sin or not. You say you know by the law that it is sin to bow down to images. I say (by your own rule), I know by the law that it is sin to do common labor on the seventh day; and you cannot deny it. And, if you know it is the duty of Roman Catholics to repent of their sins for transgressing the second command, then I know it is also your duty to repent of your sins for transgressing the fourth command. He who said, "Thou shalt not kill," "Thou shalt not steal," "Thou shalt not

The Last Trump Shall Sound: Michael Stands!   280

bow down thyself to them [images], nor serve them," etc., also said, "The seventh day is the Sabbath."

Can you not see the weakness of the argument; viz., that one seventh part of time was meant in the law, without regard to any particular day? In this you make the commandments of God of no effect through your tradition. Yea, you make void the part of the command which says, "The seventh day is the Sabbath of the Lord thy God." We read, not that the Lord blessed the seventh part of time or the Sabbath institution, as you say, but the seventh day in particular. Why do you wish to take out and make void this part of the fourth command, when Christ has said, "Till heaven and earth pass, one jot or one tittle shall in nowise pass from the law"? See Matthew 5:18. It was just as necessary that the particular day should be designated as it was that there should be a Sabbath made for man. It would not have been according to divine wisdom to say, Thou shalt keep one seventh part of time, or one day in seven, because this would have left mankind in as much confusion as your theory could make them! One might have kept one day, another the next, until seven Sabbaths were kept in one family. Thus, so much for the seventh part of time theory.

Suppose a parent should command his child to do a certain piece of labor on a certain day, and that the child should, without any just cause, neglect to perform the labor on the day specified, and should perform it on the next day. Would this show any respect for the authority of the parent? Or would the parent approve such conduct in his child? You must say, No. Or, if a governor should command all the military to do duty two days in the year, and leave each one to select his own days, there would be as much wisdom in this as in the seventh part of time for the Sabbath of the Lord. God is not; the author of confusion, but of order; while the theory of one seventh part of time, or one whole day in seven, instead of the seventh day, impeaches the divine wisdom, and makes God the author of confusion. Thus, the theory, not the law of God, leads to anarchy and confusion, and to the observance of no Sabbath; and it cannot be denied. What reasonable objection have you to the law of God? What fault can you find with it just as it stands? Have you wisdom enough to change it for the "better?" "The law of the Lord is perfect, converting the soul." See Psalm 19:7. Yea, it is so perfect that it has already converted the souls of many, even from the doctrines and commandments of men, to keep the Sabbath of the Lord, and I trust it will convert many more; because "the statutes of the Lord are right, rejoicing the heart: the commandment of the Lord is pure, enlightening the eyes.... More to be desired are they than gold, yea, than much fine gold: sweeter also than honey and the honeycomb." Verses 8-10. "Wherefore the law is holy, and the commandment holy, and just, and good.... For I [Paul] delight in the law of God after the inward man." See Romans 7:12-22.

Reader, dost thou delight in the law of God after the inward man? If not, thy soul should be converted, by praying for the law of God to be put into thy heart, and written in thy mind. But, if the law of God is already thy delight, then why not be reconciled to it? Why not be subject to it just as it stands? Why wish to make void one jot or tittle of it? I do not present the law for justification; but as a perfect rule of right in this life; first, between man and his Creator; secondly, between man and his fellow man. "Whosoever therefore shall break one of these least commandments, and shall teach men so, he shall be called the least in the kingdom of heaven: but whosoever shall do and teach them, the same shall be called great in the kingdom of heaven." See Matthew 5:19.

The Westminster divines found contradicting the writer of the Acts of the Apostles! These divines say, "From the beginning of the world to the resurrection of Christ, God appointed the seventh day of the week to be the weekly Sabbath, and the first day of the week ever since, to continue to the end of the world, which is the Christian Sabbath."

1. Luke (the writer of the Acts of the Apostles) says (Acts 13:14), Paul and his company went into a synagogue of the Jews on the Sabbath day; this was, according to our account, A. D. 45, and twelve years after the resurrection of Christ. Luke says this was on the

Sabbath day then, at that time. But the divines say this was not on the Sabbath day at that time, but on Saturday, and that the seventh day was not then the Sabbath, neither had been for twelve years. Thus, they contradict Luke plainly and pointedly.

2. Luke says (Acts 13:42, 44) that "when the Jews were gone out of the synagogue, the Gentiles besought that these words [of the gospel] might be preached to them the next Sabbath." "And the next Sabbath day came almost the whole city together to hear the word of God." This, Luke says, was on the Sabbath day at that time, twelve years after the resurrection. But the divines say that it was not on the Sabbath at that time; for Sunday had been the Sabbath for twelve years.

3. Luke says (Acts 16:13): "And on the Sabbath we went out of the city by a riverside, where prayer was wont to be made;" A. D. 53, twenty years after the resurrection, and ten years before the Acts of the Apostles was written. This, Luke says, was actually on the Sabbath day at that time; but the divines contradict him, saying this was not the Sabbath at that time, but on Saturday; for the seventh day was not then the Sabbath, neither had been for twenty years — never since the resurrection of Christ! Thus, they contradict Luke again; for all admit that Luke always called the seventh day, the day the Jews met in their synagogue, the Sabbath, in the Acts of the Apostles.

4. Luke says (Acts 17:2-4) Paul, at Thessalonica, "as his manner was," went into a synagogue of the Jews, and so preached Christ and the resurrection three Sabbath days that some Jews and a great multitude of the gentiles believed. This was twenty years after the resurrection of Christ. This, Luke says, was on three Sabbath days then, at that time. But the divines deny this also, because they say that the Sabbath had

"been changed from the seventh to the first day of the week twenty years before." Thus, they give Luke the lie.

5. Luke says (Acts 18:3, 4) Paul, at Corinth, labored with his hands, as tentmaker (on the other days, as we should understand), but "reasoned in the synagogue every Sabbath, and persuaded the Jews and the Greeks." This was A. D. 54, twenty-one years after the resurrection of Christ, and nine years before the Acts of the Apostles was written. This, Luke said, or wrote, A. D. 63, the thirtieth year after the resurrection, and the thirtieth year of the Christian church that this preaching of Paul was on every Sabbath; that is, on every seventh day, the same day that the Jews always met in their synagogue for worship. This is plain, pointed, and positive proof that the seventh day was the Sabbath, at least thirty years after the resurrection of Christ; for Luke testified again and again that those meetings of the Jews and gentiles were held on the Sabbath; and if Luke was a Christian, then the seventh day was the Christian Sabbath thirty years after the resurrection, the Westminster divines to the contrary notwithstanding. And if the seventh day was the Sabbath thirty years after the resurrection of Christ, as Luke says it was, then it is the Sabbath now; for no man, or body of men, have had any lawful right to alter or change this command of God since A. D. 63. But we find not one word in favor of the idea, not even the least hint or allusion in all the New Testament that the first day of the week was ever so much as thought of as a Christian Sabbath by any of the apostles while they lived. And you must give it up; yea, and you will give it up, if you search the Scriptures carefully and prayerfully on this subject, and if you have a spirit of discernment, and are willing to forsake error for truth, and if you are an honest Christian in the sight of God.

Now, the Scriptures are able to make one wise unto salvation, through faith in Jesus Christ; then why need I stop to examine all the various doctrines of popes, councils, and fathers, when, in searching, I should find pope against pope, council against council, and fathers against fathers? This would be like two companies fighting at great distance, with small arms. But if we wish to come to close action, let us take the armor of truth, which will most assuredly prevail; and the closer the action, the sooner the victory will be won on the side of truth.

Now, my dear reader, if you will take the Scriptures and search them as above requested, then you will find the following valuable treasures of knowledge among the many therein contained:

1. You will find Christ Himself saying, "The Sabbath was made for man," and that it was made when the first seven days were made, before man had sinned. The Sabbath was thus made not for the Jews in particular, but as a gift of God to man, i.e., to mankind universally, of all nations and of all ages of the world.

2. You will find that before the law was given at Mt. Sinai, this was a law and a commandment (Exodus 16); that it was also written by the finger of God, with the "lively oracles," which God committed to the Jews to give to us; that this law, by which is the clear knowledge of sin, is an infallible and everlasting rule by which, to know what is sin, and what is not sin; that sin is the transgression of the law; and that to act against it, or to do things contrary to it, is sin; but "where no law is, there is no transgression;" that this law Christ came not to destroy, abrogate, or make void; that the law is holy, and just, and good; and that Christians delight in it. And as Paul had not "known lust, except the law had said, Thou shalt not covet," so we had not known which day of the week was the Sabbath, except the law had said, "The seventh day is the Sabbath of

the Lord thy God." Now, we know by the law that this is the Sabbath, without the help of commentators.

3. You can find that the resurrection of our Saviour has nothing to do with changing the Sabbath, any more than His birth, His death, or His ascension had. Whether He was risen near the end of the Sabbath, or some time before the common time of beginning the first-day sabbath, so-called, has nothing to do with altering one jot or one tittle of the law of God.

4. You can find that the common reasonings of men, that Christ frequently met with His disciples on the first day of the week after His resurrection more than on other days, are false and without foundation; that He went with two of them to Emmaus, about seven and a half miles, and returned to Jerusalem, which would plainly show that He did not regard that day as a Sabbath; that He met with His disciples in the evening, which must have been after the beginning of the second day of the week (see Genesis 1:8), when they were met, but not to celebrate the resurrection, as false reasoners pretend; that He met with them again "after eight days," i.e. , near the middle of the next week; and again they were together fishing, so that the fishing day would prove a Sabbath, as much as either of the first two visits.

5. You can find that Luke had not forgotten the distinction between the "first day of the week" and "the Sabbath day" (Acts 20:7), in his recording the meeting of the disciples to break bread on that day; and that this is the only time the first day of the week is mentioned in all the Acts of the Apostles; and it is the only notice of Paul's preaching on that particular day, or rather, evening, and that on a particular occasion; viz., in order to be "ready to depart on the morrow;" that this one instance of the first day's being mentioned proves that it was not the Sabbath, and

that the many meetings of the Jews and gentiles, believers and unbelievers, where Paul preached "every Sabbath," certainly did not occur on the first day of the week.

6. You may find that Paul, in giving orders to some of the churches to lay by themselves in store something according as God had prospered them, on the first day of the week for the poor saints at Jerusalem (1 Corinthians 16:2), does not prove that to be the Sabbath day, but that it was not the Sabbath day, nor suitable to a Sabbath day's work; but rather as an offering to the Lord of "the first ripe fruits of their increase;" to be the first business attended to in the week, to reckon up their earnings and incomes, and devote a part of the same, and lay it by itself, so that it would be ready when Paul came. This was a good calculation for the first business of the week.

7. You can find that as there is no law of God against doing common labor on the first day of the week, therefore it is no sin or transgression of any law other than the laws and commandments of men.

8. You can find that the Savior said to His disciples, "If ye love Me, keep My commandments." Again, "He that hath My commandments, and keepeth them, he it is that loveth Me: and he that loveth Me shall be loved of My Father, and I will love him, and will manifest Myself to him." Again, "Jesus answered and said unto him [Judas, not Iscariot], If a man love Me, he will keep My words: and My Father will love him, and We will come unto him, and make Our abode with him."

Now, my dear reader, if you neglect or refuse to obey this fourth command of the Decalogue, are you not left without excuse? And you can plead nothing in extenuation of your neglect. "For God shall bring every work into judgment, with every secret thing, whether it be good or whether it be evil."

Appendix II: **EGW Material Abbreviated in Footnotes**

Ellen White's writings available: http://www.whiteestate.org

Sample abridged footnote entry: 4BC 1166.4
Expanded entry:
Vol. 4 S. D. A. Bible Commentary page 1166 paragraph 4

The S. D. A. Bible Commentary has 7 volumes

Manuscript Releases
1MR - Vol. 1 (1981) Thru   21MR - Vol. 13 (1993)

Testimonies for the Church
1T - Volume 1 (1855-1868) Thru 9T - Volume 9 (1909)

Books and Periodicals
1888 - The Ellen G. White 1888 Materials (1987)
1SAT - Sermons and Talks (2 volumes)
2SG - Spiritual Gifts (4 [4a & 4b] volumes)
1SM - Selected Messages Book 1 (3 volumes)
1SP - The Spirit of Prophecy (4 volumes)
AA - The Acts of the Apostles (1911)
AUCR - (Australasian) Union Conference Record
BCL - Battle Creek Letters (1928)
BEcho - The Bible Echo
BTS - Bible Training School
CC - Conflict and Courage (1970)
CD - Counsels on Diet and Foods (1938)
CE - Christian Education (1893, 1894)
CET - Christian Experience and Teachings of Ellen G. White (1922)
CH - Counsels on Health (1923)
ChS - Christian Service (1925)
CM - Colporteur Ministry (1953)
COL - Christ's Object Lessons (1900)
CTBH - Christian Temperance and Bible Hygiene (1890)
CTr - Christ Triumphant (1999)

CW - Counsels to Writers and Editors (1946)
DA - The Desire of Ages (1898)
DD - Darkness Before Dawn (1997)
Ed - Education (1903)
Ev - Evangelism (1946)
EW - Early Writings (1882)
ExV - A Sketch of the Christian Experience and Views of EGW (1851)
FE - Fundamentals of Christian Education (1923)
FLB - The Faith I Live By (1958)
GC88 - The Great Controversy (1888)
GC - The Great Controversy (1911)
GCB - The General Conference Bulletin
GH - The Gospel Herald
GW - Gospel Workers (1915)
HP - In Heavenly Places (1967)
HR - The Health Reformer
HS - Historical Sketches of the Foreign Missions of the SDA Ch... (1886)
LDE - Last Day Events (1992)
LHU - Lift Him Up (1988)
LLM - Loma Linda Messages (1981)
LP - Sketches from the Life of Paul (1883)
LS80 - Life Sketches of James White and Ellen(1880)
LS88 - Life Sketches of James White and Ellen(1888)
LS - Life Sketches of Ellen G. White (1915)
Mar - Maranatha (1976)
MB - Thoughts from the Mount of Blessing (1896)
ML - My Life Today (1952)
OFC - Our Father Cares (1991)
OHC - Our High Calling (1961)
PH068 - Rolling Back the Reproach (1900)
PH086 - Special Testimony to Battle Creek Church (1898)
PH098 - Testimony for the Church at Olcott, N. Y. (1868)
PH135 - God's Plan for the Relief of Avondale School (1900)
PH139 - The Relief of the Schools (1900)
PH154 - Special Testimony to Battle Creek Church (1896)
PK - Prophets and Kings (1917)
PP - Patriarchs and Prophets (1890)
RH - The Present Truth
RH - The Review and Herald

SD - Sons and Daughters of God (1955)
SL - The Sanctified Life (1889)
SpM - Spalding and Magan Collection (1985)
SpTA11 - Special Testimony for Ministers and Workers -- No. 11 (1898)
SpTB07 - Testimonies for the Church Containing Messages of
　Warning and Instruction to Seventh-day Adventists (1906)
SpTEd - Special Testimonies On Education (1897)
ST - The Signs of the Times
SW - The Southern Work (1898, 1901)
TDG - This Day With God (1979)
Te - Temperance (1949)
TM - Testimonies to Ministers and Gospel Workers (1923)
TMK - That I May Know Him (1964)
TSA - Testimonies to Southern Africa (1977)
TSS - Testimonies on Sabbath-School Work (1900)
UL - The Upward Look (1982)
WLF - A Word to the Little Flock (1847)
YI - The Youth's Instructor
YRP - Ye Shall Receive Power (1995)

Reference Books

Strong - Strong's Analytical Concordance
Easton – Easton's Bible Dictionary

Bibles

Douay - Douay–Rheims Bible the Latin Vulgate into English
KJV - King James Version
NASB - New American Standard Bible (1995)
NIV - New International Version
RSV – Revised Standard Version (1952)
YLT – Young's Literal Translation (1898)

www.ingramcontent.com/pod-product-compliance
Lightning Source LLC
Chambersburg PA
CBHW061718270326
41928CB00011B/2025